The Sacred in Fan

The Sacred
in Fantastic Fandom

*Essays on the Intersection
of Religion and Pop Culture*

Edited by CAROLE M. CUSACK,
JOHN W. MOREHEAD *and*
VENETIA LAURA DELANO ROBERTSON

McFarland & Company, Inc., Publishers
Jefferson, North Carolina

LIBRARY OF CONGRESS CATALOGUING-IN-PUBLICATION DATA

Names: Cusack, Carole M., 1962– editor. | Morehead, John W.,
   1964– editor. | Robertson, Venetia Laura Delano, 1987– editor.
Title: The sacred in fantastic fandom : essays on the intersection
   of religion and pop culture / edited by Carole M. Cusack,
   John W. Morehead and Venetia Laura Delano Robertson.
Description: Jefferson, North Carolina : McFarland & Company, Inc.,
   2019 | Includes bibliographical references and index.
Identifiers: LCCN 2019010186 | ISBN 9781476670836
   (paperback : acid free paper) ∞
Subjects: LCSH: Popular culture—Religious aspects. | Religion
   and culture. | Fans (Persons)
Classification: LCC BL65.C8 S226 2019 | DDC 201/.7—dc23
LC record available at https://lccn.loc.gov/2019010186

BRITISH LIBRARY CATALOGUING DATA ARE AVAILABLE

ISBN (print) 978-1-4766-7083-6
ISBN (ebook) 978-1-4766-3640-5

Front cover image © 2019 Shutterstock

Manufactured in the United States of America

*McFarland & Company, Inc., Publishers
   Box 611, Jefferson, North Carolina 28640
   www.mcfarlandpub.com*

Table of Contents

v

Part 3. Sacred Play: Performing the Text

Introduction

The Study of Fandom and Religion

CAROLE M. CUSACK *and*
VENETIA LAURA DELANO ROBERTSON

This project was originally conceived by John W. Morehead as an academic yet accessible anthology of papers that explore the sacred aspects of "fantastic" fandoms, those communities and personal engagements that celebrate texts of the fantasy and science fiction genres. When we, Carole M. Cusack and Venetia Laura Delano Robertson, were invited by John and McFarland to contribute to the volume and complete the project as editors we were excited to see the breadth and depth of the contributions. The essays selected for this volume represent innovative intellectual engagements with the relationship of religion to fandom. A considerable portion of the authors are early career researchers and, with the field being emergent and quickly evolving, the studies here are appositely fresh. While some of the fandoms and their media sources that feature in these pages have been subject to much academic assessment over the years, the following essays offer an insightful take on what these cultures can tell us about spirituality in the contemporary world.

Employing fieldwork, discourse analysis, digital ethnography, and theory from film studies, religious studies, and cultural studies among other disciplines, each essay demonstrates yet another layer of the imbrication of the religious and the fannish in participatory cultures and textual devotion. The case studies discussed in this collection will be of interest to many—consumers, scholars, fans and aca-fans—but we are proud to say that, both independently and as a whole, this work provides valuable voices in the conversation between religious studies and fandom studies on how meaning is mediated in the modern world.

The recent but blossoming field of fandom studies explores and interrogates the interactions between creators and purveyors of texts, texts themselves, and their consumers. Here "text" takes on its widest possible meaning; not only the written iteration of a story, but its visual, theatrical, filmic, and ludic manifestations all become "readable" and subject to analysis, discursive and beyond.[1] This analytical take is not as new as the arena of fandom studies but under this heading scholars bring together diverse multidisciplinary strategies, from classic forms of literary criticism, anthropological method, and theological exegesis, to the modern and postmodern realms of inquiry that focus on identity, performativity, authenticity, and the disruption of metanarratives.

With increasing vigor, religious studies has opened its own key terms up for deconstruction and redefinition. "Religion" is today studied as not exclusively a tradition-based or faith-based practice, but a rationale, an experience, a framework that is implicitly and explicitly present in a variety of cultural contexts. A spate of recent studies into the dual processes of secularization and sacralization in the contemporary Western world have produced new methodologies for interpreting shifts in our religious thinking and doing. Thus, Yves Lambert has posited that in the encounter of modernity and religion, there are four possible futures: "decline, adaptation or reinterpretation, conservation, and innovation."[2] Reinterpretation and innovation are most relevant to religions and spiritualities based on popular culture. The core characteristics of these phenomena are: "this-worldliness, self-spirituality, immanent divinity, dehierarchization, parascientific or science fiction-based beliefs, [and] loose organizational structures."[3]

There is a notable focus on how popular culture is influencing our belief structures. Christopher Partridge's notion of "popular occulture" and Emily McAvan's "postmodern sacred," for example, offer typologies for examining the convergence of texts of both "popular" and "cult" status with the contemporary metaphysical milieu and the subsequent production of eclectic and personalized faith systems that draw equally on fictional and mythical resources. Traditional religions are also affected by popular culture and the individualist and consumerist culture of the West,[4] and the existence of devoted fandoms among Christian youth, for example, has been studied.[5] Despite the influx of academic studies of how religion and fandom exist in tandem in numerous contexts, however, there still exists in the academy, and in these same studies, a tendency to differentiate between the personal and social experiences brought about by both fandom and religion; the assumption is that the two are essentially discrete phenomena. A brief argument for the necessity and merit of reversing this assumption is made here, and it is hoped that the essays in this volume persuade the reader of the validity of our stance.

Scholars of popular culture, such as the don of fandom studies, Henry

Jenkins, Cornel Sandvoss, Mark Duffett, and Sean McCloud have critiqued the comparative assessment of fandom and religion for what McCloud calls its "parallelomania," the awkward or opportunistic conflation of fan behaviors and motivations with religious ones in order to make a point that may not be there.[6] Yet, some parallels are too visible, in ways both fortuitous and causal, not to be remarked upon. The use of the word "cult" is one such example: when attached to a text—as "cult classic"—or to a following—the "cult of whatever/whoever"—the word recalls both the deviant, anti-establishment tendencies and the zealotry implicated in the sociological use of the term in religious studies.[7] Even more striking is the religious etymology of the term "fan" itself, derived from the Latin *fanaticus*, meaning an attendant of the temple (*fanus*). Once coined, it quickly came to denote those who "fanatically" adore a variety of things, from goddesses to film stars, and from politicians to baseball.[8] Henry Jenkins has complained that the negative religious connotations of the "fan"—"false beliefs, orgiastic excess, possession, and madness"—are still strongly attached to the label; but more problematic for Jenkins and company are the scholars who have read modern fandom as an inherently religious participatory culture.[9] It is Jenkins's concern that such a reading reinstates a commonly held misconception about fans being deranged in their devotions and exhibiting poor taste and defective judgment in their embarrassingly misguided attachment to "low culture" products.[10] Similarly, Duffett decries the comparative approach as an "extremely crude metaphor" with "derogatory connotations" that imposes a monolithic and hegemonic interpretation of fan experiences.[11]

This anxiety is common in media studies, wherein the discussion of religion and fandom often discredits the comparative relationship between the two by arguing that while both are devotional, religion requires a degree of faith that fandom does not, and while both can be personal, fandom delivers a kind of individualistic satisfaction that religion discourages.[12] For example, Jenkins has proposed that the difference between a religion and fandom is the fan's relationship to the stories they favor:

> They retell them, they recirculate them, they see them as revealing some deeper truth about human experience. But they don't necessarily believe them to be true. They believe them to be fabricated as an encapsulation of certain sets of values. And I believe cult texts can function as a mythology in that sense. As a religion you bring back in this notion of literal belief, and it implies that fans are unable to separate fiction from reality, or that they supposedly act on the text as if it were literally true.

For Jenkins, Sandvoss, and Duffett, the parallels drawn between fandom and religion are epistemologically flawed. Sandvoss points to the distinction in participants' relationship to their gods and idols, noting that fans wish to imitate their idols, whereas believers "do not seek to supplant God." Additionally, Sandvoss claims that, in contrast to religion "fandom lacks an absolute, other-worldly framework through which social realities are constructed and legitimized."[13] This is a claim that many of the essays in this collection confidently refute.

In the binary understanding of religion and fandom, the two concepts are made irreconcilable by attributing to each constant and essential qualities, thus reducing these innately complex and multifaceted worlds to fixities. There are numerous issues with this position. The idea that religion requires distant and inimitable gods and literal belief in cosmological narratives, whereas fandom does not require nor supply these things is, as many studies into "alternative" religions, identities, and communities have shown, quite incorrect. While much in fandom studies has been written from a position of sympathy for fans, and hoping to dispel the associations with religion that lead to a "cultish" or "fanatical" reading of fandom, or somewhat conversely, to protect religion from being associated with "profane" activities, the problematic reading of religion here has rarely been taken to task. One notable problem is that the model of religion being invoked is essentialist and tacitly Christian, which springs from an underlying ethnocentrism and cultural paternalism that plagues the academy.

In religious studies, the field in which we, the editors, primarily work, this issue is sometimes approached through a calculated dismantling of the so-called "world religions paradigm"; This paradigm posits that in order to study religion in the world, one should look at the "major" faith groups, generally understood to be those that are large in number in certain geographic regions, or that have significant cultural impact in those areas. How something is classified as a "religion" is determined through an implicit yet deeply entrenched comparative system wherein Christianity is held up as "the prototype for religion in general."[14] Treating Christianity as a monolithic whole is its own categorical minefield: the differences between Catholic, Orthodox, Protestant and post-denominational versions of Christianity in the contemporary world are significant; and the examination of Christianity throughout history and across far-flung geographical locations increases the internal diversity of the phenomenon.[15] Yet, the "basic elements" of the Christian religion—a founder, a god-figure, a place of worship, rites, and sacred scriptures—are then mapped onto religions as culturally and historically diverse as Hinduism and Judaism. Jonathan Z. Smith has observed that this approach guides us to think in reductive categorical dualisms: "our religion/their religion," "true religion/false religion," "religion/superstition," "religion/magic," and so forth.[16] Through such methods of othering, a restrictive, hegemonic, and paternalistic definition of religion emerges, and any deviating form of belief is rendered ersatz, insufficient, and unworthy of study; this includes indigenous traditions, new religions, syncretic systems, and popular cultural spiritual phenomena.

What many in the academy are trying to do now, especially those of us who work in the area of contemporary religiosity, is shift our thinking to consider the multitudinous and nuanced forms that belief, ritual, and spiritual identity take today. "Religion," for the individual and for the community, may or may not involve theism, observation of tradition, metaphysical worldviews, and experiences of the "holy," no matter what the faith system. Expanding the definition of religion beyond the "Christian" model and its normative expectations opens up the study of why people believe, what they do about it, and how they do it, in infinitely more diverse and interesting ways that befit our changing times. However, even in this field it is hard to escape the binary impulse, with taxons like David Chidester's "fake" and Adam Possamai's "hyperreal" (as opposed to "real") religion gaining traction as descriptors of contemporary and non-traditional cultural and personal beliefs and practices that have the "feel" of religion without the label.[17]

The types of religious expression that are classified under such terms are typically those that are related to fandoms, and often media or popular culture fandoms, which insinuates that these sources of enchantment and attenuating feelings of attachment are inherently deficient and transient. For example, though a useful methodological concept for this area of study, the description of the "postmodern sacred" by McAvan makes clear that this kind of spiritual experience is regarded as less "real" than that affiliated with "traditional" religion:

> I will argue that the postmodern sacred is a paradoxical attempt at accessing spirituality, using the symbols contained in explicitly unreal texts to gain a secondhand experience of transcendence and belief. This second-hand experience displaces the need for belief or real-world practice into a textual world, requiring little of its consumers. While they seem to suggest a desire for a magical world outside of capitalism, the wonder produced by these texts, however, is only temporary.[18]

In this rendering we see the theological and cultural imperialist undertones of the academy coming through, either subconsciously or intentionally, framing "religion" as inexorably "special." In this view, while texts and participatory cultures might *seem* sacred, their fans might *appear* devotional, their activities might *resemble* ritual celebration, none of this entails the same holiness as "true" religious expression.

The exceptionalist model of paradigmatic religion, as we might call it, thus continues to be held up against alternative manifestations of religious expression to devalue them. This does a serious discredit to the study of "traditional" religion as well as its alternatives. In sequestering "authentic" forms of religion from "others" we presume there is a consistent and obvious criteria for determining faith, when of course the lived reality of our beliefs, actions, and ideologies are far more culturally, socially, morally, and personally complex. Rather than tie religion to a belief in god/s, a literal understanding of a sacred text, or strict and regular adherence to an identifiable "world religion," in his book *Sacred Matters*, Gary Laderman pushes us to recognize religion as an "ubiquitous feature of cultural life, assuming many expressions though tied to an inspired by basic, universal facts of life and fundamentally biological phenomena in human experience: suffering and ecstasy, reproduction and aging, family and conflict, health and death."[19] Part of this, Laderman argues, is the "new spiritual reality" of media-influenced religion.[20] Speaking of Jediism and *Star Wars* fandom he writes:

> I can hear my New Testament and Systematic Theologian colleagues reading this with skepticism if not disgust—and indeed I've encountered these kinds of reactions in public forums. "Surely anyone identifying their religion as Jedi is just being silly," they say. Or "How do you know this is genuine religion and not just some passing fancy?" I imagine after the death of Christ members of the early Christian community may have faced the same kind of incredulity and disdain.
>
> My response: Welcome to the twenty-first century, when sacred matters are not limited to the monotheists, or confined by conventional religious traditions. Bono and Warren Buffet, Master Yoda and Obi Wan Kenobi are legitimate guiding religious lights whose words and actions stir the imagination and rally the faithful in ways those of us who study religion are only beginning to understand.[21]

That individuals and groups form their religiosity around media sources should not be deemed grounds for their dismissal as real and meaningful examples of contemporary spirituality. Jennifer Porter pertinently reminds us that being derivative is not a feature unique to such perspectives: "mainstream religions, like spiritualities expressed through and/or inspired by pop culture, draw upon pre-existing sources for inspiration, admonition, and emulation. To be referential is not to be inauthentic, it is simply to be contextualized in the cultural milieu of the times."[22] Moreover, as Carole M. Cusack has explored in her study of "invented religions"—religious movements self-consciously based on works of fiction and fantasy—exhibiting agency in the construction of one's own belief system and acknowledging the practice of pastiche and appropriation does not diminish the impact of the resultant religion, rather it foregrounds consumer choice and individualism, key values in the Western world that institutionalized religions are frequently seen to dismiss or distort. Invented religions, Cusack maintains, are able to offer followers a personalized route to the sacred, relevant to their concerns, while still sharing many of the same hallmarks we attribute to traditional religion:

> invented religions disseminate wonderful stories, filled with memorable agents, which would satisfy any seeker's desire for an imaginative and satisfying explanation of the nature of reality and the purpose of human life, and would also fulfill any cognitive science criteria to be regarded as "religious."[23]

Religious movements and individuals that adroitly merge the categories of fan and believer in their belief structures are perhaps the pinnacle case studies that represent the argument that these categories have more than simply a shared vocabulary and few superficially alike structural or social features.

A number of studies focusing on such religions have been published in recent years, looking at groups like Ilsaluntë Valion, whose beliefs are based in the work of J.R.R. Tolkien,[24] the Church of All Worlds, who were inspired by Robert A. Heinlein's 1961 science fiction novel *Stranger in a Strange Land*,[25] and individuals who have mystical relationships with, or even identify *as*, fictional entities, such as soulbonders, tulpamancers, and Otherkin.[26] These investigations build on earlier studies of the religious tendencies of fandoms that have blazed trails in the field, such as Michael Jindra's work on *Star Trek* fandom,[27] Daniel Cavicchi on Springsteen fans,[28] and Matt Hills' lens of "neo-religiosity" as a way to view fan engagement.[29] Hills has been especially constructive in expanding the definition of "religion" beyond the paradigmatic strictures of the classifications applied by scholars like Jenkins and Sandvoss, aptly noting that "religiosity is itself sociohistorically reconstructed and reconfigured (as neoreligiosity) through 'cult media' and associated fan practices and experiences in such a way as to suggest that there is no essential thing which can be referred to as 'religiosity.'"[30] The essays collected in this volume illustrate the ongoing fascination with, and existence of, the coalescing of religious and fannish interests and how this continues to make us question, deconstruct, and reconfigure the hegemonic cultural assumptions that reduce and devalue meaningful, world-building, and enchanted experiences with media sources.

Overview of Essays

This volume is divided into three sections based generally on the type of interactions respondents have with their chosen texts. The first is titled "Sacred Reading: Analyzing the Text," and is comprised of investigations into the ways fans "read" and "read into" the plots, characters, and implications of novels and television shows. This section opens with Carole M. Cusack's "Harry Potter and the Sacred Text: Fiction, Reading and Meaning-Making," which looks at a project run out of Harvard Divinity School that seeks to use the exegetical practice of *lectio divina* to interpret J.K. Rowling's *Harry Potter* books (1997–2007). Cusack argues that in their contextualization of these works as sources of scripture, containing sacred truths and moral imperatives, this development indicates a "radical democratization of the sacred," both by wresting the traditional art of hermeneutics from scholiasts and theologians and handing it to the lay-reader, and by substituting young adult novels for the Bible or a similarly ancient and revered text. Continuing with this theme, Rhiannon Grant's essay, "Doctrine and Fanon: George Lindbeck, Han's Gun and Sherlock's Gay Wedding," addresses the notions of "canon" (key aspects of the original text) and "fanon" (additional aspects contributed by fans) in the fandoms surrounding *Star Wars* (1977–) and the BBC's *Sherlock* (2010–2017). The doctrinal fervor that consuming and interpreting stories inspires in fans is a particularly telling sign of the significant role played by media in our lives. Furthermore, how the fannish imagination has impacted the creators of the texts (be they the original auteurs or those responsible for later adaptations) shows that the audience is now responsible for *in*-world building, and not merely relegated to the margins. In the third contribution, "*Supernatural's* Winchester Gospel: A Fantastic Midrash," Linda Howell makes this interaction a central theme of her argument. Howell analyzes fan reactions and "fannotations" to television's *Supernatural* (2005–) to demonstrate that, through this pattern of influence, the fans and show-writers together produce a "symbiotext." The final essay in this section, Greg Conley's "'Seizing the Means of Perception': The Use of Fiction in Chaos Magic and Occultural Fandom," explores the explicitly religious use of fiction, in particular that of H.P. Lovecraft, by Chaos Magicians. As a type of "occultural fandom," Chaos Magic represents one of the most stark and interesting modes of sacralizing media forms by mining them for symbols, rituals, and deities. Whether it is by reading god into the text, or moving from disciple to dogmatist, these essays demonstrate the varied and productive ways that fandom effects belief structures.

The second section, "Sacred Viewing: Watching the Text," focuses on experience, affect, and transformative texts. The experiential aspect of fandom is undoubtedly acutely powerful for some participants, and here a combination of fieldwork, theory, and analysis provide bounteous evidence in support of this statement. Marc Joly-Corcoran, in "Cinephany, the Affective Experience of the Fan: A Typology," offers a unique framework for understanding profound audience reactions to visual texts with his neologism "cinephany." Drawing on Mircea Eliade's concept of "hierophany," encounters with the sacred, Joly-Corcoran uses cinephany to categorize the motivations and responses of *Star Wars* fans who have made fanfilms based on George Lucas's beloved space-western. Following this essay is "Experiencing the Sacred: *The Hobbit* as a Holy Text" by Jyrki Korpua, Maria Ruotsalainen, Minna Siikilä-Laitila, Tanja Välisalo and Irma Hirsjärvi, researchers affiliated with the international World Hobbit Project, which has surveyed thousands of viewers of Peter Jackson's filmic version of J.R.R. Tolkien's classic novel. With reference to the Finnish responses to this global research exercise, the authors point to the value-laden notions of authenticity and originality, nostalgia, and awe to demonstrate how sacrality is implicated in the relationship of fan to text. In his analysis of Joss Whedon's eminently popular *Buffy* and *Angel* television series, James Reynold's essay, "Transformative Souls and

Transformed Selves: *Buffy, Angel* and the Daimonic Tale," offers a change of tack, here examining in detail the narratives of these texts and what they communicate about ensouled selfhood. Reynolds posits that audiences are, in part, so enthralled by these stories because of this existential theme, which he dubs "the daimonic tale." The emotional depths and spiritual sentiment of what Anne Jerselv calls "sacred viewing"[31] is evident in the discussions of this section.

The final part of the book, "Sacred Play: Performing the Text," looks to fan-text encounters that involve identification with and personalization of the roles and themes present in the medium. Jovi L. Geraci, in "Until the End of the World: Fans as Messianic Heroes in *World of Warcraft*," explores this avenue through the immensely popular computer game *World of Warcraft*, wherein by participating in this immersive multiplayer universe, the individual becomes interpolated into the mythology that sustains the narrative and the game. Here, the player can take up the mantle of not just the hero but the messiah in the apocalyptic landscape of Azeroth. Juli L. Gittinger brings the physical embodiment of religion and fandom to the fore in her essay "Muslim Women Cosplayers: Intersecting Religious, Cultural and Fan Identities." Using her fieldwork among Muslim cosplayers from America, Asia, and Europe, Gittinger investigates the experiences of female fans whose outwardly visible dedication to both their faith and their fandom is challenged by this practice. In the final essay, "Magical Matrimony: Romance and Enchantment in *Harry Potter*–Themed Weddings," Venetia Laura Delano Robertson draws on interviews with engaged and married couples who have integrated *Harry Potter* themes into the décor and rituals of their weddings and wedding receptions.

As Cusack demonstrates in the opening essay of this volume, *Harry Potter* has become an important site for the convergence of spirituality and fandom, and as life events like weddings become increasingly secular people are looking to fun yet meaningful alternatives to express their feelings about love, community, and the power of fantasy. In three different but intriguing ways, these essays demonstrate the interpolation of the sacred and the secular in playful and performative ways.

John W. Morehead's "Afterword: Fantastic Fan Conventions and Transformational Festivals" examines fan conventions and postmodern ritual spaces including Burning Man to argue that fandoms, far from being trivial or unimportant, offer paths to the sacred through the shared crafting of mythos and ritual, and especially in large-scale gatherings where community is fostered. Morehead's heartfelt expression of his own journey as a fan is a rousing conclusion to the book, touching as it does on many themes explored by contributors.

Conclusion

Ultimately, while some of the essays in this volume are focused first and foremost on the exploration of fan labor, identities, and philosophies, whereas others privilege the reading of religiosity into the texts and their reception, the main theme that is repeated throughout the discussion is that of sacralization; the motivations, processes, and outcomes of setting apart certain products, authors, actors, and activities as special, meaning-laden, even mystical. The "sacred" here is, as Gary Laderman observes, a potent word like "religion" that nonetheless has no "fixed universal meaning," but can be understood as emotional, cognitive, spiritual, and material moments and actions: "vital rituals, living myths, indescribable experiences, moral values, shared memories, and other commonly recognized features of religious life."[32] The sacralization of cultural products is a fundamental component in the religious landscape of many contemporary societies, which indicates that secularization and sacralization, rather than being two distinct roads that diverge from the waning influence of the well-trod path of mainstream institutions of religion, need to be understood as intertwined, and perhaps symbiotic. The academy needs to embrace a more dynamic, deregulated, and possibly more secular definition of religion if it wants to fully grasp the profundity with which many fans engage with their media, and the degree to which concepts like the sacred, the divine, scripture, dogma, gnosis, and enchantment are embedded in their experiences.

NOTES

1. Donna E. Alvermann and Margaret C. Hagood, "Fandom and Critical Media Literacy," *Journal of Adolescent & Adult Literacy* 43, no. 5 (2000), 436–446.

2. Yves Lambert, "Religion in Modernity as a New Axial Age: Secularization or New Religious Forms?" *Sociology of Religion* 60, no. 3 (1999), 311.

3. Carole M. Cusack, *Invented Religions: Imagination, Fiction and Faith* (Farnham: Ashgate, 2010), 9.

4. David Lyon, *Jesus in Disneyland: Religion in Postmodern Times* (Cambridge: Polity, 2000), 1–19.

5. Andrew Crome, "Reconsidering Religion and Fandom: Christian Fan Works in *My Little Pony* Fandom," *Culture and Religion: An Interdisciplinary Journal* 15, no. 4 (2014), 399–418.

6. Sean McCloud, "Popular Culture Fandoms, the Boundaries of Religious Studies, and the Project of the Self," *Culture and Religion* 4, no. 2 (2003), 188.

7. See James T. Richardson, "Definitions of Cult: From Sociological-Technical to Popular-Negative." *Review of Religious Research* 34, no. 4 (1993), 348–356.

8. Victoria Nelson, *Gothicka* (Cambridge, MA: Harvard University Press, 2012), 51–2.

9. Henry Jenkins, *Textual Poachers: Television Fans & Participatory Culture* (New York: Routledge, 2005), 12, 13.

10. Jenkins, *Textual Poachers*, 17.

11. Mark Duffett, "False Faith or False Comparison? A Critique of the Religious Interpretation of Elvis Fan Culture," *Popular Music and Society* 26, no. 4 (2003), 520.

12. J. Otter Bickerdike, *The Secular Religion of Fandom* (London: Sage, 2016), 8–15.
13. Cornel Sandvoss, *Fans: The Mirror of Consumption* (Cambridge: Polity Press, 2005), 63.
14. Catherine Bell, "Paradigms Behind (and Before) the Modern Concept of Religion," *History and Theory* 45, no. 4. (2006), 29.
15. Mark MacWilliams, Joanne Punzo Waghorne, Deborah Sommer, Cybelle Shattuck, Kay A. Read, Selva J. Raj, Khaled Keshk, Deborah Halter, James Egge, Robert M. Baum, Carol S. Anderson and Russell T. McCutcheon, "Religion/s Between Covers: Dilemmas of the World Religions Textbook," *Religion Studies Review* 31, nos 1–2 (2005), 1–35.
16. Jonathan Z. Smith, "Religion, Religions, Religious," in *Critical Terms for Religious Studies*, ed. Mark C. Taylor, 269–284 (Chicago: University of Chicago Press, 1998), 276.
17. MacWilliams, Waghorne, et al., "Religions/s Between Covers," 1–35.
18. Emily McAvan, *The Postmodern Sacred: Popular Culture Spirituality in the Science Fiction, Fantasy and Urban Fantasy Genres* (Jefferson, NC: McFarland, 2012), 19.
19. Gary Laderman, *Sacred Matters: Celebrity Worship, Sexual Ecstasies, the Living Dead, and Other Signs of Religious Life in the United States* (New York: New Press, 2009), viii–ix.
20. Gary Laderman, "Sacred & Profane: From Bono to the Jedi Police—Who Needs God?" *Religion Dispatches*, June 22 (2009). http://religiondispatches.org/isacredi-from-bono-to-the-jedi-police-who-needs-god/.
21. Laderman, "Sacred & Profane."
22. Jennifer Porter, "Implicit Religion in Popular Culture: The Religious Dimensions of Fan Communities," *Implicit Religion* 12, no. 3 (November 2009), 275.
23. Cusack, *Invented Religions*, 24.
24. Markus Altena Davidsen, "The Elven Path and the Silver Ship of the Valar: Two Spiritual Groups Based on J.R.R. Tolkien's Legendarium," in *Fiction, Invention, and Hyper-Reality*, ed. Carole M. Cusack and Pavol Kosnáč (London: Routledge, 2017), 15–30; see also Gwineth, "Appendix 1.2 Ilsaluntë Valion," in *Fiction, Invention, and Hyper-Reality*, 34–36.
25. Cusack, *Invented Religion*, 53–82.
26. Venetia Laura Delano Robertson, "Salvation and Animation: Religion, Fandom and Identity in the Romantic Narratives of Mystics and Soulbonders," in *Fiction, Invention, and Hyper-Reality*, 58–78; Samuel Veissière, "Varieties of Tulpa Experiences: Sentient Imaginary Friends, Embodied Joint Attention, and Hypnotic Sociality in a Wired World," *Somatosphere*, April 3 (2015), http://somatosphere.net/2015/04/varieties-of-tulpa-experiences-sentient-imaginary-friends-embodied-joint-attention-and-hypnotic-sociality-in-a-wired-world.html; Danielle Kirby, *Fantasy and Belief: Alternative Religions, Popular Narratives, and Digital Cultures* (Durham, UK: Acumen, 2013).
27. Michael Jindra, "*Star Trek* Fandom as a Religious Phenomenon," *Sociology of Religion* 55, no. 1 (1994), 27–51; see also Jindra, "'*Star Trek* to Me Is a Way of Life': Fan Expressions of *Star Trek* Philosophy." In *Star Trek and Sacred Ground: Explorations of Star Trek, Religion, and American Culture*, ed. Jennifer E. Porter and Darcee L. McLaren, 217–230 (Albany: State University of New York Press, 1999).
28. Daniel Cavicchi, *Tramps Like Us: Music and Meaning Among Springsteen Fans* (Oxford: Oxford University Press, 1998).
29. Matt Hills, "Media Fandom, Neoreligiosity, and Cult(ural) Studies," *The Velvet Light Trap* 46 (2000), 73–84.
30. Hills, "Media Fandom, Neoreligiosity, and Cult(ural) Studies," 74.
31. Anne Jerslev, "Sacred Viewing: Emotional Responses to *The Lord of the Rings*," in *The Lord of the Rings Popular Culture in Global Context*, ed. Ernest Mathjis (London: Wallflower Press, 2006), 206–221.
32. Laderman, *Sacred Matters*, ix.

Bibliography

Alvermann, Donna E., and Margaret C. Hagood. "Fandom and Critical Media Literacy." *Journal of Adolescent & Adult Literacy* 43, no. 5 (2000): 436–446.

Bell, Catherine. "Paradigms Behind (and Before) the Modern Concept of Religion." *History and Theory* 45, no. 4 (2006): 27–46.

Cavicchi, Daniel. *Tramps Like Us: Music and Meaning Among Springsteen Fans*. New York: Oxford University Press, 1998.

Crome, Andrew. "Reconsidering Religion and Fandom: Christian Fan Works in *My Little Pony* Fandom." *Culture and Religion: An Interdisciplinary Journal* 15, no. 4 (2014): 399–418.

Cusack, Carole M. *Invented Religions: Imagination, Fiction, and Faith*. Farnham: Ashgate, 2010.

Davidsen, Markus Altena. "The Elven Path and the Silver Ship of the Valar: two Spiritual Groups Based on J.R.R. Tolkien's Legendarium." In *Fiction, Invention, and Hyper-Reality*, edited by Carole M. Cusack and Pavol Kosnáč, 15–30. London: Routledge, 2017.

Duffett, Mark. "False Faith or False Comparison? A Critique of the Religious Interpretation of Elvis Fan Culture." *Popular Music and Society* 26, no. 4 (2003): 513–522.

Gwineth. "Appendix 1.2 Ilsaluntë Valion," in *Fiction, Invention, and Hyper-Reality*, edited by Carole M. Cusack and Pavol Kosnáč, 34–6. London: Routledge, 2017.

Hills, Matt. "Media Fandom, Neoreligiosity, and Cult(ural) Studies." *The Velvet Light Trap* 46 (2000): 73–84.

Jenkins, Henry. *Textual Poachers: Television Fans & Participatory Culture*. New York: Routledge, 2005

Jerslev, Anne. "Sacred Viewing: Emotional Responses to *The Lord of the Rings*." In *The Lord of the Rings Popular Culture in Global Context*, edited by Ernest Mathjis, 206–221. London: Wallflower Press, 2006.

Jindra, Michael. "*Star Trek* Fandom as a Religious Phenomenon," *Sociology of Religion* 55, no. 1 (1994): 27–51

_____. "'*Star Trek* to Me Is a Way of Life': Fan Expressions of *Star Trek* Philosophy." In *Star Trek and Sacred Ground: Explorations of Star Trek, Religion, and American Culture*, ed. Jennifer E. Porter and Darcee L. McLaren, 217–230. Albany: State University of New York Press, 1999.

Kirby, Danielle. *Fantasy and Belief: Alternative Religions, Popular Narratives, and Digital Cultures*. Durham, UK: Acumen, 2013.

Laderman, Gary. "Sacred & Profane: From Bono to the Jedi Police—Who Needs God?" *Religion Dispatches*, June 22, 2009. http://religiondispatches.org/isacredi-from-bono-to-the-jedi-police-who-needs-god/ (accessed May 20, 2018).

_____. *Sacred Matters: Celebrity Worship, Sexual Ecstasies, the Living Dead, and Other Signs of Religious Life in the United States*. New York: New Press, 2009.

Lambert, Yves. "Religion in Modernity as a New Axial Age: Secularization or New Religious Forms?" *Sociology of Religion* 60, no. 3 (1999): 303–333.

Lyon, David. *Jesus in Disneyland: Religion in Postmodern Times*. Cambridge: Polity, 2000.

MacWilliams, Mark, and Joanne Punzo Waghorne, Deborah Sommer, Cybelle Shattuck, Kay A. Read, Selva J. Raj, Khaled Keshk, Deborah Halter, James Egge, Robert M. Baum, Carol S. Anderson and Russell T. McCutcheon. "Religion/s Between Covers: Dilemmas of the World Religions Textbook." *Religion Studies Review* 31, nos 1–2 (2005): 1–35.

McAvan, Emily. *The Postmodern Sacred: Popular Culture Spirituality in the Science Fiction, Fantasy and Urban Fantasy Genres*. Jefferson, NC: McFarland, 2012.

McCloud, Sean. "Popular Culture Fandoms, the Boundaries of Religious Studies, and the Project of the Self." *Culture and Religion* 4, no. 2 (2003): 187–206.

Nelson, Victoria. *Gothicka*. Cambridge, MA: Harvard University Press, 2012.

Otter Bickerdike, J. *The Secular Religion of Fandom*. London: Sage, 2016.

Porter, Jennifer. "Implicit Religion in Popular Culture: The Religious Dimensions of Fan Communities." *Implicit Religion* 12, no. 3 (November 2009): 271–280.

Richardson, James T. "Definitions of Cult: From Sociological-Technical to Popular-Negative." *Review of Religious Research* 34, no. 4 (1993): 348–356.

Robertson, Venetia Laura Delano. "Salvation and Animation: Religion, Fandom and Identity in the Romantic Narratives of Mystics and Soulbonders," In *Fiction, Invention, and Hyper-Reality*, edited by Carole M. Cusack and Pavol Kosnáč, 58–78. London: Routledge, 2017.

Sandvoss, Cornel. *Fans: The Mirror of Consumption*. Cambridge: Polity Press, 2005.
Smith, Jonathan Z. "Religion, Religions, Religious." In *Critical Terms for Religious Studies*, edited by Mark C. Taylor, 269–284. Chicago: University of Chicago Press, 1998.
Veissière, Samuel. "Varieties of Tulpa Experiences: Sentient Imaginary Friends, Embodied Joint Attention, and Hypnotic Sociality in a Wired World." *Somatosphere*, April 3 (2015). http://somatosphere.net/2015/04/varieties-of-tulpa-experiences-sentient-imaginary-friends-embodied-joint-attention-and-hypnotic-sociality-in-a-wired-world.html.

PART 1

Sacred Reading
Analyzing the Text

Harry Potter and
the Sacred Text

Fiction, Reading and Meaning-Making

CAROLE M. CUSACK

Introduction

Since the mid-twentieth century fictional narratives have been used to affirm what theologian Paul Tillich termed "ultimate concern"[1] for certain people, making fiction fulfill the roles and functions of religious texts. Tillich stated that "religion is being ultimately concerned about that which is and should be our ultimate concern ... faith is the state of being grasped by an ultimate concern."[2] It is clear that Tillich did not intend secular ideas, popular culture, or any other "profane" things to replace Christianity's sacred narrative. Yet, by the start of the twenty-first century, institutional Christianity in the West is in retreat, and in the individualist landscape of late capitalism, imaginative practices, such as visual and performing arts, reading and viewing fiction, can provide alternative meaning templates that are now understood by some to meet requirements that were once considered unique to religion.[3] For this to occur, the fictional text must draw upon and reflect human concerns, and afford space for contemplation, so individuals can devise or extract personal meaning from the story.[4] In some cases, knowledge of, repeated immersion in, and social approval of affective narratives, for example, science fiction and fantasy novels and films, that feature new worlds and have significant impact in experiential terms, or art practices and experimental lifeways, may trigger a spiritual response or even, when collectively shared, result in the formation of a new religion.[5]

Harry Potter fans have engaged with the sacred in various ways in the two decades since Harry Potter and the Philosopher's Stone (1997) was first published. First, the act of reading engages the imagination in constructing an "otherworld" that transcends the reader's mundane reality. Second, immersion in books tends to lead to exegetical readings and the assertion that even the most innocent of texts have hidden meanings that are available to the dedicated, devout seeker.[6] Third, the formation of fandom communities creates a "church" of "believers" with common commitments and interests across the world. Fourth, enacting elements of the *Harry Potter* story through cosplay, attendance at conventions, and tourism resembles the religious activity of going on pilgrimage. These parallels between fandom and religion have been noted with reference to a number of popular cultural forms, like *Star Trek* and *Star Wars*.[7] The *Harry Potter* fandom has not yet developed into a religion, as is the case with Jediism in relation to the *Star Wars* films, and it is possible that it never will.[8]

A small number of invented or fiction-based religions based on novels and films have emerged in the twentieth century, the chief of which is the Church of All Worlds (CAW), a Pagan religion started in 1962 by Tim (now Oberon) Zell (b. 1942) and Lance Christie (1944–2010) while students at Westminster College, Fulton, Missouri. In the twenty-first century, CAW is a major voice in ecological spirituality and remains true to its fictional roots. In 2004 Oberon Zell, inspired by the *Harry Potter* novels, founded the Grey School of Wizardry, a seven-year magical education system. Zell has emulated J.K. Rowling's Hogwarts: the Grey School has houses "named for the Elementals associated with the Four Quarters, Sylphs, Salamanders, Undines and Gnomes" and a curriculum that includes "magickal arts, conducting rituals, wizards of history … and a multitude of other subjects."[9] This enthusiastic adoption of *Harry Potter* by modern Paganism is not unproblematic, as will be discussed later.

That Rowling's novels are popular and influential is beyond doubt; the Potter books have been translated into more than sixty languages, have sold more than 450 million copies, and were made into eight films that "brought in more than $7 billion … [and if] revenue tied to book sales, DVD and digital sales is factored in, that number soars to nearly $25 billion."[10] *Harry Potter* is passionately loved by an enormous fanbase that has taken the boy wizard to heart. As noted above, there is no religion based on Rowling's books, but as Laura Feldt has argued, the novels

are more than "mere fiction," even if they are not used by religious practitioners in rituals, and even if they are not ascribed reality status. They provide virtual worlds as arenas to inhabit for a while, to reflect on different planes of reality … and to seek individualised insights in religion, myth and magic.[11]

This essay discusses a Potter-related podcast phenomenon, *Harry Potter and the Sacred Text*; I argue that the approach of *Harry Potter and the Sacred Text* is a radical democratization of the sacred, in which Potter fans are enabled to construct a personal spirituality that is based on Rowling's fictional world.

Harry Potter and the Sacred Text is a collaboration between Harvard Divinity School graduates Caspar ter Kuile and Vanessa Zoltan, and producer Ariana Nedelman, a current student. This project is subtitled "Reading Something We Love As If It Were Sacred," and it commenced in mid–2016. Each chapter of the Potter novels (199 in all) is analyzed by ter Kuile and Zoltan using *lectio divina*, a traditional mode of interpretation of Christian religious texts, in order to draw out the sacred nature of Rowling's books. This approach involves: trusting the text; rigorous ritual reading; and consciousness of reading in community. I situate this development in the fan culture of *Harry Potter* and its capacity to evoke the sacred in a historical perspective that interrogates the specific cultural value of writing and reading as once-rare practices and capabilities that are no longer special.[12] Projects such as *Harry Potter and the Sacred Text* draw attention to the possible sacred qualities inherent in reading not just an acknowledged scripture, but potentially any text, including novels, comics and film scripts, and also to the impact of fiction on contemporary religions and spiritualities.

The Harry Potter *Phenomenon*

Joanne Kathleen (J.K.) Rowling's first novel, *Harry Potter and the Philosopher's Stone*, was published in 1997 by Bloomsbury and the American edition appeared as *Harry Potter and the Sorcerer's Stone* the following year. By 1999 Rowling's books had won several awards, and the first three Potter novels "were in ranked in the first three positions on the *New York Times Bestseller* list," a distinction rarely achieved by children's literature.[13] The seventh and final installment, *Harry Potter and the Deathly Hallows*, was released in July 2007. The film series commenced in 2001, and the two-part adaptation of *Deathly Hallows* debuted in cinemas in 2010 and 2011 respectively. *Harry Potter* won fans among children (and adults) worldwide, and the films brought to life the alternative England known as the "Potterverse." The Potter phenomenon was not without controversy: conservative Christians objected to Rowling's portrayal of magic and argued that children were being lured into occult practices through their enthusiasm for the education in wizardry that Harry and his friends Ron Weasley and Hermione Granger experienced at Hogwarts.[14] The interest from Pagan groups like CAW, referred to above, fanned the flames of this debate. Rowling's response was to stress her own faith, and the compatibility of Harry's story with Christian values.[15]

The conclusion of Harry's story in *Deathly Hallows*, was not, however, the end of the Potter phenomenon. Three supplementary books were published: *Fantastic Beasts and Where to Find Them* (2001), *Quidditch Through the Ages* (2001), and *The Tales of Beedle the Bard* (2008). The first of these was released as a feature film in 2016 with a script by Rowling, and a series of film prequels to Harry's adventures is in the works.[16] The same year also saw the release of the stage play *Harry Potter and the Cursed Child*, based on an original story by Rowling, Jack Thorne, and John Tiffany. The published play is accepted as the eighth Potter narrative by fans.[17]

The *Harry Potter* series draw upon a number of literary genres: the boarding school tale that stretches from Thomas Hughes' *Tom Brown's School-days* (1857) to Enid Blyton's Malory Towers novels, the magic-filled world of the fantasy genre defined by works such as J.R.R. Tolkien's *Lord of the Rings* (1954–1955)—which has been the most fertile genre, along with science fiction, for inspiring new religions—and the coming of age narrative in which a protagonist undergoes trials and is victorious over enemies and evil, developing into a hero or heroine. In the Potter novels, the realist trials of the coming of age novel combine with the universal conflict between good and evil, as the young witches and wizards who become Harry's friends at Hogwarts learn to defend themselves against the dark magic of the resurgent villain Lord Voldemort.

Markus Altena Davidsen has studied religious and spiritual groups inspired by Tolkien and his legendarium, and suggests that fantasy is a genre that has more religious affordances (mechanisms and motifs that resemble or function like elements in mythology or scriptures). He states that the religions or spiritualities that such texts inspire differ depending on whether the "story-world" is anchored "in the actual world" (meaning the text can be taken as historical, as is the case with most Tolkien religionists)[18] or whether concepts that are not so anchored are the focus (the text is not assumed to be historical, as is the case with Jediism, the religion based on George Lucas' *Star Wars* films). The fictional world of *Harry Potter* splices the magical world of Hogwarts with the everyday English world of "muggle" or mundane life. Moreover, there is a strong sense of historical time: Harry is born on July 31, 1980, and is eleven when the series commences; he turns seventeen in the final book and the apocalyptic Battle of Hogwarts that provides the climax to *Harry Potter and the Deathly Hallows* can be dated precisely to May 2, 1998. Each book reflects the structure of the school year, with Harry at his uncle and aunt's house in the summer holidays, then at Hogwarts over the school terms, which are punctuated by familiar real-world events such as the Christian festivals of Christmas and Easter.

Yet, for all this historical specificity, Harry is a classic hero of mythology or legend. He has a mysterious origin, an orphan born to two brave young lovers, James and Lily, who died fighting evil when he was a baby; his upbringing with his cruel and cold relatives the Dursleys is intended by his headmaster and patron Albus Dumbledore to protect him from Voldemort and his army of Death Eaters. This invites comparisons with King Arthur, brought up in obscurity as the foster-son of Sir Ector, his greatness only revealed when he pulled the sword Excalibur from the stone. Even a casual reading of the Potter books reveals Rowling's extensive use of motifs from myths and legends, religions and magical traditions, all of which combine to increase the attractiveness of Harry as a hero and of the fictional world in which he lives.[19] Hogwarts students study Care of Magical Creatures with Hagrid, the friendly half-giant, and the protagonists interact with dragons, a unicorn, a three-headed dog, centaurs, a hippogriff, and other creatures from the bestiaries of legend (to which Rowling adds her own magical beasts, including Kneazles, Nifflers, Bowtruckles, Grindylows, Hinkypunks, and Blast Ended Skrewts, among others). Dumbledore recalls archetypal wizards such as Merlin and Gandalf, and other Hogwarts teachers bear the names of mythological figures like Professor Minerva MacGonagall and Sybill Trelawney, or are legendary beings like Remus Lupin, the benevolent werewolf and Defense Against the Dark Arts teacher.[20]

It is, however, qualitatively different to say that characters and creatures in the Potter novels are derived from, or evoke, mythology and legend, and to argue that the texts authored by Rowling are scriptures. This is because historically a distinction has been made between texts that have religious authority and texts that record events that have taken place (history) or that are imaginative constructions (fiction). Those texts that are revered as scriptures were usually composed in a bygone era when the ability to read or write was limited to a priestly elite, and there were very few written texts. Yet recently it has been recognized that when religion is approached naturalistically, the distinction between scriptures and fictions becomes blurred. Ander Klostergaard Petersen argues that, "there is much evidence supporting the claim that … [human] thinking is, in fact, narratively organised."[21] He concludes that the "epistemological stance" of the reader/ believer is what distinguishes whether a text is read and internalized as religious or as a diverting fiction.[22]

This perspective enables readers to view the *Harry Potter* novels as being of ultimate significance in certain circumstances. The context in which such a valuation becomes possible is the modern West, in which institutional Christianity has been in retreat since the 1960s at least, and "seekers" experiment with a variety of spiritual beliefs and practices, which are accepted or rejected according to whether they accord with personal orientation.[23] An increasing number are non-religious, yet interestingly many non-religious people are inclined to be interested in values and to view themselves as spiritual people.

Harry Potter and the Sacred Text

Harry Potter and the Sacred Text began as "a reading group … at the Humanist Hub, where Zoltan [was] an assistant chaplain."[24] Zoltan, ter Kuile and Nedelman explored various texts, including the respected literary novel *Jane Eyre* (1846) by Charlotte Bronte, before deciding on *Harry Potter* as the focus for their *lectio divina* exercise. Nedelman has expressed discomfort with critical hierarchies that rank certain types of literature above others, and Zoltan has affirmed that Rowling's series is "duly complicated"; that is, it invites complex analysis and offers interpretations that are open-ended and rich. All three understand America as a deeply religious country, and are committed to the need for spiritual nourishment even for those who identify as atheist, non-religious, or secular. The podcast series began in May 2016 and the established pattern has been to examine each book in sequence. The first episode, "Commitment: The Boy Who Lived (Book 1, Chapter 1)," set the scene, with ter Kuile and Zoltan saying, "We are going to ask ourselves, what if we take this seriously? What gifts is it going to give us if we love something, and we love it with rigour, and we love it with commitment?" The pattern of the podcasts is that a chapter is selected and a theme identified that will enable a reading that opens up questions of meaning: "love, and fear, death, and even resurrection," as ter Kuile observes. The discussions range across the presenters' family backgrounds, historical events, and the way that gifts and goodness are often concealed in the most unpromising people and situations.

Ter Kuile and Zoltan, both desirous of bringing the sacred into the lives of the non-religious, have stressed in interviews that they seek to persuade listeners that:

> If you love something, and it's complicated enough, we encourage you to practice treating something as sacred. What you're doing is practicing *loving* something, and practicing loving things can only be a good thing. You get better at loving, and it's a time in which you're having a positive emotional experience. We just think that is always good … if you pick these things with intention, and apply practice to it, a lot of things can end up being sacred texts.[25]

In order to bring out the sacred qualities of Rowling's novels, Ter Kuile and Zoltan situate their exegesis in a recognizable genealogy of scriptural interpretation that originated in the Benedictine monastic tradition, and they include practices that are explicitly religious, such as the selection of a character to bless at the close of each episode. This is intended

> to call out people's goodness that isn't entirely obvious. So you reread a positive quality on a character that we had negative associations with … or draw attention to secondary or tertiary characters, pointing out that just because somebody isn't a

primary character in your life doesn't mean they don't have an entire inner life ... the secondary purpose is that we're hoping, in some ways, that we're offering blessings to our listeners.[26]

Thus, in the first episode of the second season, the first chapter "The Worst Birthday" of *Harry Potter and the Chamber of Secrets* (1998) is discussed with reference to the theme of disappointment, and at the conclusion Zoltan blesses Hedwig, Harry's owl and faithful companion, whereas ter Kuile blesses Harry. In the fifteenth episode of the third season, the chapter "The Quidditch Final" from *Harry Potter and the Prisoner of Azkaban* (1999) is analyzed using the theme of pain, and Zoltan blesses Lavender and Parvati, whereas ter Kuile blesses Percy Weasley. The rationale for the blessings is explained, and ways that the blessing might impact the "real world" are also teased out.

To accompany the four seasons that presently exist each have a featured video that tackles some of these issues. Season One, *Harry Potter and the Sorcerer's Stone* (the title used in the United States), has a video entitled "Can You Forgive Petunia Dursley?" In two-and-a-half minutes listeners are invited to accept that the young Petunia Dursley loved her husband Vernon and her son Dudley, was conflicted about yet still loved her more attractive and talented sister Lily, and that her life was ruined by the responsibility of caring for her dead sister Lily's child, Harry. Ter Kuile asks gently, "What if you were the villain in someone else's story?" The video for the second season is "Who Is Your Ginny Weasley?" The question here is "Who are we not listening to?" This animation is even briefer, and suggests that the eleven-year-old Ginny's near-fatal "friendship" with Tom Riddle (who later becomes Lord Voldemort, Harry's mortal enemy) via the diary she was surreptitiously given by Lucius Malfoy, occurred because family and friends failed to listen to her and take her seriously, in particular with reference to her "crush" on Harry.[27]

The Season Three trailer, "Harry Potter: How To Be Brave" is barely two minutes in length, but asks a key question for the whole series, "What do you do with your good intentions?"[28] The tone of the novels is darker and more adult in *Harry Potter and the Prisoner of Azkaban* (1999), in which Harry meets his godfather Sirius Black (the "prisoner" of the title), learns of the horrors of Azkaban and the Dementors who guard it, and Ron's elderly rat Scabbers turns out to be the Animagus Peter Pettigrew, a Death Eater who betrayed James and Lily Potter and framed Sirius Black for these crimes.[29] The latest video, "In Harry Potter, Who's Your Knight in Shining Armor?" celebrates the aid given by Stanley Shunpike, the conductor of the Knight Bus, a minor character in the series who nevertheless assists Harry at crucial times.

It is especially interesting to see how the first two novels, which are shorter than later books and addressed to a readership that is Harry's particular age, eleven in his first year at Hogwarts, then twelve in his second, nevertheless repay the detailed and moral exegesis that ter Kuile and Zoltan apply to them. The podcast on Chapter 18 of *Harry Potter and the Chamber of Secrets*, "Dobby's Reward," is particularly poignant. The pitiable house-elf Dobby, abused by the Malfoy family to whom he is indentured, is a mysterious and somewhat frustrating figure in this novel, as the backstory of house elves has not yet unfolded. When he dies in *Harry Potter and the Deathly Hallows* he has become beloved of all, and many fans identify Dobby's death as one of the most moving and powerful episodes in the whole narrative. The theme of this episode is love, and fascinating parallels are teased out between Ginny Weasley who is returned to life after being "dead," and Moaning Myrtle, the melancholy ghost who haunts the first floor girl's toilet at Hogwarts, who like Ginny, fifty years earlier encountered the basilisk in the Chamber of Secrets, but died as a result having no loving friends to rescue her. The closeness of the Weasley family is discussed in detail, and the way that Harry contrives to get Lucius Malfoy to give Dobby a sock that sets him free is identified as a truly selfless act of love. This act is recalled, many volumes later, when Ron takes off his socks to place them on Dobby's feet before he, Harry, Hermione, and their friends bury the brave little elf who died saving Harry's life, setting him free to fight on, just as Harry had set Dobby free years ago.[30]

It is worth mentioning that this description of *Harry Potter and the Sacred Text* is flat and lifeless compared to the experience of listening to it. Each episode contains the competition between ter Kuile and Zoltan called "Thirty Second Recap," where each attempts to summarize the plot of the chapter in thirty seconds, and then listeners are asked to vote for the winner in the recap race. These recaps can be very funny, and Zoltan tends to have the edge. Each episode involves at least one presenter relating an anecdote about their personal life that illuminates the theme in question, and also a discussion of a spiritual practice. The practice in "Dobby's Reward" is *florilegia*, the anthologization of textual extracts by Christians in Late Antiquity and the Middle Ages in a book called a *florilegium* (collection of flowers). *Florilegia* are new texts created from "bits and pieces" of old texts.[31] Ter Kuile and Zoltan relate this practice to contemporary tweets and blogs that are comprised of quotations. At the end of each episode both presenters bless a character, and explain their reasoning for selecting that person. Listeners send in audio files that expand on various aspects of the podcasts, and there are teaser and wrap-up podcasts for each season. *Harry Potter and the Sacred Text* has proved popular; four months after its debut it was at "the number one spot on iTunes's religion and spirituality charts, ahead of best-selling author and televangelist Joel Osteen," and had approximately 100,000 listeners per week.[32]

Ter Kuile and Zoltan's family backgrounds in Christianity and Judaism impact the style and content of the podcasts significantly, and they explicitly address this in the "Frequently Asked Questions" section of the website:

Given that we are Jewish and Christian, and that is what we studied, we only want to teach and lead that which is authentically ours. We have hosted people of different faiths (Seja Patel and Marya Bangee, for example, have both been on the show speaking about Hinduism and Islam respectively) and we plan to have more guests representing different faiths as well. However, we will never lead in practices that are not of our traditions.[33]

Over two years, *Harry Potter and the Sacred Text* has become a richer and more complex fan phenomenon. The site now contains transcriptions of all the podcasts and a selection of "Spiritual Practice Resources," live events have been added to the program, and fifteen "real world" study groups have been established.[34] The resources list Jewish interpretive methods, including *havruta* (friendship), a method of reading the Talmud, and PaRDeS (a four-tier method of textual interpretation). A second subtitled has been added: "Reading Fiction Doesn't Help Us Escape the World, It Helps Us Live in It," and the live events have drawn sizeable audiences. Ter Kuile and Zoltan host weekly meetings in Harvard Square, and toured America gaining a rapturous reception in the summer of 2017.[35]

Harry Potter and the Sacred Text is a fan project, but it is one that is explicitly directed to the creation of meaning and the articulation of morals in the contemporary world; and it is significantly more adult, despite what some critics think, than most fan activities. Ter Kuile and Zoltan have never contacted Rowling, and their methods are those of the divinity school classroom. They explicitly state that they do not wish to start a religion; rather, "the goal of treating the text as sacred is that we can learn to treat each other as sacred. If you can learn to love these characters, to love Draco Malfoy, then you can learn to love the cousin you haven't spoken to for 30 years, then the refugee down the street."[36] Their target audiences include Potter fans, Millennials, and those who identify as "spiritual but not religious."

The Potter Fandom, Religion and Spirituality

Serious fans might be termed "devotees" as they manifest a deep, almost religious, attachment to their popular cultural text of choice. This devotion is expressed by going on "pilgrimage" to popular culture conventions (Leaky-Con, PotterVerse and PotterCon are all devoted to *Harry Potter*), and to film studios and sites that feature in the films.[37] Online surveys to determine which Hogwarts house fans would be assigned by the Sorting Hat abound. There are official *Harry Potter* stores selling wands, cauldrons, house scarves, collectables, and a multitude of Potter related merchandise. Fans engage in activities to insert themselves into the Potter story, such as cosplay at conventions and writing fanfiction. The importance of websites like Mugglenet and The Leaky Cauldron cannot be overestimated, in that they and other similar sites supplied fans with a near-inexhaustible amount of Potter-related information. A keen fan, Swanhilda (pseudonym), who discovered *Harry Potter* in 2000 aged eight, and was deeply involved in the online Potter world for nine years, recalls carrying

> wands in the pockets of our high school blazers, learning to play the film soundtrack on guitar and piano, posting YouTube videos of us re-enacting scenes from the films, dressed up in wizarding robes, and casting spells on J.K. Rowling from afar to include an Australian exchange student as a character so that we could audition for the films.[38]

Swanhilda graduated from Mugglenet to writing fanficton, in particular "Dramione" stories, that explored romance between Hermione and Draco Malfoy, in part due to dissatisfaction with the black and white moral code of the novels, in which Slytherins are almost uniformly evil. Writing about Hermione and Draco satisfied her desire to be a "Slytherin apologist" and also her identification with Hermione; "since I most closely associated myself with her as a character, I was writing her as a Mary Sue. My Hermione was always a magical version of myself." Swanhilda's passion for the Potterverse was definitely that of a serious fan, and it contributed to her identity as a high school student, but it waned as she matured; her love of Rowling's series is now a happy memory.[39]

Her experience contrasts with that of Mikhail (pseudonym) who also took refuge in *Harry Potter* as an adolescent, reading and re-reading the novels and discovering fansites between the publication of *Harry Potter and the Order of the Phoenix* (2003) and *Harry Potter and the Half-Blood Prince* (2005).[40] He found the adult sites, Harry Potter for Grown-Ups (HP4GU) and Snapedom, and was inspired by "theorizing and speculation … capable of creating from some scant references to past events in the text a workable history of the universe and a theory of magic."[41] He eagerly awaited *Harry Potter and the Half-Blood Prince* but suffered disillusionment after reading it, later appreciating the view of those fans who claimed that Rowling was a channel for the story, not an author or creator (a view that Tolkien religionists hold about Tolkien), and had got parts of the story wrong. Mikhail's account is framed in the language of religion:

> After I received the book I went into a sort of blackout state where I secluded myself and semi-ritually and with heightened awareness read through it in one breath. As I progressed in my reading I started to become … alarmed and after finishing I was in a state of shock and disillusionment. I'll spare you my specific reasons for disliking it, but suffice to say I deeply felt that it was a great betrayal of my trust in the author and for some time I withdrew from the fandom…. When *Deathly Hallows* was released it was almost an afterthought for me, my involvement in the series had me

emotionally drained and I read it with the expectation of disappointment in the story resolution, a disbelief that Rowling could adequately resolve the various story lines in such a way that it would do justice to the great amount of care and thought put into it by some parts of fandom.

Mikhail is suspicious of the idea that the Potterverse can be the basis of a system of values, and is inclined to the revisionist interpretation that understands it as a dystopia. He describes these interpretations, found on sites like the now-deleted LiveJournal of Swythyv and the webpage Red Hen, as an "anti-fandom," and notes their focus on the "(dubious) morality" and "plot inconsistencies" of Rowling's series. Swythyv and Joyce Odell of Red Hen contributed to John Granger's volume of fan-theories *Who Killed Albus Dumbledore? What Really Happened in Harry Potter and the Half-Blood Prince*.[42] Granger's own site, *Hogwarts Professor: Thoughts for Serious Readers*, is a forum for "academic" interpretations of the Potter novels to this day, and he is one of the strongest Christian supporters of Rowling's fictions. Mikhail, however, concludes "the idea that people would treat the book as a sacred text that could impart messages of moral value both intrigues and horrifies me, because I did not think that ultimately the series was worthy of this devotion."

This assessment is far from the position taken by the *Harry Potter and the Sacred Text* team. The "duly complicated" nature of the Potter novels that Vanessa Zoltan noted above is such that they can be read in community with an attitude of love as texts that can teach ultimate values and function as a guide to life. Yet, they can be denounced in community as false "scriptures" that fascinate and "convert" young fans to a version of "faith" that is cozy and fails to meet the complex ethical challenges of present-day life. Christine Emba, reporting on a *Harry Potter and the Sacred Text* gathering attended by five hundred in July 2017, notes that Millennials (young adults in the early twenty-first century) are more likely to have no religion than older generations, but still experience the need for meaning. Emba criticizes ter Kuile and Zoltan's invitation to "practice faith with something we already love: Harry Potter" as values drawn from children's novels are a retreat to a "childhood comfort zone."[43] Those fans who outgrew Rowling's novels experienced disillusionment in maturity, and lost faith in Rowling as an author and the series as a meaningful world to immerse themselves in; Emba's assessment of the goal of *Harry Potter and the Sacred Text* is that everyone should reach a point in life where they put away childish things.

Conclusion

Reading is an imaginative activity; readers create in their minds images of the worlds they encounter through immersion in books. Sociologist Colin

Campbell regards the Romantic movement of the eighteenth century as the seedbed of individualism. The emergence of the romantic novel and marriage for love, and the consumer revolution dependent on the Industrial Revolution, are all traceable to the eighteenth century, the era of the Enlightenment. Yet they represent the affective and imaginative "other" to the reason advocated by Enlightenment thinkers. Campbell argues that day-dreaming and fantasy are crucial for modern Western people; they permit individuals to imagine themselves in other worlds and with other lives.[44] When this historical perspective is combined with secularization and the decline in influence of institutional Christianity in the twentieth century, what emerges is a changed understanding of the sacred. In the past religion was uniquely regarded as the source of the sacred, and morality and values, ideas of virtue and vice, were all derived from Christian theology. In the contemporary West, religion has become only one possible source of the sacred, which now manifests in a multitude of phenomena previously regarded as profane, such as sport and music, film and television, novels and comic books.[45]

In the case of fictions in which magic, and the supernatural more broadly, plays a role like the *Harry Potter* novels, the imaginative exercise of realizing that world is extremely attractive, in that it is more exciting and exotic to participate in than the everyday world of realistic novels, which is familiar to the reader. Magic, and its religious counterpart miracle, are what István Czachesz calls "mental candies," sweets that are more cognitively pleasurable than the bread and butter of reality.[46] This is one reason why speculative fiction (fantasy and sci-fi) is the genre that most often inspires religious and spiritual groups. The otherworlds in such novels have similar ontological status as heaven and hell in traditional religions; that is, they are places of the imagination that are accessed via reading.[47] Despite Rowling's professed Christianity, much of the power of the *Harry Potter* series lies in the universal conflict between good and evil, and the appeal of a hero who is small and insignificant, yet able to find reserves of courage, resilience and strength when necessary.

It is true that Harry has qualities that align him with Jesus Christ, including miraculous birth and resurrection from the dead, but as Signe Cohen has observed, he is a "human being with very human flaws."[48] For the non-religious this humanity is a strength, not a weakness, and in *Harry Potter and the Sacred Text*, which is explicitly addressed to the non-religious, ter Kuile and Zoltan extract moral lessons, meaning and comfort from the tale of the boy wizard who battled through to victory against a powerful and terrifying adversary, Lord Voldemort. Near the end of *Harry Potter and the Chamber of Secrets*, Harry asks Dumbledore what separates him from Tom Riddle, whose life choices led him to become Voldemort. Dumbledore acknowledges that there are similarities between the two (they both have one

Muggle and one Wizard parent, their wands are twins, their magical talents are comparable, and there are other connections that emerge only in later novels) but he reassures Harry that, "It is our choices, Harry, that show what we truly are, far more than our abilities."[49] Fans, too, choose to direct their devotion, and fandom communities increase the knowledge of, and practices relating to, the beloved character or series, contributing to its fame and social importance.

Serious fans have extraordinary psychological relationships with *Harry Potter* and other characters in Rowling's novels, and Harry's journey from outsider to hero makes him a role model; it is more difficult to establish that fans adopt values and behaviors from the novels, however. Yet that is precisely what ter Kuile, Zoltan, and Nedelman intend to happen with listeners to *Harry Potter and the Sacred Text*. Their project is more adult and less "fanlike" than many other online sites devoted to *Harry Potter*, and their techniques are conservative. Thus, they adopt a devotional reading strategy, a respectful stance toward the text, and urge a moral interpretation of it. Their aim is that the reader will be transformed by the reading. This is arguably a spiritual aim, perhaps even a religious aim, and it urges the consideration of the *Harry Potter* series of novels as a legitimate entry into the experience of the sacred.

NOTES

1. Paul Tillich, *Theology of Culture* (Oxford: Oxford University Press, 1959), 40, 42.

2. Tillich, *Theology of Culture*, 40.

3. Richard Shusterman, "Art and Religion," *The Journal of Aesthetic Education* 42, no. 3 (2008): 1–18.

4. Markus Altena Davidsen, "The Religious Affordances of Fiction: A Semiotic Approach, *Religion* 46, no. 4 (2016): 521–549.

5. Jesse Walker, "Inside the Spiritual Jacuzzi: What JewBus, Unitarian Pagans, and the Hot Tub Mystery Religion tell us about traditional faiths," *Reason* (2003): 32–40.

6. Henry Jenkins, "'Cultural Acupuncture': Fan Activism and the Harry Potter Alliance," in *Popular Media Cultures: Fans, Audiences and Paratexts*, ed. Lincoln Geraghty (London: Palgrave Macmillan, 2014), 206–229.

7. See Michael Jindra, "*Star Trek* Fandom as a Religious Phenomenon," *Sociology of Religion* 55, no. 1 (1994), 27–51; and Jennifer E. Porter, "Pilgrimage and the IDIC Ethic: Exploring *Star Trek* Convention Attendance as Pilgrimage," in *Intersecting Journeys: The Anthropology of Pilgrimage and Tourism*, eds. Ellen Badone and Sharon R. Roseman (Urbana and Chicago: University of Illinois Press, 2004), 160–179.

8. This is a contentious claim; Zoe Alderton has claimed that a short-lived phenomenon involving three women who believed they were in mystical sexual relationship with Severus Snape from the Potter novels constituted a religion, whereas I would argue that it was an example of a personal spirituality that failed to establish either community or institutions such as are required for a religion. See Alderton, "'Snapewives' and 'Snapeism': A Fiction-Based Religion Within the Harry Potter Fandom," *Religions* 5 (2014): 219–67.

9. Carole M. Cusack, *Invented Religions: Imagination, Fiction and Faith* (Farnham and Burlington, VT: Ashgate, 2010), 75.

10. Michelle Coffey, "This is how much money Daniel Radcliffe's 'Harry Potter' films have grossed," *Market Watch*, November 13 (2015), http://www.marketwatch.com/story/this-is-how-much-money-daniel-radcliffes-harry-potter-films-have-grossed-2015-11-13.

11. Laura Feldt, "Contemporary Fantasy Fiction and Representations of Religion: Play-

ing with Reality, Myth and Magic in *His Dark Materials* and *Harry Potter," Religion* 46, no. 4 (2016): 570.

12. David R. Olson, *The World on Paper: Conceptual and Cognitive Implications of Writing and Reading* (Cambridge: Cambridge University Press, 1994), 91–114.

13. Elizabeth D. Schafer, *Exploring Harry Potter* (London: Ebury Press, 2000), 14.

14. Adam Possamai, *Religion and Popular Culture: A Hyperreal Testament* (Brussels: Peter Lang, 2005), 147–53.

15. Jonathan Petre, "J.K. Rowling: 'Christianity Inspired Harry Potter,'" *The Telegraph*, October 20 (2007), https://www.telegraph.co.uk/culture/books/fictionreviews/3668658/J-K-Rowling-Christianity-inspired-Harry-Potter.html.

16. Nicholas Barber, "Film Review: Is Fantastic Beasts a Rowling Triumph?," *BBC Culture*, November 17 (2016), http://www.bbc.com/culture/story/20161117-film-review-is-fantastic-beasts-a-rowling-triumph.

17. This five-hour theatrical production has received positive reviews, although the casting of Noma Dumezweni, a black actress, as Hermione has been controversial. Susannah Clapp, "*Harry Potter and the Cursed Child* Review—The Spell-Binding Is Utterly Theatrical," *The Observer*, July 31 (2016), https://www.theguardian.com/stage/2016/jul/31/harry-potter-and-the-cursed-child-review-palace-theatre.

18. Markus Altena Davidsen, "Fiction and Religion: How Narratives About the Supernatural Inspire Religious Belief," *Religion* 46, no. 4 (2016): 492.

19. J'annine Jobling, *Fantastic Spiritualities: Monsters, Heroes and the Contemporary Religious Imagination* (London and New York: T&T Clark, 2010), 33–35.

20. Signe Cohen, "A Postmodern Wizard: The Religious Bricolage of the Harry Potter Series," *The Journal of Religion and Popular Culture* 28, no. 1 (2016): 54–66.

21. Anders Klostergaard Petersen, "The Difference Between Religious Narratives and Fictional Literature: A Matter of Degree Only," *Religion* 46, no. 4 (2016): 500–20.

22. Petersen, "The Difference Between Religious Narratives and Fictional Literature: A Matter of Degree Only," 518.

23. Carole M. Cusack, "Play, Narrative and the Creation of Religion: Extending the Theoretical Base of 'Invented Religions,'" *Culture and Religion: An Interdisciplinary Journal* 14, no. 4 (2013): 371.

24. John Michael Baglione, "The Sacred in Harry Potter," *Harvard Gazette*, September 14 (2016), http://news.harvard.edu/gazette/story/2016/09/the-sacred-in-harry-potter/.

25. Sara Boboltz, "Why Two Harvard Academics Talk About 'Harry Potter' Like It's the Bible," *The Huffington Post*, August 27 (2016), http://www.huffingtonpost.com.au/entry/why-two-harvard-divinity-experts-talk-about-harry-potter-as-if-it-were-the-bible_us_57bf3bdae4b02673444f1511.

26. Boboltz, "Why Two Harvard Academics Talk About 'Harry Potter' Like It's the Bible."

27. J.K. Rowling, *Harry Potter and the Chamber of Secrets* (London: Bloomsbury, 1998), 31.

28. ter Kuile, Caspar and Vanessa Zoltan (with Ariana Nedelman), *Harry Potter and the Sacred Text* (2016–2018), http://www.harrypottersacredtext.com.

29. J.K. Rowling, *Harry Potter and the Prisoner of Azkaban* (London: Bloomsbury, 1999).

30. J.K. Rowling, *Harry Potter and the Deathly Hallows* (London: Bloomsbury, 2007), 388.

31. Henry Chadwick, "Florilegium." *Reallexikon fur Antike und Christentum* 7 (1950): 1131–59.

32. Cristela Guerra, "Could 'Harry Potter' Give Rise to a New Religion?," *The Boston Globe*, September 22 (2016), https://www.bostonglobe.com/lifestyle/2016/09/22/could-harry-potter-give-rise-new-religion/WIAWQ431SNS2E8KFNlOaiP/story.html.

33. ter Kuile and Zoltan (with Ariana Nedelman), "Frequently Asked Questions," *Harry Potter and the Sacred Text.*

34. ter Kuile and Zoltan (with Ariana Nedelman), "Local HPST Groups! Start One or Join One!" *Harry Potter and the Sacred Text.*

35. Julie Zauzmer and Michelle Boorstein, "Hundreds pack DC Hall to discuss podcast

exploring Harry Potter as a sacred text," *The Washington Post*, July 19 (2017), https://www.washingtonpost.com/news/acts-of-faith/wp/2017/07/19/harry-potter-and-the-sacred-text-podcast-draws-non-believers-who-find-meaning-in-magical-fiction/?utm_term=.fee4cfd 24482.

36. Zauzmer and Boorstein, "Hundreds pack DC Hall to discuss podcast exploring Harry Potter as a sacred text."

37. Christina Lee, "'Have Magic, Will Travel': Tourism and Harry Potter's United (Magical) Kingdom," *Tourism Studies* 12, no. 1 (2012), 56–59.

38. Personal correspondence with Swanhilda (pseudonym) who discovered Harry Potter in 2000, aged eight, and was deeply involved in the online Potter world for nine years.

39. This essay was first given as a lecture at Radboud University in Nijmegen, the Netherlands on December 1, 2016. Mikhail (pseudonym) was in the audience and sent me a lengthy e-mail detailing his experiences with *Harry Potter*. I later gave a shorter presentation at the Studies in Religion research seminar at University of Sydney on March 28, 2017, which elicited a similar e-mail from Swanhilda.

40. J.K. Rowling, *Harry Potter and the Order of the Phoenix* (London: Bloomsbury, 2005) and J.K. Rowling, *Harry Potter and the Half-Blood Prince* (London: Bloomsbury, 2005).

41. Personal correspondence with Mikhail who discovered Harry Potter in adolescence, and was deeply involved in the online fandom until reading *Harry Potter and the Half-Blood Prince* (2005), after which he became disillusioned.

42. John Granger, ed., *Who Killed Albus Dumbledore? What Really Happened in Harry Potter and the Half-Blood Prince: Six Expert Harry Potter Detectives Examine the Evidence* (Cheshire, CT: Zossima Press, 2006).

43. Christine Emba, "Millennials are turning to Harry Potter for meaning. That's a mistake," *The Washington Post.* July 24 (2017), https://www.washingtonpost.com/opinions/millennials-are-turning-to-harry-potter-for-meaning-thats-a-mistake/2017/07/24/ca0a7f42-7097-11e7-9eac-d56bd5568db8_story.html?utm_term=.a3934ad3a4e5 (accessed May 9, 2018).

44. Colin Campbell, *The Romantic Ethic and the Spirit of Modern Consumerism* (York: Alcuin Academics, 2005 [1987]), 95.

45. Cusack, *Invented Religions: Imagination, Fiction and Faith*, 19.

46. István Czachesz, "How to Read Miracle Stories with Cognitive Theory: On Harry Potter, Magic, and Miracle," in *Hermeneutik der frühchristlichen Wundererzählungen: Geschichtliche, literarische und rezeptionsorientierte Perspektiven* ed. Bernd Kollmann and Ruben Zimmermann (Tübingen: Mohr Siebeck, 2014), 545.

47. Anthropologist Maurice Bloch says that the "capacity to imagine other worlds" is a key human evolutionary adaptation, which contributes to the development of religions. See Bloch, "Why Religion Is Nothing Special but Is Central," *Philosophical Transactions of the Royal Society B* 363 (2008): 2055–2061.

48. Cohen, "A Postmodern Wizard: The Religious Bricolage of the Harry Potter Series," 60.

49. J.K. Rowling, *Harry Potter and the Chamber of Secrets* (London: Bloomsbury, 1998), 245.

BIBLIOGRAPHY

Alderton, Zoe. "'Snapewives' and 'Snapeism': A Fiction-Based Religion Within the Harry Potter Fandom." *Religions* 5 (2014): 219–67.

Baglione, John Michael. "The Sacred in Harry Potter." *Harvard Gazette* (September 14, 2016). http://news.harvard.edu/gazette/story/2016/09/the-sacred-in-harry-potter/ (accessed May 9, 2018).

Barber, Nicholas. "Film Review: Is *Fantastic Beasts* a Rowling Triumph?" *BBC Culture* (November 17, 2016). http://www.bbc.com/culture/story/20161117-film-review-is-fantastic-beasts-a-rowling-triumph (accessed May 9, 2018).

Boboltz, Sara. "Why Two Harvard Academics Talk About 'Harry Potter' Like It's the Bible." *The Huffington Post* (August 27, 2016), http://www.huffingtonpost.com.au/entry/why-two-harvard-divinity-experts-talk-about-harry-potter-as-if-it-were-the-bible_us_57bf3bdae4b02673444f1511 (accessed May 9, 2018).

Campbell, Colin. *The Romantic Ethic and the Spirit of Modern Consumerism.* York: Alcuin Academics, 2005 [1987].

Chadwick, Henry. "Florilegium." *Reallexikon fur Antike und Christentum* 7 (1950): 1131–59.

Clapp, Susannah. "*Harry Potter and the Cursed Child* Review—The Spell-Binding Iis Utterly Theatrical." *The Observer* (July 31, 2016). https://www.theguardian.com/stage/2016/jul/31/harry-potter-and-the-cursed-child-review-palace-theatre (accessed May 9, 2018).

Coffey, Michelle. "This is how much money Daniel Radcliffe's 'Harry Potter' films have grossed." *Market Watch* (November 13, 2015). http://www.marketwatch.com/story/this-is-how-much-money-daniel-radcliffes-harry-potter-films-have-grossed-2015-11-13 (accessed May 9, 2018).

Cohen, Signe. "A Postmodern Wizard: The Religious Bricolage of the Harry Potter Series." *The Journal of Religion and Popular Culture* 28, no. 1 (2016): 54–66.

Cusack, Carole M. *Invented Religions: Imagination, Fiction and Faith.* Farnham and Burlington, VT: Ashgate, 2010.

Cusack, Carole M. "Play, Narrative and the Creation of Religion: Extending the Theoretical Base of 'Invented Religions.'" *Culture and Religion: An Interdisciplinary Journal* 14, no. 4 (2013): 363–77.

Czachesz, István. "How to Read Miracle Stories with Cognitive Theory: On *Harry Potter,* Magic, and Miracle." In *Hermeneutik der frühchristlichen Wundererzählungen: Geschichtliche, literarische und rezeptionsorientierte Perspektiven,* edited by Bernd Kollmann and Ruben Zimmermann, 391–404. Tübingen: Mohr Siebeck, 2014.

Davidsen, Markus Altena. "Fiction and Religion: How Narratives About the Supernatural Inspire Religious Belief." *Religion* 46, no. 4 (2016): 489–99.

_____. "The Religious Affordances of Fiction: A Semiotic Approach." *Religion* 46, no. 4 (2016): 521–549.

Emba, Christine. "Millennials are turning to Harry Potter for meaning. That's a mistake." *The Washington Post* (July 24, 201). https://www.washingtonpost.com/opinions/millennials-are-turning-to-harry-potter-for-meaning-thats-a-mistake/2017/07/24/ca0a7f42-7097-11e7-9eac-d56bd5568db8_story.html?utm_term=.a3934ad3a4e5 (accessed May 9, 2018).

Feldt, Laura. "Contemporary Fantasy Fiction and Representations of Religion: Playing with Reality, Myth and Magic in *His Dark Materials* and *Harry Potter.*" *Religion* 46, no. 4 (2016): 550–74.

Granger, John. *Who Killed Albus Dumbledore? What Really Happened in Harry Potter and the Half-Blood Prince: Six Expert Harry Potter Detectives Examine the Evidence* (Cheshire, CT: Zossima Press, 2006).

Guerra, Cristela. "Could 'Harry Potter' Give Rise to a New Religion?" *The Boston Globe* (September 22, 2016). https://www.bostonglobe.com/lifestyle/2016/09/22/could-harry-potter-give-rise-new-religion/WIAWQ43lSNS2E8KFNlOaiP/story.html (accessed May 9, 2018).

Jenkins, Henry. "'Cultural Acupuncture': Fan Activism and the Harry Potter Alliance." In *Popular Media Cultures: Fans, Audiences and Paratexts,* ed. Lincoln Geraghty, 206–229. London: Palgrave Macmillan, 2014.

Jindra, Michael. "*Star Trek* Fandom as a Religious Phenomenon." *Sociology of Religion* 55, no. 1 (1994): 27–51.

Jobling, J'annine. *Fantastic Spiritualities: Monsters, Heroes and the Contemporary Religious Imagination.* London and New York: T&T Clark, 2010.

Lee, Christina. "'Have Magic, Will Travel': Tourism and Harry Potter's United (Magical) Kingdom." *Tourism Studies* 12, no. 1 (2012): 52–69.

Olson, David R. *The World on Paper: Conceptual and Cognitive Implications of Writing and Reading.* Cambridge: Cambridge University Press, 1994.

Petersen, Anders Klostergaard. "The Difference Between Religious Narratives and Fictional Literature: A Matter of Degree Only." *Religion* 46, no. 4 (2016): 500–20.

Petre, Jonathan. "J.K. Rowling: 'Christianity Inspired Harry Potter.'" *The Telegraph* (October 20, 2007). https://www.telegraph.co.uk/culture/books/fictionreviews/3668658/J-K-Rowling-Christianity-inspired-Harry-Potter.html (accessed May 9, 2018).

Porter, Jennifer E. "Pilgrimage and the IDIC Ethic: Exploring *Star Trek* Convention Attendance as Pilgrimage." In *Intersecting Journeys: The Anthropology of Pilgrimage and Tourism*, edited by Ellen Badone and Sharon R. Roseman, 160–179. Urbana and Chicago: University of Illinois Press, 2004.

Possamai, Adam. *Religion and Popular Culture: A Hyperreal Testament*. Brussels: Peter Lang, 2005.

Rowling, J.K. *Harry Potter and the Philosopher's Stone*. London: Bloomsbury, 1997.

_____. *Harry Potter and the Chamber of Secrets*. London: Bloomsbury, 1998.

_____. *Harry Potter and the Prisoner of Azkaban*. London: Bloomsbury, 1999.

_____. *Harry Potter and the Goblet of Fire*. London: Bloomsbury, 2000.

_____. *Harry Potter and the Order of the Phoenix*. London: Bloomsbury, 2003.

_____. *Harry Potter and the Half-Blood Prince*. London: Bloomsbury, 2005.

_____. *Harry Potter and the Deathly Hallows*. London: Bloomsbury, 2007.

Schafer, Elizabeth D. *Exploring Harry Potter*. London: Ebury, 2000.

Shusterman, Richard. "Art and Religion." *The Journal of Aesthetic Education* 42, no. 3 (2008): 1–18.

ter Kuile, Caspar, and Vanessa Zoltan (with Ariana Nedelman). *Harry Potter and the Sacred Text: Reading Something We Love as If It Were Sacred* (2016–2017). http://www.harry pottersacredtext.com (accessed May 9, 2018).

Tillich, Paul. *Theology of Culture*. Oxford: Oxford University Press, 1959.

Walker, Jesse. "Inside the Spiritual Jacuzzi: What JewBus, Unitarian Pagans, and the Hot Tub Mystery Religion tell us about traditional faiths." *Reason* (2003): 32–40.

Zauzmer, Julie, and Michelle Boorstein. "Hundreds pack DC Hall to discuss podcast exploring Harry Potter as a sacred text." *The Washington Post* (July 19, 2017). https://www.wash ingtonpost.com/news/acts-of-faith/wp/2017/07/19/harry-potter-and-the-sacred-text-podcast-draws-non-believers-who-find-meaning-in-magical-fiction/?utm_term=.fee4 cfd24482 (accessed May 9, 2018).

Doctrine and Fanon

George Lindbeck, Han's Gun and Sherlock's Gay Wedding

Rhiannon Grant

Introduction

This essay argues that our understanding of the interaction between fans and their canons—the core texts which are the focus of their fandom— is enhanced by a comparison with the interaction between religious believers in scripturally-focussed traditions and their canons.[1] In order to structure this comparison (there are many points of comparison and to explore them all in a single essay is impossible), I leverage George Lindbeck's cultural-linguistic approach to doctrine, as it provides a way of considering the ongoing and developing relationship between a religious tradition, and its core texts and claims, rather than regarding either of them as static. This is a better fit for the fandoms considered here, which, unlike some religious groups, make no claim to have always held the same views. In particular, the Lindbeckian comparison between religion and language, and the idea that to learn to "speak Christian" is to be absorbed into the world of Christian narrative (that is, into the biblical text or its descendants), are useful analytical tools for understanding a range of different groups of fans.

This essay develops in three interlocking stages. First, Lindbeck's work will be introduced and related to religious examples for clarity. Second, two fandoms, those attached to the *Star Wars* film franchise (1977–) and the figure of Sherlock Holmes, most notably in the BBC series *Sherlock* (2010–), will be introduced, and considered carefully through the Lindbeckian lens I have developed.[2] Finally, I bring the question around full circle, testing the fruitfulness of the comparison by asking what insights the development of fandom, especially online, might bring to our understanding of religion; especially the "fictionalist" position of Don Cupitt and others.[3]

Lindbeck: Religion, Language and Community

In Lindbeck's classic work *The Nature of Doctrine*, he develops the "cultural-linguistic" approach to religion, with particular attention to Christianity. In contrast to the cognitive-propositional, which treats religion as a series of belief claims to be accepted or rejected, and the experiential-expressivist, which regards religious acts (including speech) as expressions of feeling with no propositional content, Lindbeck treats religion as analogous to language or culture.[4] Doctrine can develop, as a culture changes over time, without ceasing to be the same culture. Doctrine is also heavily context-dependent; Lindbeck draws on Wittgenstein's ideas about the nature of language and treats doctrine as something that needs to be understood within the community that develops and uses it. Lindbeck sees doctrine as closely related to scripture, and within the Christian communities in which he is mainly interested, thinks that people who are "competent speakers" of Christianity will draw their core vocabulary and grammar from biblical sources.[5]

The idea that some individuals within a community are more fluent, and therefore more authoritative about what is acceptable and what is not, is one of the most useful products of the analogy between religion and language. In religion this might mean, for example, that ordinary believers who are steeped in the faith and "think, feel, act, and dream"[6] in it are better able to judge whether a new formulation of their faith—whether a fresh theological idea or a trendy advertising campaign—is a true representation of their tradition than someone who, for example, analyzes it to see whether it contains the same propositional content (on the cognitive-propositional model) or asks whether it expresses the same emotions (on the experiential-expressivist model).[7] The answers this produces may not be obviously logical, and the language comparison makes it clear that such believers can be following rules that are detectable but rarely explicit. (Readers who doubt this are invited to consider the ordering of adjectives in English. Almost all native speakers agree that a fat, old, yellow cat is not under any circumstances a yellow, fat, old cat, but almost none of them—without specific training in linguistics and/or the use of Google—can explain *why* that should be the case.) The idea that a fluent speaker of a language or a religion—or, I will argue, a fannish canon—may have a sense of what is "grammatical" or "correct" which goes beyond logic and emotion is one of the central ideas I take from Lindbeck's work and apply in my analysis of fans and their relationships to canon.

A second central idea is that a language, like a doctrine, needs to be understood within its community context. To explore this idea I will turn briefly to the source of some of Lindbeck's ideas: the later work of Ludwig Wittgenstein. Throughout his life, Wittgenstein was fascinated by problems of language and communication, and in his later work he put forward the idea that language can only be understood by observing it in its "native habitat," so to speak: as Wittgenstein said, "the meaning of a word is its use in the language."[8] Although Wittgenstein's work is enigmatic in some ways, I follow Lindbeck in taking his point here to be: words and other signs (which are just sounds, gestures or symbols, without intrinsic value) acquire meaning only when they are used; and use is always contextual, by a particular person, in a particular place and time, drawing on the prior experiences of speaker and hearer. In short, we always communicate within a community and our language only has meaning within that framework of established but changeable patterns of use.

Thirdly, one further concept that arises from Lindbeck's work must be introduced. This is the idea, used by other Christian thinkers, especially in the narrative theology tradition, that to enter the Christian worldview and linguistic community is also to be drawn in to the story-world of the Bible: to have one's spiritual grammar and vocabulary inflected and influenced, if not completely formed, by biblical sources. In Lindbeck's view, it is the development of "an intimate and imaginatively vivid familiarity with the world of biblical narrative" which makes it "possible to experience the whole of life in religious terms."[9] This idea is not so easy to transfer across all religions. Something similar can probably be said about the other Abrahamic monotheisms, Judaism and Islam, but there are other traditions, such as Chinese folk religion, which do not have a single written scripture, and where the linguistic world is created entirely by the accumulation of material over time.[10] Since Christianity also has the accumulation of tradition, even if some Protestant groups disavow portions of it, a comparison between them is possible, but for the purposes of this essay, it will be helpful to focus on Christianity as Lindbeck's key example which, because of its particular relationship to scripture, turns out to be especially comparable to the fandom cases discussed herein.

Star Wars: *"Han Shot First" and Other Doctrinal Claims*

I own a t-shirt which says, in the same font as the *Star Wars* opening scrolls, HAN SHOT FIRST, a reference to a notoriously controversial edit made to a scene from the first *Star Wars* film, *Episode IV: A New Hope*.[11] I am also a Quaker in the so-called liberal tradition, and as such, I do not often make creedal or other doctrinal statements.[12] It is possible that this t-shirt is the closest I get.

I will now explore some attitudes to canon among *Star Wars* fans, and two approaches to canon in particular: first, the perspective on the nature of canon which makes my t-shirt both true (from a certain point of view) and non-trivial; and second, the perspective of spiritually-motivated viewers who take the canon of *Star Wars* as religious inspiration, that is, those who consider themselves to be following the Jedi path. In choosing these two perspectives I have focused on positions that are philosophically and theologically interesting. If one examined majority views among committed fans, or the perspectives of casual fans, or views officially supported by the copyright holders, very different approaches to canon would unfold. Here, all I require is that some fans who hold these views exist, and that these views are comparable to the Lindbeckian view of religion outlined above.

Did Han shoot first? This depends on which print of the film originally released as *Star Wars*, and now known as *Star Wars Episode IV: A New Hope*, the viewer watches. In the initial version, as shown in cinemas in 1977, there is a scene in which Han Solo, not yet associated with the "good guys," is challenged by a former business partner, Greedo. In the words of fan commentator James T, Han "takes advantage of Greedo's monologuing by shooting him, while Greedo bangs on about how he's going to kill him."[13] However, in the "Special Editions" produced in 1997, before the release of *Episode I: The Phantom Menace*, this scene is re-cut. Greedo now shoots first, as Ben Kirby writes for *Empire Online*: "inexplicably missing at point blank range, and allowing Han to return fire in "self-defence."[14]

To answer the question, then, the viewer must take a position on which of these is "true," or accepted as canon. There is no convenient, or even widely-discussed but far-fetched, in-universe way of accepting both as somehow having happened (unlike the problem about the location of Watson's war wound and many other examples in the Holmes canon discussed in the next section). In response to a change by the creator, the fan must either accept that George Lucas was somehow "wrong the first time," and showed Han shooting first even though that was not "true," or reject this, and assert that Han did shoot first, and the later version is a "cover up" which disguises what viewers of the initial film took to be Han's "true nature." The qualifying "scare quotes" in this sentence reveal that the nature of the "truth" involved here is a tricky one. The truth in plain terms is that: there just are two versions of the scene, created at different stages in the long process of the making of the *Star Wars* film series.

That truth, however, cannot satisfy the fan, who—in order to understand the story as a narrative whole—needs to know what "really" happened. Fans in this position do not for a moment think that Han, or Greedo, or their meeting is anything but fictional: but they do understand that a fiction, in order to be aesthetically and emotionally complete, needs to be coherent. These fans are comparable to people seeking to understand a religion using Lindbeck's cultural-linguistic model: they suspend judgment on whether the items described by the story are "real" and ask whether the story as a whole makes sense, hangs together, follows the rules of its internal grammar. In the case of Han and Greedo, many fans review the evidence and conclude that in "truth," Han must have shot first. There are two grammatical "rules" of the *Star Wars* universe that support this. Firstly, Han's character development, from amoral smuggler to heroic rebel, requires the demonstration of his lack of heroism at the early point in the story when the scene with Greedo takes place. Secondly, for Greedo to be a credible threat, and worth shooting at all, he has to be able to injure Han; which, if he misses at point-blank range as shown in the later versions, he is not.

This application of narrative logic in order to determine which of many possibilities is true often echoes Christian approaches to scripture. Choosing between original and remastered prints of *A New Hope* is relatively simple compared to the issues involved in the consideration of the four gospels, but both ordinary Bible readers and scholars of the New Testament ask similar questions, either questions from outside the canon like "Which version was produced first?" or "in universe" questions which take with them the assumptions of the story-world, like "Is this how this person would usually act?" More subtly, the need to ask the in-universe question is an example of the way that compelling narratives draw us into their worlds, so that not only can we ask questions which only make sense if we accept the premises of the universe within which the problem is set, but we feel we have to ask these questions and to assert their answers such that those who do not agree with us—or even worse, show a lack of interest in the question—are excluded from our communities. This is not always a clear demarcation within *Star Wars* fandom (although if I wore my t-shirt to a convention, for example, I would be placing myself on one side of a debate), but I will return to the question when I consider the Sherlock Holmes canons, where those who refuse to "play the Great Game" (that is, participate in using Holmes' methods to explore the Holmesian canon, usually within a framework where Conan Doyle is regarded as a "literary agent" and Holmes and Watson are assumed to have existed) are often not regarded as fans at all.

In Lindbeck's vision of Christians being absorbed into the narrative of the Bible, this not only causes them to take positions on questions which can only be asked within the framework of the story (such as, "Did Jesus give that sermon on a mount or on a plain?"), but also to change their behavior. It could be argued that many stories have this effect to some extent, and there are obviously changes of behavior which the owners of the *Star Wars* narrative set out to promote (encouraging people to buy cinema tickets, themed merchandise, DVD and Blu-ray box sets, and so on being the most prominent of those). However, there are also fans who have decided to change their behavior in other ways as a result of their absorption into the *Star Wars* universe, and two examples of this which have attracted some publicity are considered here.

The first appears minor at first glance. In 2001, the British government ran a regular census, but they included a new question about religion. In response, almost 0.8 percent of the total population said that they were a "Jedi" or a "Jedi Knight."[15] There is little evidence that any of them changed their life as a result of identifying as Jedi except in this one way: they wrote it on their census form. This was repeated in census results from a number of other countries, with 53,000 people in New Zealand and 70,000 in Australia listing themselves as Jedi in the religious categories of their 2001 forms. It is a joke, on one level; however, I want to suggest that the very existence of this joke, and its scale, reveals something about the relationship the British population to the *Star Wars* canon and to religion. Firstly, when British respondents were asked this question they had a desire to joke, either just for fun, to annoy people, or in response to a hoax campaign that claimed that a sufficient number of responses would require legal recognition of Jedi as a real religion. The game-playing desire, probably present in all humans and most animals, is strong in this population. Secondly, and more significantly for this essay, the answer Jedi was readily available to large numbers of people as a possible answer. They knew that Jediism was a fictional religion, but they had coded it as a case of a religion (as opposed to, for example, a military force or a political position). Beth Singler has argued that "invented religions" like Jediism create tradition and thus legitimize themselves through the use of social media—supported, I would add, by the availability of the term, which in turn is created by the popularity and accessibility of the original fictional source.[16] In order to be able to make this joke, census respondents have to be in, and know that others will be in, at least a minimal relationship to the *Star Wars* canon.

It seems that a small number of people take their adoption of Jediism as a religion more seriously. This does not mean that it is recognized as such, nor—and this is where it becomes interesting for my purposes—that these people are in an especially close relationship to the *Star Wars* text. As of December 2016, the Charity Commission in Britain does not treat it as a religion for tax purposes,[17] and in interviews with the BBC, leading members of online Jedi orders have suggested that not only has the faith adopted aspects of other religions, but that Jediism as now practiced reaches beyond the *Star Wars* script. On the one hand, Jedi Michael Kitchen says he believes in "the

Force," as mentioned in the films, which "might be an energy field or it might be relationship between objects and people in the universe," but on the other hand says that it is not really about the films. "We don't take inspiration from *Star Wars* but from what George Lucas was inspired by in creating *Star Wars*— a range of much older spiritualist beliefs."[18]

The name is still based on the *Star Wars* canon, but perhaps these Jedi are in a similar position to some post–Christian religious seekers: having explored one tradition, they find a need to move on and explore other traditions while also retaining what was most useful in their home tradition. For the Jedi, this is the name, a rallying cry around which people who are intrigued by the idea—their imaginations fired by the films and their curiosity aroused by the mixture of real life and fiction—can gather, forming a community, while the content of the faith needs to be supplemented from other sources. For Christians such as Don Cupitt, to whose fictionalist views about religion I will return, there is often a move to reject propositional content (especially claims generally regarded as incompatible with the current scientific understanding of our world, such as belief in miracles), while retaining moral or aesthetic content.

In this section, three possible relationships to the *Star Wars* canon were outlined, each of which can be related to Lindbeck's understandings of the nature of religion. The fan is drawn into the text, needing to hold opinions on in-universe questions, as the Christian is drawn into the narrative world of scripture. The census–Jedi uses the availability of Jedi as a possible, although fictional, religious category in order to make a joke, thereby incidentally demonstrating the extent to which the term "Jedi" has entered the vocabulary of the population. This might be compared to the way that some Christian terms are available in popular culture for jokes and references: Slimming World, a UK-based dieting club, can refer to some foods as "syns" and everyone knows that these are the foods which have been declared "bad" without necessarily understanding the theological weight that this comparison carries. In Lindbeckian terms, these words and ideas are being played with by speakers who might not be at all fluent in the "languages" from which they came, like English speakers using the Japanese word *ninja* and imposing their own rules of pluralisation onto it.

Finally, the practitioners of Jediism enter the thought-world of the Jedi only to find that they need to reach beyond the *Star Wars* canon to sources that inspired George Lucas and are available to anyone interested in comparative religions. Like the fans, they have been drawn into the world but, seeking actual spiritual inspiration rather than merely in-universe answers, they are also drawn out again to explore the sources of the film's ideas. I compare this to the situation of the post–Christian believer who has found Christianity unsatisfactory but is still a spiritual seeker. Particularly interesting from a

Lindbeckian point of view is the way that this approach draws on several "vocabularies" and tries to bring them together into a single "grammar," in the Jedi case, incorporating various understandings of impersonal powers into the concept of "the Force." After my consideration of *Sherlock*, I draw some of these insights together into a consideration of fictionalist approaches to religion.

BBC Sherlock *and Other Holmeses: Ways of Playing the Great Game*

"Another, and perhaps the greatest of the Sherlock Holmes mysteries is this: that when we talk of him we invariably fall into the fancy of his existence" wrote T.S. Eliot.[19] This section considers fans' reactions to various versions of the Sherlock Holmes character, and explores the relationships they hold to their texts. In particular, I examine two distinct "canons" and their fandoms: first, the writings of Arthur Conan Doyle about Sherlock Holmes and the people who "fall into the fancy of his existence," or, as they might put it, play the Great Game; and second, the BBC drama series *Sherlock*, in which a version of Holmes appears in modern London, and the (small group) of fans, who call themselves The Johnlock Conspiracy or TJLC, who became convinced that a sexual and/or romantic relationship between Sherlock Holmes and John Watson would become canon. Players of the Great Game are "mainstream" Holmes fans, and, I argue, give an insight into how certain extra claims about the canon can become "orthodoxy" or "fanon" (fan-produced canon). Members of The Johnlock Conspiracy are a small "sect" of the fandom but nevertheless, I argue, operate with a very particular and interesting relationship to canon, one which encompasses both a great deal of devotion to existing materials and a passionate desire to see certain future developments.

It is well known that Sherlock Holmes has been an audience favorite almost since his invention; that Conan Doyle was persuaded to "rescue" the hero from the Reichenbach Falls and continue writing stories about him is one among many pieces of evidence of this. It is also striking that, as Eliot noted, fans "fall into the fancy of his existence," and, even more, are inspired to copy his methods. This has sometimes happened in the real world (Conan Doyle wrote in a science fiction mold and sometimes correctly predicted scientific developments, such as the increasing sophistication of blood type analysis), but more interestingly for the purposes of this essay, his methods have been widely adopted by fans for application to the Holmes canon itself. Like biblical scholars who examine every word of the text, and sometimes like midrash, as a form of exegesis in which someone can take a stray word and build from it a whole new story, fans of Holmes treat every word as significant and assume that there is a logical explanation for everything. Indeed, this comparison was made by Ronald Knox, who began to analyze the canon before Conan Doyle had stopped writing it, and was also a biblical scholar.[20] Notably, he ends his paper with Holmes' own words: "You know my methods, Watson: apply them."

Since the available evidence about Conan Doyle's writing style suggests that the most logical explanation for many puzzles about the canon (from the dual location of Watson's war wound to the reuse of names) is that he was in a hurry and wanted to get paid for the story rather than build a coherent narrative, the application of Higher Criticism to the text requires a step which should make a Lindbeckian proud: entering the story universe. In my discussion of *Star Wars*, above, this is termed seeking in-universe explanations; in this case, there are specific words for the process. Fans talk about "Doyleist" (outside the text) and "Watsonian" (inside the text) explanations, and when they take the latter to its fullest extent, referring to Conan Doyle as Watson's "literary agent," they call it "playing the game" or, borrowing a phrase from the canon, "playing the great game."[21]

Once a fan has accepted the move into the text and started playing the game, all kinds of debates become possible within the community of interpretation they have now joined (not dissimilar to the fan who, having accepted that Han shot first, becomes a member of a particular part of the *Star Wars* fan community). For example, while the reader regards Watson as fictional, it makes no sense to ask whether or not he was actually a woman; but within the game, this is a question which has been considered repeatedly.[22] Similarly, as hinted above, a Doyleist perspective on the question of whether Watson's war wound was in his shoulder or his leg must simply say that Conan Doyle forgot what he specified before, and invented something else for a later story. From a Watsonian perspective, however, it is both necessary and difficult to explain this. That being so, conjectures have abounded, with variants of a story in which Watson is shot while bending over seeming most popular. I will return shortly to the idea that some such explanations might become accepted as "extra canon" or "fanon."[23]

This process of stepping into the text looks close to the situation described by Lindbeck with relation to religious conversion: "the logic of coming to believe, because it is like that of learning a language, has little room for argument, but once one has learned to speak the language of faith, argument becomes possible."[24] Similarly, once one has accepted the particular relationship with the text that comes with playing the game, one can argue "within" it. To separate out the two metaphors I am drawing from Lindbeck here: one can learn to speak Holmesian, and once fluent, hold debates in it, as one does in a new language; and one can come to be a Holmesian, and once a believer, discuss issues within the community, as one does when converted to a new religion.

However, it is also clear that players of the Great Game know that they are merely playing, and are able to separate their Holmesian hobby from the rest of their lives. Even if they sometimes seek to apply a little of his method to their everyday problems, they do live acting consistently as if Holmes were real. This, therefore, requires a comparison not to religion as a whole, but to particular understandings of religion that value the stories while admitting that their content is fictional. This will form the basis of the final section.

The Johnlock Conspiracy can be explained, briefly, as the claim that the creators of the BBC television show *Sherlock* intend to, eventually, enter a sexual and/or romantic relationship between Sherlock Holmes and John Watson into the canon. This has been an element of fanon—something which is widely accepted as true or possible by fans but never expected to be reflected by official creators—for many versions of Holmes and Watson, but this particular group of fans of this particular version take it a step further.

The *Sherlock* canon is already well removed from Conan Doyle's original, set mainly in the twenty-first century and containing much modern technology alongside jokes and call-backs to previous versions of the characters as meta-references to the show's existence in a wider franchise framework. The idea that Holmes and Watson might have a relationship which is not just a friendship is an old one (underlying the argument that Watson may have been a woman, besides many other pastiches and new versions of which the most notable is probably Billy Wilder's 1970 film *The Private Life of Sherlock Holmes*), but it found new strength among a group of fans, mainly on social media, after the first series of *Sherlock* was broadcast in 2010.[25] It is worth disentangling carefully some of the claims that are involved, as they shed light on these fans' complex relationship with the text. A fuller analysis has been conducted by Diana W. Anselmo, and here I select only those aspects of the situation which form a relevant comparison to the situation in *Star Wars* fandom.[26]

First, these fans do not make the leap into the text involved in playing the Great Game.[27] They do not operate with the assumption that Holmes and Watson are real and can be analyzed as such. They use both in-universe and out-of-universe evidence in support of their theories, using photographs taken during the film as clues and spending a lot of time debating things said by the writers, directors, and cast (often, it must be said, taking these comments considerably out of their original context).

Second, despite these caveats, these fans do assert that the characters of Sherlock and John as depicted in this particular show must be internally consistent with the clues they locate within the canon. In particular, they extrapolate from Sherlock's lack of interest in women to the idea that he is gay, perhaps even asexual, and from John's obvious interest in both women and spending time with Sherlock that he is bisexual. None of these "observations" are the only possible readings of canon, but, like so many other fans of Holmes, they seek to use his methods, and "observations" are the firm basis for later "deductions." They have not made the leap into the text, but they do draw the method out and turn it back to apply to the text itself. This might be compared to someone who asks whether the acts of Jesus described in the gospels live up to the maxim that one should "love your neighbor as yourself." This question might equally well be posed by a Christian or by a non-believer, but in some ways, it comes more naturally to the latter since the former is likely to assume that all of Christ's actions are in line with, indeed examples of, his teaching. Johnlock Conspiracy fans approve of Sherlock's methods, but also think they know something that he may not even know himself (depending the reading of key scenes): that he is, or will be, in love with/attracted to John.

Third, Johnlock fans—assisted by the ease with which ideas are circulated from one hand to another within social media sharing functions such as tumblr's "reblog" option—build a community consensus around what will happen. Within a Lindbeckian analysis this is a good illustration of the importance of community: fans build on each other's work, using the Holmesian method as grammar and drawing on more and more elaborate clues to extend their vocabulary. This process was at its clearest in late 2016, as the broadcast of the fourth series in January 2017 was getting closer: Johnlock Conspiracy fans had agreed, not on everything, but on certain key elements of the narrative which they expected to see. They wrote "meta" (literary analysis, albeit in an informal format) arguing the details of their case, and devised theories to predict what would happen.[28]

They were correct about little or nothing. In particular, the thing they were hoping for did not happen in any meaningful way: if John and Sherlock are in a gay relationship, this remains as much subtext as ever. There has always been this possible subtextual reading, and one which has produced a large quantity of slash fanfiction (homoerotic fan-written stories) but *Sherlock*'s 2017 run did not do anything to bring it closer to surface text. If anything, the knowing winks given to the possibility of a romantic or sexual relationship between the male leads were teasing and could be seen as leading fans on to expect something which was never going to occur; or as mocking, making a joke of homosexuality without treating it as a real possibility. Fairly quickly, as the new series was airing, new fanon formed which predicted that there would be an extra, secret episode in which it all came true, but as of April 2018, this has not happened.[29]

Johnlock Conspiracy fans are left with three possible relationships to the text, especially if, as seems increasingly likely at this point, this is now a closed canon. A few might have concluded that they were wrong, and if so they have left the community quietly. Some are simply angry and assume that the BBC either backed out of showing a queer relationship or "queer-baited," taunted fans by placing queer-coded clues with no intention of making it canon.[30] Within fandom, the pronouncements of authority figures are sometimes called "the Word of God" (as in, J.K. Rowling said that Dumbledore was gay, so Word of God makes it so, even if not even Sherlock Holmes himself could find a clue to it in the text of the books or films).[31] This fits neatly into a comparison between the position of these angry fans and those sometimes called "moral atheists," those who might believe in God's existence but refuse to worship a deity who permits all the evil visible in the world. Others persist in their interpretation of the text, either holding out hope for a future "revelation" in which the relationship will materialize or falling back on older fan strategies: claim that it is happening but it is subtext because the creators could not/did not want to make it obvious, or step into the text and become creators themselves, writing fanfiction and creating art which accepts without debate the fanon fact of the relationship.

Religion as Fiction: Lindbeck, Cupitt and the Fans

Throughout this essay I have offered examples of possible comparisons between the ways that fans of *Star Wars* and Sherlock Holmes approach their texts and the ways that religious believers, especially Christians, approach their scriptures. In particular, I have suggested that the most apt comparison is between these fans and religious thinkers who take a fictionalist approach to scripture and doctrine. While there are other fruitful comparisons that could be explored—I already mentioned Knox's straightforward application of the methods of biblical criticism to the Holmes canon and I could add Rachel Barenblat's comparison of the methods of midrash and fanfiction[32]—in this final section, I want to turn the question around and ask what the methods of the fans might have to offer to the Christian, especially the fictionalist theologian and believer.

Don Cupitt is an example of such a theologian, someone who takes the view that God is a useful story and that Christians should reject straightforward faith in the reality of miracles and divinity in favor of a focus on the teachings offered by the Christian narratives. In *Reforming Christianity*, Cupitt writes:

> church Christianity is in terminal decline and its divine Christ is (a) a muddle, and (b) never existed. I have for some years tried to argue that fortunately the historical Jesus and his kingdom religion are on the contrary alive and intellectually very inter-

esting. But in a number of ways the evidence is against me. The church and the church's divine Christ *are* indeed fading away—but the historical Jesus is not yet catching on.[33]

Cupitt then outlines his attempts to "save" Jesus, "not as a god who can't be wrong, but as a man who might be right."[34] However, perhaps what is unhelpful here is the emphasis on the term "historical." That sounds like a claim of fact, open to doubt and discussion and being proven wrong by one of the historical critics whom Cupitt himself holds in high regard. Instead, the position might be on firmer ground if it accepted that historical evidence is hardly the point and, copying the move of the fans who set aside the Doyleist perspective in favor of stepping into the Great Game, looked for answers to the questions the text raises strictly within the text.

Drawing moves from the other groups of fans might also be helpful. The Johnlock Conspiracy community sometimes take on aspects of religion which Cupitt and other fictionalists would doubtless find distasteful, such as the belief in a seemingly endlessly delayed "final revelation." However, their intellectual and emotional commitment to their reading of the text, at odds with many others, highlights the ways in which a community can come together to support a particular perspective and to try and convince others, through the use of evidence. Perhaps they sympathize with those who, more or less seriously, call themselves Jedi, whether in all of life or just for a census form. The widespread appeal of this joke, and the consequent awareness that fictional categories are available to answer questions about religion, might indicate that the time is ripe for a strong argument to be put in favor of a fictionalist position.

Conclusion

In conclusion, can the approach to narrative suggested by the Han Shot First t-shirt give a richer fictionalist perspective? Typically, as I suggested in my description of Cupitt's position, fictionalist views hold that God is something like a useful story. If that story is not entirely consistent or coherent, believers, like fans, will have to take a stance on which parts are to be accepted and which rejected. In the case of scripture, this is sometimes assumed to rest on Doyleist questions like which text is older, which text more accurately reflects a historical situation, and so on. If the issue of "truth" were dropped, as it is by necessity in the case of an obvious fiction like *Star Wars*, the focus could shift to Watsonian questions like which narrative is more satisfying and whether the actions of characters and their reported speech are aligned. This enables ordinary fictionalist believers, as well as theologians who are already familiar with the use of literary analysis of scripture, to participate in discussions about biblical questions in a way in which they might reject without the change of emphasis. Within their Watsonian perspective, they may have as good a grasp of the internal logic or grammar of a narrative as any other reader, and the rejection of confusions about Doyleist questions might lead to greater clarity that what matters is the truth of the text and its teachings and not its origin.

NOTES

1. My thanks to organizers Clive Marsh and Isobel Woodcliffe, and the many attendees, for conversations at the 2015 Fandom and Religion conference at the University of Leicester where I began to explore these ideas. Many thanks also to Martel Reynolds for years of debate, *Star Wars* appreciation, and typo-spotting.

2. The *Star Wars* franchise includes films I–VI, written and directed by George Lucas (USA: 20th Century Fox, 1977, 1980, 1983, 1999, 2002, 2005) as well as the spin-off films, animations, games, and related merchandise. *Sherlock*, created by Mark Gatiss and Stephen Moffat, and loosely based on the eponymous hero of Arthur Conan Doyle's detective novels, has 4 seasons with only 13 episodes (UK: BBC, 2010–2017).

3. Don Cupitt, *Reforming Christianity* (Santa Rosa, CA: Polebridge Press, 2001).

4. George A. Lindbeck, *The Nature of Doctrine: Religion and Theology in a Postliberal Age* (London: SPCK, 1984), 16–17.

5. Lindbeck, *The Nature of Doctrine*, 82.

6. Lindbeck, *The Nature of Doctrine*, 100.

7. Lindbeck, *The Nature of Doctrine*, 100.

8. Ludwig Wittgenstein, *Philosophical Investigations*, eds G.E.M. Anscombe, P.M.S. Hacker, and Joachim Schulte (Chichester: Blackwell, 2009), section 43.

9. Lindbeck, *The Nature of Doctrine*, 132–3.

10. Wai Yip Wong, "Reconstructing John Hick's theory of religious pluralism: a Chinese folk religion's perspective" (Ph.D. thesis, University of Birmingham, 2012).

11. *Episode IV: A New Hope*, writer and dir. George Lucas (U.S.: 20th Century Film, 1977).

12. Pink Dandelion, *An Introduction to Quakerism* (Cambridge: Cambridge University Press, 2007).

13. James T, "The 10 Worst Crimes Against the Original *Star Wars* Trilogy," *Den of Geek*, April 4 (2011), http://www.denofgeek.com/movies/star-wars/17281/the-10-worst-crimes-against-the-original-star-wars-trilogy.

14. Ben Kirby, "Who Shot First? The complete list of *Star Wars* changes," *Empire Online*, January 31 (2017), http://www.empireonline.com/movies/features/star-wars-changes/.

15. "Census 2001 Summary theme figures and rankings—390,000 Jedi There Are," *Office for National Statistics*, February 13 (2003), http://webarchive.nationalarchives.gov.uk/2016 0105160709/http:/www.ons.gov.uk/ons/rel/census/census-2001-summary-theme-figures-and-rankings/390-000-jedis-there-are/jedi.html.

16. Beth Singler, "'See Mom It Is Real': The UK Census, Jediism and Social Media," *Journal of Religion in Europe* 7, no. 2 (2014): 150–68.

17. "Jedi is not a religion, Charity Commission rules," *BBC News*, December 19 (2016), http://www.bbc.co.uk/news/uk-38368526.

18. Laurence Cawley, "The Jedi and the Bishop: Two Men from Essex, Two Religious Outlooks," *BBC News*, March 23 (2015), http://www.bbc.co.uk/news/uk-england-essex-3179 5408.

19. T.S. Eliot, "Sherlock Holmes and His Times. A review of The Complete Sherlock Holmes Short Stories, by Sir Arthur Conan Doyle; and The Leavenworth Case, by Anna Katharine Green," in *The Complete Prose of T.S. Eliot: The Critical Edition—Literature, Politics, Belief, 1927–1929*, eds. Frances Dickey, Jennifer Formichelli, and Ronald Schuchard (Baltimore: Johns Hopkins University Press, 2015), 603.

20. R.A. Knox, "Studies in the Literature of Sherlock Holmes," *Blackfriars* 1, no. 3 (1920): 154–72.

21. See, for example, the webpage of the *Baker Street Journal*, which publishes both in- and out-of-universe articles: http://www.bakerstreetjournal.com/.

22. An early, perhaps the first, example is Rex Stout, "Watson Was a Woman," *The Saturday Review of Literature* (1941).

23. A brief summary of the options can be found in Dennis Simanaitis, "Watson's War Wound," *Simanaitis Says*, January 24 (2017), https://simanaitissays.com/2017/01/24/watsons-war-wound/.

24. Lindbeck, *The Nature of Doctrine*, 132.

25. Within social media, the main hub of activity is on tumblr: http://tjlc.tumblr.com/about, which provides a starting point for exploration.

26. Diana W. Anselmo, "Gender and Queer Fan Labor on Tumblr: The Case of BBC's *Sherlock*," *Feminist Media Histories* 4, no. 1 (2018).

27. For a more general consideration of the fan relationship to the text of BBC *Sherlock*, see Ashley D. Polasek, "'Winning the grand game': *Sherlock* and the Fragmentation of Fan Discourse," in Sherlock *and Transmedia Fandom: Essays on the BBC Series*, ed. Louisa Ellen Stein and Kristina Busse (Jefferson, NC: McFarland, 2012), 41–54.

28. See, for example: Junejuly15, "The Six Thatchers: What You Need to Know," *Sherlockbuddy* (2016), https://sherlockbuddy.tumblr.com/post/150962020284/the-six-thatchers-what-you-need-to-know.

29. This possibility was discussed in various ways, and when it did not happen, fans began to hunt for explanations about why. See, for example, the alternate storylines posited on the *Deducing* Sherlock tumblr, n.d. http://deducing-sherlock.tumblr.com/.

30. The BBC denies this. See an email response to just this complaint, posted by an angry fan: eggmancustard, *eggmancustard* (2017), http://eggmancustard.tumblr.com/post/156446238353/okay-but-like-my-complaint-was-about. For analysis of queerbaiting as a concept in fan cultures, see Cassandra M. Collier, "The Love That Refuses to Speak Its Name: Examining Queerbaiting and Fan-Producer Interactions in Fan Cultures" (MA thesis, University of Louisville, 2015).

31. For more examples of this usage, see "Word of God," *TV Tropes*, http://tvtropes.org/pmwiki/pmwiki.php/Main/WordOfGod.

32. Rachel Barenblat, "Fan fiction and midrash: Making meaning," *Transformative Works and Cultures* 17 (2014).

33. Cupitt, *Reforming Christianity*, 134.

34. Cupitt, *Reforming Christianity*, 135.

Bibliography

Anselmo, Diana W. "Gender and Queer Fan Labor on Tumblr: The Case of BBC's *Sherlock*." *Feminist Media Histories* 4, no. 1 (2018): 84–114.

Barenblat, Rachel. "Fan Fiction and Midrash: Making Meaning." *Transformative Works and Cultures* 17 (2014). DOI: https://doi.org/10.3983/twc.2014.0596.

Cawley, Laurence. "The Jedi and the Bishop: Two Men from Essex, Two Religious Outlooks." *BBC News*, March 23 (2015). http://www.bbc.co.uk/news/uk-england-essex-31795408 (accessed May 6, 2018).

"Census 2001 Summary Theme Figures and Rankings—390,000 Jedi There Are." *Office for National Statistics*, February 13 (2003). http://webarchive.nationalarchives.gov.uk/20160105160709/http://www.ons.gov.uk/ons/rel/census/census-2001-summary-theme-figures-and-rankings/390-000-jedis-there-are/jedi.html (accessed May 6, 2018).

Collier, Cassandra M. "The Love That Refuses to Speak Its Name: Examining Queerbaiting and Fan-Producer Interactions in Fan Cultures." MA thesis, University of Louisville, 2015.

Cupitt, Don. *Reforming Christianity*. Santa Rosa, CA: Polebridge Press, 2001.

Dandelion, Pink. *An Introduction to Quakerism*. Cambridge: Cambridge University Press, 2007.

Deducing Sherlock (2012–2016). http://deducing-sherlock.tumblr.com/ (accessed May 6, 2018).

eggmancustard. *Eggmancustard* (2017). http://eggmancustard.tumblr.com/post/156446238 353/okay-but-like-my-complaint-was-about (accessed May 6, 2018).

Eliot, T.S. "Sherlock Holmes and His Times. A Review of the Complete Sherlock Holmes Short Stories, by Sir Arthur Conan Doyle; and the Leavenworth Case, by Anna Katharine Green." In *The Complete Prose of T.S. Eliot: The Critical Edition—Literature, Politics, Belief, 1927–1929*, edited by Frances Dickey, Jennifer Formichelli, and Ronald Schuchard, 601–610. Baltimore: Johns Hopkins University Press, 2015.

"Jedi Is Not a Religion, Charity Commission Rules." *BBC News*, December 19 (2016). http://www.bbc.co.uk/news/uk-38368526 (accessed May 6, 2018).

Junejuly15. "The Six Thatchers: What You Need to Know." *Sherlockbuddy* (2016). https://sherlockbuddy.tumblr.com/post/150962020284/the-six-thatchers-what-you-need-to-know (accessed May 6, 2018).

Kirby, Ben. "Who Shot First? The Complete List of *Star Wars* Changes." *Empire Online*, January 31 (2017). http://www.empireonline.com/movies/features/star-wars-changes/ (accessed May 6, 2018).

Knox, Ronald A. "Studies in the Literature of Sherlock Holmes." *Blackfriars* 1, no. 3 (1920): 154–72.

Lindbeck, George A. *The Nature of Doctrine: Religion and Theology in a Postliberal Age*. London: SPCK, 1984.

Polasek, Ashley D. "'Winning the Grand Game': *Sherlock* and the Fragmentation of Fan Discourse." In Sherlock *and Transmedia Fandom: Essays on the BBC Series*, edited by Louisa Ellen Stein and Kristina Busse, 41–54. Jefferson, NC: McFarland, 2012.

Sherlock. Seasons 1–4. Created by Mark Gatiss and Stephen Moffat. UK: BBC, 2010–2017.

Simanaitis, Dennis. "Watson's War Wound." *Simanaitis Says*, January 24 (2017). https://simanaitissays.com/2017/01/24/watsons-war-wound/ (accessed May 6, 2018).

Singler, Beth. "'See Mom It Is Real': The UK Census, Jediism and Social Media." *Journal of Religion in Europe* 7, no. 2 (2014): 150–68.

Star Wars Episode IV: A New Hope. Written and directed by George Lucas. U.S.: 20th Century Film, 1977.

Stout, Rex. "Watson Was a Woman." *The Saturday Review of Literature* (1941): 3–4.

T, James. "The 10 Worst Crimes against the Original *Star Wars* Trilogy." *Den of Geek*, 4 April (2011). http://www.denofgeek.com/movies/star-wars/17281/the-10-worst-crimes-against-the-original-star-wars-trilogy (accessed May 6, 2018).

Wittgenstein, Ludwig. *Philosophical Investigations*. Edited by G.E.M. Anscombe, P.M.S. Hacker, and Joachim Schulte. Chichester: Blackwell, 2009.

Wong, Wai Yip. "Reconstructing John Hick's Theory of Religious Pluralism: A Chinese Folk Religion's Perspective." Ph.D. thesis, University of Birmingham, 2012.

"Word of God." *TV Tropes*. http://tvtropes.org/pmwiki/pmwiki.php/Main/WordOfGod (accessed 8 May, 2018).

Supernatural's Winchester Gospel

A Fantastic Midrash

LINDA HOWELL

> "Interpretation always assumes some kind of lack, need, gap to be filled, even rabbinic interpretation. For even repetition is a kind of interpretation."—Susan Handelman[1]

> "One day, these books—they'll be known as the Winchester Gospel."—Castiel, *Supernatural*[2]

Introduction

In April 2009, *Supernatural* introduced what would become one of the show's long-standing tropes: the story within the story. Episode 18 in Season 4, "Monster at the End of this Book," inserts a metanarrative into the show's fictional world-building with the character named Chuck Shurley, who pens a series of fictional books called, fittingly, *Supernatural*, which foretell the lives of the protagonists, the demon-hunting brothers Sam and Dean Winchester.[3] The tongue-in-cheek nod to Shurley's books as "the Winchester Gospel" and Shurley as "god" or a "prophet" work as a parody on multiple levels, referencing the show's overt religious themes, the devotion of its fanbase, and the active role fans take, in their own way, in determining and passing judgment over the actions and consequences of the Winchesters in their fight against evil.

At the time of the episode's airing, the metafictional move was both familiar and strange for television audiences. Science fiction and fantasy narratives, especially on television, have never been particularly afraid of metafiction; however, this episode creates a new avenue of "meta" whereby the text's creators slyly and insidiously begin to acknowledge and respond to the consumption and interpretation of their text by the audience. This creates a hazardous precedent that Laura Felschow notes in her critical review of the episode's presence in the show's canon:

> It is precisely this privileged status of the cult fan that producers have begun to tap into to help secure the success of their product. Yet while the cult fan may be viewed as a powerful tool for those producers, the cult fan is not merely a mindless consumer machine.[4]

Felschow's observation here is essential to understanding how the insertion of fan and other paratextual objects demonstrate an emerging symbiotic relationship between textual producers and consumers, and how those relationships are pushing back against the consumer-as-repository conceit. Instead, consumers are producers, and surely producers are consumers. This consumption model transition not only challenges the distribution streams and mass marketing campaigns, but it also introduces the problems inherent to continuous and congruent interactivity between authorized writers and producers and the consumers for whom they produce—but we have similar models of production/consumption available to us outside of economic models, for example, the midrashic tradition made famous by the deep interpolative practice of reading of the scriptures by ancient rabbis. Midrash provides a novel yet germane context through which to understand this transition, which marks a death, not so much of the author but of the authority of the text, and confuses who exactly gets to alter its meaning. Such a death exacerbates the interpretive crisis that this essay explores.

This essay addresses two main areas: fanwork as metacritical, and the metatextuality of the canonical source which directly addresses fanwork and in doing so creates a site for a potential hermeneutic crisis, demonstrated this study of *Supernatural*. For the purpose of this essay, the term "text" will stand in for a variety of types of works, from traditional print-based artifacts to visual and media arts, and beyond. The term "fanwork" will represent a range of generative activities—fanfiction, fanart, fanvidding, fan interactions, which all lead to a pluralistic and polyvocal space. Fanworks create a multiverse, in a very poignant way, where the text becomes a tesseract of entry points that provide consumers with limitless points of certified entrance that do not necessarily begin with the "real" story.

By using the midrash tradition as a correlative, this essay proposes that the reading of *Supernatural's* metacontent and the fandom's production of metawork neglects the agonistic process between show and fan that inspires, fuels, and certifies seemingly extra-textual activities (from metacommentary to metacreative) as authoritative and instructive. While Kristina Busse might argue fan works should be seen as "objects of study"[5] (a claim with which I agree), this essay deprioritizes the products of both show and fan to reprioritize process and method. Rather, it frames fanwork as a type of textual methodology that aligns with many religious exegetical practices but also transforms its "gloss" or "paratext" into primary source material that can yes, stand on its own as object of study, but goes further than simply creating parallel creative marginalia to creating authorized portals to meaning but subversively, unlike a text like *Homestuck*[6] that deeds the entire ownership of creating to its consumers.

Metacommentary[7] and metacreativity provide a place for fans to perform what I would call a type of phenomenological criticism that employs art, fiction, and other forms of creative criticism to compile a gnostic (or esoteric) branch of the source material. Gnostic here refers to a type of special knowledge keeping, where those fans who reach different levels of practice and study unlock hidden meanings or secret rituals that provide more meaningful and functional interpretations of the text. Given the availability of fanwork and the ease of accessing the digital archives of fanworks, these gnostic texts can become primary avenues of consumption. This structure, in return, affects the expectations of the text. These forms of creative criticism interlace with interpretive approaches and the resulting confusion about meaning making emerges as a place of contention, specifically about authorship. As the fanwork expands, the scholarship of the fandom and its study of the text can eclipse the source material.

That eclipse can be seen in the distribution machine of fandom, such as in *Supernatural,* where the show has colonized much of fan scholarship and its viral presence on social media platforms, which one blogger, Nil, affectionately called "secondhand fandom syndrome."[8] Nil writes, "I know too much about the Winchesters for someone who has never watched a single episode of the show. I know quite a bit about the fandom, and the ships and stuff like that, and I've even read a fanfic or two."[9] Nil's story is not uncommon. In fact, one might argue that *Supernatural* has lent fodder to the field of contemporary fan studies like no other fictional work has done, even *Harry Potter*, *Star Trek*, *Star Wars*, and *Lord of the Rings*. Its televisual and serial format creates a consistently living text that can change in the presence of its annotations so as Brigid Cherry points to in her critique of the Becky character in *Supernatural*, the inclusion of fan materials runs the risk of fans believing their works are canon.[10] This pseudo-institutionalization provides the area of contention that pits meaning-making against authority-making.

Fan communities produce and facilitate an emergent hermeneutic wherein ideas of authorship, ownership, and creation coincide with concepts of interaction, simultaneity, and customization. This kind of native methodology is localized, based on the organic growth of marginalia and annotation from the origin text, a text that becomes destabilized under the pressure of such expansion. *Supernatural's* integrated "meta" episodes demonstrate the contrary conflation of the story's origin text with its fandom text. We will see that consolation, comfort, ease in the face of life's challenges share a common ground in much metacommentary. This essay examines *Supernatural's* metatextual work through the lens of hermeneutics, but more specifically through a postmodern reading of the midrash tradition, a form of methodology that began with rabbis in the early common era but that represents both the product and the practice of study, interpretation, and commentary.[11]

Terms of Interpretation

A long, complicated history of scholarship addresses the place of Jewish midrash and Talmudic traditions in religious study, as well as other traditions of interpretation. This essay foregrounds the work of the midrash since it applies metacommentary as exegetical practice, drawing out the meaning of otherwise authoritative sources like the Tanakh (the canonical assembly of Jewish scriptural texts), through reading, interpreting, and commenting. Midrashim were composed by rabbis, Judaism's class of religious scholars, to provide expositions of the texts, traditions, and practices, both orally and literally transmitted.[12] In the first five centuries of the common era, such literature was meant to support and supplement their teachings, and then became part of a central hermeneutic tradition.

As David Stern points out, though, using midrash as a comparison can present problems for a scholar because understanding the tradition relies on a complex set of questions and contexts[13]; however, this essay employs Stern's notion of the inherent polysemy of the midrash and its place in the margins as a way to view fan space; the essay also relies on Susan Handelman, Daniel Boyarin, and Robert Alter, as scholars of note in studying how midrash operates and how midrashists can be viewed as textual workers and scholars who created authoritative texts for each other and other consumers of the text. It is important to note that I situate this conversation in an area of scholarship that was under hot debate between these parties, especially Stern and Handelman, in the mid–1980s, when the postmodern ethos in literary criticism began invading and penetrating interdisciplinary textual studies.[14]

In his 1956 essay "The Philosophy Implicit in the Midrash," Henry Slonimsky describes the midrash as the "faith" alongside the "work," and for him that work is a labor of consolation for a people under tremendous difficulty.[15] Slonimsky's observations augment my understanding of what sacred texts might mean for the faithful, no matter the religion or creed. I continually return to this idea of consolation. Consolation takes the place here of a series of interpretive moves that provide the framework for this essay that sees fanwork as consolation but also as the site of interpretative authority.

As Boyarin muses in his analysis of midrash as site of intertextuality, these texts produce other texts that are coded to the interpretation and not only the canonical text.[16] As with any deployment of postmodern technique such as intertextuality or pastiche, there is resistance and skepticism. Concerns may be raised, for example, over the diminishing of historical significance in service to the emphasizing of play over purpose. To best meet these challenges, we will consider the merits of exegesis as a creative practice of interpretation.

Exegesis is a kind of close reading wherein various apparatuses are employed to understand a text, from grammatical and sentence-level examination through thematic and historical critiques. I choose the term exegesis over hermeneutics here to clearly delineate a practice that focuses on how a text works over what it may or may not represent. As a practice, exegesis presumes a sustained familiarity with the text that comes from reiterative engagement. The return to a text, again and again, will produce analyzes that augment the understanding of the text, especially if they produce marginalia or gloss.

Furthermore, exegesis provides a site for the forming of congregations of interpreters doing this work. In her study of women and biblical "interpretive communities," Elisabeth Schüssler Fiorenza argues that they "are not just scholarly investigative communities but also authoritative communities. They possess the power to ostracize or to embrace, to foster or to restrict membership, to recognize and to define what "true scholarship" entails."[17] While she focuses on the conventional division between gendered understandings of Schüssler Fiorenza's advocacy for what she calls a "rhetorical-emancipatory" ethos in biblical scholarship informs this essay's argument, for the analogy of fan communities of textual practice clearly align with interpretive communities and the concept of communities of practice which build expertise and experts, and that often happens in the annotative spaces, or "fannotations."

Gloss is a formal word for annotations, such as you find in biblical, legal, or literary studies, and which can be both redactive or an amplification of a text's work. Mikhail Bakhtin's concept of heteroglossia, where language, narrative, writing, and speech are not monolithic or static but multilithic and mobile, aligns well with the polysemic notion of midrash this essay employs.[18] This ability to enliven the gloss, give breath to the marginalia, per se, aligns the works of fans with the work of midrash. In her work on midrash and fanfiction, Rachel Barenblat notes the many similarities between the two textual traditions, listing off each aspect with a refrain of "In fanfiction, as in midrash…"[19] These similarities include the ability to answer the text, to speculate about the text, to fill in the gaps of the text, and to give a platform to voices neglected by the text. Barenblat perfectly frames the conceits upon which this essay is built; however, I would further Barenblat's assertions by adding "In fanwork, as in midrash, we can replenish the authority of the text. In fanwork, unlike in midrash, the text can be altered by our work." In this process, the authoritative voices on the text are no longer exclusively those of God and his prophets, scholars, and other mouthpieces, but the lay-person, or in this case, the fan.

Fannotations can become an authority on the text, which provides an auxiliary access point for additional readers to engage in meaning-making. In this case, much as in most annotations of source materials, the gloss becomes doubly a record of textual engagement and instructional for those encountering the text. However, the danger is in reading the gloss as just marginal, especially when it begins to carry the weight of authority, which is the fine line between what we call paratext and what I would like to begin thinking about as symbiotext.

In his work *Paratexts: Thresholds of Interpretation,* Gerard Genette defines the paratext as an attachable (and detachable) text to a source text, such as prefaces, introductions, and so forth. He defines the process of identifying a paratext as locating it in time and place in relation to the source text, its mode or form, its writer, and finally, its purpose.[20] Genette's project examines the possible iterations of a text as it meets its audience, yet the prefix of "para-" troubles this concept as it denotes a positioning alongside or beside. This is why I would argue for a *symbio*textual approach where we can see the esoteric layer of texts within the text's psyche or its life breath. Symbiotext includes metatexts such as marginalia, glossia, annotations, and other commentary or creative endeavors, which can become, independently, the primary source material in fandom.

I want to avoid, in this essay, falling back on trying to see fandom or fanwork as constituting a religion or categorizing fan activity into parts of a sociological debate about cults and cultish behaviors which can lead to a punitive characterizing of the fan as a celebrated victim of prejudice, as a fledgling neophyte, or worse, as a cultist. Fantext is neither barnacle nor potential parasite. While auxiliary texts can augment reading, so can those texts that go unannounced, which this essay seeks to unpack. The fantext is, here, the symbiotext, the secretly vital text, the vascular text. In the case of *Supernatural,* the vitality of the fantext transforms into an essential component for reading part of its canon.

Scholarship on *Supernatural* and its fans is a fairly saturated area of study. As I stated earlier, one could argue that the show has given an intellectual grant to fan studies just by virtue of its complex and expansive fan universe. The most notable scholar, Lynn Zubernis, has written and edited several books on the show and its relationship with fans, as well as fans' relationship with the show. Zubernis's and Kathy Larsen's *Fandom at the Cross-roads: Celebration, Shame, and Fan/Producer Relationships* tackles the gray lines between the show and its fans through the theme of shame, which has been a thematic component of both fandom and academic fandom, aka "aca-fans." The two scholars have produced other versions of this scholarship and have indeed given fans skin in the game, inviting fans to submit works about their experience of the show and its fandom in texts such as *Fangasm* to their edited collection from *Fan Phenomena.*

The scholarship reaches back through the show's long run but climbs to its apex in Seasons 4 through 10, when the show's meta threads become permanent parts of the landscape. *Transformative Works and Cultures* has dedicated a volume to the show in 2010, edited by Catherine Tosenberger, and several texts beyond Zubernis and Larsen, have been published looking at spirituality, psychology, and folklore as applied to the show and its fandom. In recent years, well-known fan scholars such as Chin, Booth, and Jones, have used *Supernatural* as examples of the interplay between actors and fans, the inherent contradictions between the show's often white masculinist canon text and its diverse fandom, and how both fail and succeed at engaging fans. Coincidentally, the show's popularity as an object of study occurs alongside its metanarrative evolution, which coincides with the increasing popularity of social media forums like Twitter, Facebook, tumblr, and LiveJournal, forums which allow fans to communicate with each other, but even more importantly, allow producers, scholars, and other fans to participate and observe these interactions in public spaces.

Supernatural's fan workers, in this essay, emerge as kind of rabbinic authoritative and missionary figures. They become not only curators of knowledge but producers of knowledge that can be used to inform and sustain communities of practice. While the show's turn toward meta infuriated some fans and enchanted others, the problem the theme would eventually expose offers an access point for scholars to understand how fans perceive and perform consumption of texts through a process of expertise building. This expertise building clashes violently with the canonical (or authorized) text and with other sects of experts within the fandom. Two different forms of methodology in fandom contend with each other—that of considering the text to be allegorical versus the text as socio-literal, a contention that for *Supernatural* is best represented in the "shipping" division of its fandom.

Supernatural, *Fandom and Symbiotext*

Supernatural provides a potent case study for it has a large capacity of fanworks that have produced various schools of thought about the text, which are implied in the types and genres of work that gets produced. For example, at the time of the writing of this essay, a simple search on the popular fanwork archive, *Archive of Our Own*, produces over 195,000 works in the "*Supernatural*" tag.[21] The popularity of the show in fandom has generated a community of participants and creators that extends far beyond the scope of the source material, establishing reconfigurations of the story that discharge the narrative across genres and forms. In a similar search on deviantart.com, which is an archive of visual art, the term "SPN" produces a result of over 56,000 hits.

We will consider the show in two ways—first the methodology of shipping as an esoteric part of the scholarship produced by fans and then the show's move toward self-iconoclasm with the insertion of the fan figure, which directly challenges the text's sacrality. The inherent violence of this insertion can lead to a hermeneutic crisis when the fan becomes sacred figure to be painted. The idea of faith as work alongside source materials is relevant to the study of fans and their products since fan works rely on exegesis and creative criticism to unpack the meaning of the text. The creative criticism, here, includes kinds and forms of textual re-interpretation and re-presentations that challenge transcendentalizing texts, where the story, the actors, and the world building, become readily available to its recipients not as a lesson or fully formed, but rather as a partially-formed opportunity to construct iterations and reiterations that travel outward from the source material, paving roads for other participants who can travel back to the text via these avenues. Fans also act as counselors of the text, as well as consolers when the text stops delivering the emotive, psychological, or other affective forms of satisfaction. For example, a popular genre or tag on *Archive of Our Own*, called "fix it" has over 27,500 listed. Additionally, there are approximately 5000 variations of the term "fix it" in an AO3 tag search. The notion of fixing adjoins this notion of comfort, as fans tasks themselves and are tasked with fixing the problems of the canon.[22] The comfort of annotated work demonstrates how fans intervene in meaning-making.

One of the most popular subcategories of iconic and textual production comes from the fanwork focused on romantic and/or sexual relationships between characters, most of them centering on two main "couplings": Sam and Dean Winchester or Dean Winchester and the angel, Castiel. There are other couplings, for sure, but the popularity of these two relationships somewhat override other possibilities. "Shipping," a shortened form of "relationshipping," has become a standardized slang term in fandoms for fans who place characters, generally those who are not romantically involved in the source material, into romantic and/or sexual relationships, specifically "slash," which is a transient term that deals with pairings of same-sex partnerships.

The term "shipping" began in *The X-Files* fandom to describe fans of the Mulder and Scully relationship, and was originally a derogatory term. However, the term has been re-purposed by fans and turned into an accepted, even celebrated, nomenclature. On any given day, you can see the bifurcation between fans about this issue, which is best seen in the ways fans speak to each other or how fans read each other.[23] Shipping has been a point of scholarship, but for this essay, the way fans interact with each other, especially online and in the comments sections and as translated by uber-fans, constitute a more meaningful contribution to understanding the sectionalism that can occur.

One contingent seeks to hide the activity from producers and authors, while the other contingent seeks to make it public, and have it celebrated and addressed. For *Supernatural,* the convention circuit becomes a venue of contention since fans have direct access to the actors, which has led to tense interactions, but this need to be seen also extends into the text. In the episode "Fan Fiction," which also happened to be the show's 200th episode, the brothers find out that a young woman, who attends an all-girl high school, has adapted the Chuck Shurley books into a musical.[24] During the episode, the show throws various glances toward the fourth wall, and incorporates both the Dean/Sam relationship and the Dean/Castiel relationship as fodder. The moral of the story, if there was one, distinctly places fan interpretations and creations, transformations, outside the realm of the show. It tries to erect a barrier between the two spaces, to what good has been a topic of debate.

If a user searches the comments sections on various episode reviews for "Fan Fiction," they will find a host of mixed emotions. For example, in the *Spoiler TV* review of "Fan Fiction," a thread started by a user named Mindy noted that "As much as I love this show, I couldn't help but cringe through this entire nightmare load of meta-crap episode," with responses from other users ranging from affection for the episode to a type of meta-meta comment, "I'm definitely expecting this episode to garner a lot of pretty strong reactions—both negative and positive."[25] These types of conversations can be found in many review sections, which indicate the emergent debate about the show's direct address to its audience within text. Another avenue of discussion happened on the Reddit board devoted to the episode, and it provides a good exemplar of the positive reactions, with one user proclaiming that "Dean Winchester is judging the ENTIRE FANDOM" to another user stating "The best part of this is that it means someone involved with shows is at least monitoring places like this sub and fanfiction.net. Everybody just think about that for a sec."[26] That intuition about being seen reaffirms the show's possible symbiotextual move since the reading of the episode was almost entirely dependent on knowing the paratextual landscape.

The actors are prolific convention stars and attendees, the shipping element has become a thematic element in their interactions with fans, which has led to some controversial events. These include Jensen Ackles, who plays the hyper-masculine Dean, specifically stating how concerned he was when he first saw the script for "Fan Fiction," and his blatant repudiation of both the homoerotic reading of his character[27] and a fan favorite ship.[28] This controversy represents the eventful and discomforting back-and-forth contest between the show and its fans with various participants—the actors, fan-authors, the episode writers, even the characters—being intermittently made responsible as the authorized faces and voices of the show.

Shipping has become a contentious area of debate between fans and between fans and producers. For example, the executive producer of the science-fiction drama television program, *The 100*, engaged with fans of a particular ship—a lesbian relationship between two characters—which was then actualized on screen, only to be destroyed immediately after by the death of one of the women. The outrage reached far beyond the isolated community of the fans, leading to articles about queerbaiting (when a show or text seems to promise a same-sex romance but either defers the relationship or quickly ends it such as in *The 100*) and the responsibility of television and representation of marginalized communities, in this case queer women.[29] The accessibility of shipping fanwork, in particular, has increased in the social media environment, making it much more a part of a story's branding opportunities, as can be seen in various interactions between producers and fans, such as Julie Plec and the very popular pairing of Elena and Damon on *The Vampire Diaries*. When the show was in its nascent seasons, Plec retweeted fan videos of the couple, which would put her in an interesting contrary position in later seasons when the relationship fell apart and the actress who played Elena exited the show.[30]

The textual play with external fanwork such as conventions creates a vibrant heteroglossia for *Supernatural*. When Bakhtin writes about heteroglossia, he notes that it is congregation of different speeches or languages coming together in a text, which provides the baseline presumption for ideas like translanguage and code-switching where speech, writing, and storytelling are not monolithic but rather vehicles of translation and reside on context.[31] The number of voices in a text, from the characters to the writer to the reader, vary in tone, form, and content. So, as the conventions, social media, and the show converge into a shared space the boundaries of what constitutes the sacred text become blurred, if not totally dissolved.

Subsequently, forms of creative criticism, such as fanfiction, fanart, and other fan-driven interruptions, interlace with interpretive agendas. The resulting confusion about meaning making emerges as a place of contention, specifically about authorship. Given the distribution of fanwork and its almost immersive presence in the lives of digital denizens, these gnostic texts become the primary avenues of consumption. This structure, in return, affects the expectations of the text. Fandom works act to augment the text for readers but they can also become the entry points to the text's meaning, and depending on where one enters, the text could be forever altered by the expectations set forth by the interpretation.

We can read fan activity as annotative, however, wide-ranging "fannotations" have the potential to move authority and authorship from the traditional primary text, i.e., the show, to the marginalia, making the fanwork a primary source itself. The source material then is presumed to have to meet the expectations of the interpretation rather than being the text to be interpreted. That shift is catastrophic in many ways because it prevents accountability in narrative construction. But at the same time, the shift enables fans. It can be an act of empowerment, for now the annotations are not by-stander texts, they assume as much importance, if not more, than the primary text. A singular cosmology implodes to be replaced by multiple universes. The crisis, then, emerges when there is a dissipation of distinction between the source material and the fannotations, or the faith that resides alongside the work. Marginalia, glosses, contingent commentary, and other extratextual works often act to situate a source text within certain interpretive spaces, which returns fanwork to a midrashic space where the text provides an infinite landscape of iterations that can stand as guides and teachers for other fans, both new and old.

The show resists reader attempts to sacralize it, and does so in a couple of ways, which begin with self-insertion. The insertion of both writer and fan, which has been read in many ways, can be interpreted as a reluctance to being made holy. It reminds the reader, by disrupting a suspension of disbelief, that the text is performance and narrative, that it is fictional. The caricaturizing of these two actors, writer and fan, serves to reposition the viewer in a metatextual space, external to the text. The introduction and portrayal of Charlie Bradbury, for example, becomes the placeholder for an idealized fan (which makes her gruesome murder a particularly grotesque wound). Charlie is introduced in from Season 7 in "The Girl with the Dungeons and Dragons Tattoo" as a smart computer hacker who loves Comic Con and *Harry Potter*. Additionally she is identified as a lesbian, which ticks off many boxes for fan representation.[32]

As she evolves in the show, Charlie becomes part of the extended Winchester hunting community and family, and is the character who reminds the brothers and the fans, by extension, of the Shurley books in Season 10's "Slumber Party" when she reveals she has discovered not only the original Chuck Shurley books but the unauthorized sequels that were written by Becky Rosen Winchester (who happens to be the fangirl from the fifth and seventh seasons who Sam married under the influence of a spell).[33] The episode (written by writer Robbie Thompson, who also wrote "Fan Fiction") plays with intertextuality in many ways as it is also the episode inspired by *The Wizard of Oz,* which entered the public domain in 2015 and thus available for adaptation and reinterpretation. While Charlie becomes the fully integrated fan figure, Chuck's journey moves from that of marginal prophet to "The God" in—and of—*Supernatural.* In this way the show returns the gaze of its viewers and closes a loop, such as in the eleventh season finale arc, which begins with Thompson's "Don't Call Me Shurley," in which he confirms his omniscience, through the season finale episode "Alpha and Omega" where he disappears and relinquishes the world back to the Winchesters.[34]

As metatextual reminder, the self-awareness responds to a danger of a literal reading; however, the counternarrative of fan influence or fan inclusion actually extends the hermeneutic confusion, for now you have a double wound with which to contend—the text as fictional and the reader as character. In a text that already heavily relies on supernatural and religious symbols, imagery, and content, the text risks acerbic heresy. The contradictions can be interpreted as a way of moderating the often profane or heretical story arcs the show gestures to, including the inclusion of angels in the fourth season, which coincidentally is the first metatextual explication the show indulges in.

The parodic move, then, reduces the potential sacrilegious content but, as a result, produces another layer of interpretive perplexity, for now the reader is part of the mystical text. I would not argue that this is causal but I am interested in the correlation of the timeline, and how at each juncture when fan and writer appear, they provide a metatextual and satirical catharsis to the content that skirts close to heretical narrative. Here, Linda Hutcheon's work on parody might provide an insight into how this metatextual parody works, since it subverts from the inside, invoking a conversation with the consumer about the instability of the text and its dependence on continuity.[35]

The show continues to resist the external pressures of sacrament in other ways. For instance, in the Season 8 episode "The Great Escapist," the show introduces the character of Metatron, who is purported to be the scribe of God, and is later confirmed to be the scribe in the "Don't Call Me Shurley."[36] Metatron's introduction is interesting in a variety of ways, but most particularly *how* he is introduced. He has hidden himself away in a library where he can appreciate God's real gift, the human story and the human storyteller. At one point he says, "But really? Really? It was your storytelling. That's the true flower of free will. At least how you've mastered it so far. When you create stories, you become gods of tiny, intricate dimensions unto themselves." Given the show's already running metacommentary, this character introduction can be read as not only self-commentary but also commentary to its fans and its fan creators. This season, coincidentally, evolved at the same time that the show entered into Netflix streaming rights and its viewership spiked over 20 percent, and so did the interest from fandom platforms like tumblr.[37] While not causal, the correlations are worthy of note.

Metatron's introduction and place in the text is a constant reminder of how story is story but also how corrupting the need to claim authorship or originality can be since his character development is based primarily on greed and envy. He revolts and takes over heaven, punishes angels, and eventually tries to assume the mantle of God. The commentary can be construed as the show's internal struggle with what it means to author a world that has too many authors, or gods, already.

Conclusion

The tension between the private and public spheres of fandom presents a nonsensical debate, in many ways, because the distribution of fanwork is often open source and open access. There are few borders to access unless a participant creates boundaries via locking an account or requiring a certain level of access before reading, such as in the option in *Archive of Our Own* where authors can restrict viewing to only logged members of the community. Other apparatuses of restriction exist, but the economy of feedback, sharing (reblogging, retweeting, and so forth), and sectional unity within groups of fans (shippers, character fans, and so forth), make restriction counterproductive.

As social media and other forms of mass distribution have made it possible to *see* and *take note of* more fanwork and fan behaviors, the labor of fans has emerged in a landscape where authorship is a performative (and not implicit) dialogic. What happens then is that the once hidden or rarely highlighted multiverse implied in close reading practices and protocols becomes public through publishing, and the product of such publication is a sense of authentication wherein the polyphony threatens to become a cacophony without centralized organization. This multivocality is a kind of protestant rebellion against distributers as the only avenue of access because all readers become all rabbis, all priests, prophets, all scholars and scholiasts, all authorities, and thus authors, of the text. However, the catastrophe comes when the primary text becomes a destabilized teller of stories that bends under the weight of its interpretation, which I would argue happens in *Supernatural.* The risk is in the radicalization of the hermeneutic space, a sectionalizing that turns readers against readers, readers against text, text against text. Furthermore, this radical reorganization of authority reframes canonical episodes as dependent on external texts, especially in the show's later seasons, creating a symbiotic reliance on knowledge of fandom to understand moves in canon.

Supernatural's world building extends far beyond the source material, which allows readers to study how texts become sacred to those who deem them so. Uniquely, this text in particular recognizes the encroachment of fan and fan text as an attempt to sanctify the narrative, and in that recognition, takes measures to self-deprecate, even make itself carnivalesque and grotesque, to frustrate consecration. The push and pull between these two impetuses—reverence and irreverence—provide a glimpse into the way fanwork can influence the structure of a narrative, and points to how fragile the walls between writer and reader truly are, in bright, performative, interactive, mediated, twenty-first century high-definition detail. The show bears the burden of its fandom in a visible way, and becomes its own iconoclastic vehicle, that tries again and again to dispel its own authority while reasserting it, which creates a space of irredeemable postmodern violence.

Beyond *Supernatural*, though, there are the questions the show presents about the place of fan methodologies that lead to worlds, even galaxies, of annotations surrounding the source text. Do these methodologies place so pressure on those fictional central walls or borders that the sacred text then collapses? Also, if we read fanwork as scholarship or the training work toward expertise, how do the avenues of access (and the gatekeeping mechanisms that restrict access) change under the inchoate possibilities of digital and social media technologies? In its struggle to define itself and its borders, *Supernatural* and its fandom presents and begins to answer what I would argue are rather important existential and epistemological questions. *Supernatural* and its fandom is, above all else, supertextual, subtextual, metatextual, and ultimately, symbiotextual.

NOTES

1. Susan Handelman, "Fragments of the Rock: Contemporary Literary Theory and the Study of Rabbinic Texts—A Response to David Stern," *Prooftexts* 5, no. 1 (January 1985): 75–95.

2. "Monster at the End of this Book," Season 4: Episode 18, *Supernatural*, writer Julie Siege, dir. Mike Rohl (U.S.: Warner Bros Television, 2009).

3. *Supernatural*, Seasons 1–14, created by Eric Kripke (U.S.: Warner Bros Television, 2005–).

4. Laura Felschow, "'Hey, Check It Out, There's Actually Fans': (Dis)empowerment and (Mis)representation of Cult Fandom in *Supernatural*," *Transformative Works and Cultures* 4 (2017), http://dx.doi.org/10.3983/twc.2010.0134.

5. Kristina Busse, "Introduction: In Focus: Fandom and Feminism: Gender and the Politics of Fan Production," *Cinema Journal* 48, no. 4 (Summer 2009): 104–107.

6. *Homestuck* was a webcomic written by Andrew Hussie that ran from 2009 to 2012 and 2013 to 2016. The comic has following in the millions and has opened itself up to a multitude of fan interventions and reconfigurations. It can be viewed here: https://www.homestuck.com/.

7. This essay uses "meta" in its prefix sense, meaning self-referential.

8. Nil, "The Secondhand Fandom Syndrome," *The Book Window*, December 20 (2016), https://bookwindowcom.wordpress.com/2016/12/20/the-secondhand-fandom-syndrome/.

9. There is a long running fandom joke about how *Supernatural* is part of most tags on tumblr.

10. Brigid Cherry, "Sympathy for the Fangirl: Becky Rosen, fan identity and interactivity in *Supernatural*," in *TV Goes to Hell: An Unofficial Roadmap of Supernatural*, ed. Stacey Abbott and David Lavery (Toronto, ON: ECW Press, 2011), 203–218.

11. David Stern, "Midrash and Midrashic Interpretation," *Jewish Study Bible* (New York: Oxford University Press, 2004), 1863–1875.

12. Stern, "Midrash and Midrashic Interpretation."

13. David Stern, "Midrash and Indeterminacy," *Critical Inquiry* 15, no. 1 (Fall 1988): 132–161.

14. To understand the contention between schools of interpretation of midrash traditions, a reader should look at the debate between Handelman and Stern in "Fragments of the Rock," as well as the resistance to postmodern criticism that Boyarin would face in *Critical Inquiry*.

15. Henry Slonimsky, "The Philosophy Implicit in the Midrash," *Hebrew Union College Annual* 27 (1956): 237.

16. Daniel Boyarin, "The Sea Resists: Midrash and the (Psycho)dynamics of Intertextuality," *Poetics Today* 10 (1989): 661–677.

17. Elizabeth Schüssler Fiorenza, *Rhetoric and Ethic: The Politics of Biblical Studies* (Minneapolis: Fortress Press, 1999).

18. *Heteroglossia* comes from Bakhtin's work on discourse, the dialogic, and most specifically how novels perform this concept. See Mikhail Bakhtin, *The Dialogic Imagination: Four Essays*, trans. Carly Emerson and Michael Holquist (Austin: University of Texas Press, 1981).

19. Rachel Barenblat, "Transformative Work: Midrash and Fanfiction," *Religion & Literature* 43, no. 2 (Summer 2011): 171–77.

20. Gerard Genette, *Paratexts: Thresholds of Interpretation* (New York: Cambridge University Press, 1987): 6–7.

21. *Archive of Our Own*, or AO3, is among a number of fan fiction archive sites. This number does not include LiveJournal, which was a popular fanfiction exchange site for many *Supernatural* fans, especially in earlier seasons. Nor does the number include works from tumblr or fanfiction.net.

22. *Archive of Our Own* tags searches can combine different tags and when combining *Supernatural* and the "fix it" tag, a user can drill down to about 5,000 fanworks.

23. Shana O'Neil, "Everybody Ships: Why Shipping Is More than Fandom's Dirty Little Secret," *blastr*, February 25 (2016), http://www.syfy.com/syfywire/everybody-ships-why-shipping-more-fandoms-dirty-little-secret.

24. "Fanfiction," Season 10: Episode 5, *Supernatural*, writer Robbie Thompson, dir. Phil Sgriccia (2014).

25. Comments on Lisa Macklem, "*Supernatural*—Fan Fiction—Review—Supersize 200th Episode Edition," *Spoiler TV*, November 12 (2014), https://www.spoilertv.com/2014/11/supernatural-fan-fiction-review.html.

26. "[Episode Discussion] S10E05 Fan Fiction," r/supernatural, November 11 (2014), https://www.reddit.com/r/Supernatural/comments/2lzn0j/episode_discussion_s10e05_fan_fiction/.

27. Aja Romano, "How 1 Question Triggered a 'Supernatural' Fandom Meltdown," *Daily Dot*, May 6 (2013), https://www.dailydot.com/society/jensen-ackles-homophobia-supernatural-fandom/.

28. Uve, "JIB5: Destiel, the PR nightmare and the potential queerbaiting." *Daily Fandom*, May 25 (2014), https://thedailyfandom.com/jib5-destiel-the-pr-nightmare-and-the-potential-queerbaiting/.

29. Maureen Ryan, "What TV Can Learn from 'The 100' Mess," *Variety*, March 1 (2016), http://variety.com/2016/tv/opinion/the-100-lexa-jason-rothenberg-1201729110/.

30. Edward Vkanty, "The *Vampire Diaries*' E.P. Julie Plec Reacts to Online Haters and Bullies," *Inquistr*, October 15 (2015), www.inquisitr.com/2525170/the-vampire-diaries-e-p-julie-plec-reacts-to-online-haters-and-bullies/.

31. Mikhail Bakhtin, *The Dialogic Imagination*.

32. "The Girl with the Dungeon and Dragons Tattoo," Season 7: Episode 20, *Supernatural*, writer Robbie Thompson, dir. John MacCarthy (2012).

33. "Slumber Party," Season 9: Episode 4, *Supernatural*, writer Robbie Thompson, dir. Robert Singer (2013).

34. "Don't Call Me Shurley," Season 11: Episode 20, *Supernatural*, writer Robbie Thompson, dir. Robert Singer (2016); "Alpha and Omega," Season 11: Episode 23, *Supernatural*, writer Andrew Dabb, dir. Phil Sgriccia (2016). Chuck Shurley's evolution from prophet to god is nodded to in the 200th episode when he appears at the end of the episode to grant legitimacy to the young protagonist's version of his books. His status as God is confirmed in Season 11.

35. Linda Hutcheon, *A Theory of Parody: The Teaching of Twentieth-Century Art Forms* (Urbana: Illinois University Press, 1985).

36. "The Great Escapist," Season 8: Episode 21, *Supernatural*, writer Robert Duncan McNeill, dir. Robert Duncan McNeill (2013).

37. Gavia Baker-Whitelaw, "*Supernatural* can thank its fandom for its audience growth," *Daily Dot*, June 16 (2014), https://www.dailydot.com/parsec/fandom/supernatural-ratings-spike-queerbaiting/.

Bibliography

Alter, Robert. *The Art of Bibilical Narrative*. New York: Basic Books, 1981.

Baker-Whitelaw, Gavia. "*Supernatural* can thank its fandom for its audience growth." *Daily Dot*, June 16 (2014). https://www.dailydot.com/parsec/fandom/supernatural-ratings-spike-queerbaiting/ (accessed May 9, 2018).

Bakhtin, Mikhail. *The Dialogic Imagination: Four Essays*. Translated by Carly Emerson and Michael Holquist. Austin: University of Texas, 1981.

Barenblat, Rachel. "Transformative Work: Midrash and Fanfiction." *Religion & Literature* 43, no. 2 (Summer 2011): 171–77.

Boyarin, Daniel. "Old Wine in New Bottles: Intertextuality and Midrash." *Poetics Today* 8, nos 3/4 (1987): 539–556.

———. "The Sea Resists: Midrash and the (Psycho)dynamics of Intertextuality." *Poetics Today* 10, no. 4 (1989): 661–77.

Busse, Kristina. "Introduction: In Focus: Fandom and Feminism: Gender and the Politics of Fan Production." *Cinema Journal* 48, no. 4 (Summer 2009): 104–07.

Cherry, Brigid. "Sympathy for the Fangirl: Becky Rosen, fan identity and interactivity in 'Supernatural.'" In *TV Goes to Hell: An Unofficial Roadmap of Supernatural*, edited by Stacey Abbott and David Lavery, 203–218. Toronto: ECW Press, 2011.

Dufrene, Mikel. *Phenomenology of Aesthetic Experience*. Evanston, IN: Northwestern UP, 1973.

"[Episode Discussion] S10E05 Fan Fiction." r/supernatural, November 11 (2014). https://www.reddit.com/r/Supernatural/comments/2lzn0j/episode_discussion_s10e05_fan_fiction/ (accessed May 9, 2018).

Felschow, Laura. "Hey, check it out, there's actually fans": (Dis)empowerment and (Mis)representation of Cult Fandom in *Supernatural*." *Transformative Works and Cultures* 4 (2017). DOI: https://doi.org/10.3983/twc.2010.0134.

Genette, Gerard. *Paratexts: Thresholds of Interpretation*. New York: Cambridge University Press, 1987.

Handelman, Susan. "Fragments of the Rock: Contemporary Literary Theory and the Study of Rabbinic Texts—A Response to David Stern." *Prooftexts* 5, no. 1 (January 1985): 75–95.

———. *The Slayer of Moses: The Emergence of Rabbinic Interpretation in Modern Literary Theory*. Buffalo: State University Press of New York, 1983.

Hills, Matt. *Fan Cultures*. London: Routledge, 2002.

Hutcheon, Linda. *A Theory of Parody: The Teaching of Twentieth-Century Art Forms*. Urbana: Illinois University Press, 1985.

Jindra, Michael. "*Star Trek* Fandom as a Religious Phenomenon." *Sociology of Religion* 55, no. 1 (Spring 1994): 27–51.

Knibbs, Kate. "How Horny *X-Files* Lovers Created a New Type of Online Fandom." *Gizmodo*, May 5 (2015). http://gizmodo.com/how-horny-x-files-lovers-created-a-new-type-of-online-f-1702083417 (accessed May 6, 2018).

Macklem, Lisa. "*Supernatural*—Fan Fiction—Review—Supersize 200th Episode Edition." *Spoiler TV*, November 12 (2014). https://www.spoilertv.com/2014/11/supernatural-fan-fiction-review.html (accessed May 6, 2018).

Nichols, Bill. *Ideology and the Image.* Bloomington: Indiana University Press, 1981.

Nil. "The Secondhand Fandom Syndrome." *The Book Window*, December 20 (2016). https://bookwindowcom.wordpress.com/2016/12/20/the-secondhand-fandom-syndrome/ (accessed May 6, 2018).

O'Neil, Shana. "Everybody Ships: Why Shipping Is More Than Fandom's Dirty Little Secret." *Blastr*, February 25 (2016). http://www.syfy.com/syfywire/everybody-ships-why-shipping-more-fandoms-dirty-little-secret (accessed May 6, 2018).

Romano, Aja. "How 1 Question Triggered a *Supernatural* Fandom Meltdown." *Daily Dot.* May 6 (2013). https://www.dailydot.com/society/jensen-ackles-homophobia-supernatural-fandom/ (accessed May 6, 2018).

Ryan, Maureen. "What TV Can Learn from *The 100* Mess." *Variety*, March 14 (2016). http://variety.com/2016/tv/opinion/the-100-lexa-jason-rothenberg-1201729110/ (accessed May 6, 2018).

Schüssler Fiorenza, Elizabeth. *Rhetoric and Ethic: The Politics of Biblical Studies.* Minneapolis: Fortress Press, 1999.

Slonimsky, Henry. "The Philosophy Implicit in the Midrash." *Hebrew Union College Annual* (1956): 235–290.

Stern, David. "Midrash and Indeterminacy." *Critical Inquiry* 15, no. 1 (Autumn 1988), 132–161.

_____. "Midrash and Midrashic Interpretation." In *Jewish Study Bible*, edited by Barry Rubin, 1863–1875. New York: Oxford University Press, 2004.

Supernatural. Seasons 1–14. Created by Eric Kripke. U.S.: Warner Bros Television, 2005–2018.

Uve. "JIB5: Destiel, the PR nightmare and the Potential Queerbaiting." *Daily Fandom.* May 25 (2014). https://thedailyfandom.com/jib5-destiel-the-pr-nightmare-and-the-potential-queerbaiting/ (accessed May 6, 2018).

Vkanty, Edward. "The Vampire Diaries E.P. Julie Plec Reacts to Online Haters and Bullies." *Inquistr*, October 15 (2015). http://www.inquisitr.com/2525170/the-vampire-diaries-e-p-julie-plec-reacts-to-online-haters-and-bullies/ (accessed May 6, 2018).

"Seizing the Means of Perception"

The Use of Fiction in Chaos Magic and Occultural Fandom

Greg Conley

Introduction

In the twentieth and twenty-first centuries new cultural practices and currents, such as fandom and occulture, have emerged to supplement the social, personal, and philosophical affordances of traditional religion. While it is not accurate to say that fandoms replace religion, they provide similar outlets for ontological and epistemological inquiry, imaginative expression, and community building for many people, including those who do not find such things in religious adherence—either as "nones" or those left unsatisfied by their institutions of faith. Occulture, the merging of popular culture and magical subcultures, again offers individuals attractive beliefs and practices beyond the norm. In both fandom and occulture we may witness the sacralization of fiction and fictional figures, an important factor in their ability to produce religious-like feelings and behaviors in participants. Both are to some degree countercultural; both produce the sacred for their practitioners; and both blur the boundaries between fiction and reality. Thus, it is helpful to consider fandom as a kind of occulture, and in turn, magical practices that rely on fiction like Chaos Magic can he helpfully thought of as a kind of fandom, as this comparison, or "occultural fandom," reveals something of the internal methods and motivations in sacralizing media.

In fandom and occulture, the method of sacralization is just as important as the end results, because both contemporary fans and occultists are taking personal control over their belief structures, rather than acceding control to external agencies. To borrow a phrase from Erik Davis, they are both "seizing the means of perception."[1] If we look at practitioners of Chaos Magic, occultists who typically take a postmodern approach to concepts of "truth" and readily sacralize fiction, this assertion becomes especially evident. Like fans who engage in hyperdiegetic world-building, Chaos magicians invest their perception with symbolic power and intentionally bend the parameters of their subjective reality to live in more emotionally satisfactory spaces and, in their magical practice, effect change in cooperation with their will.

This essay will refer primarily to science fiction and fantasy fandoms as they are utilized by Chaos magicians or "Chaotes," in particular, the influence of the work of nineteenth-century author H.P. Lovecraft (1890–1937) on magical practices. As Emily McAvan has noted, our present postmodern crisis undermines the usefulness and authority of traditional religious structures, and with the fall of their metanarratives we find new ways to comprehend what is sacred and what is profane.[2] The resultant "postmodern sacred," however, is not necessarily atheistic, rather it plays with the sacred by combining metaphysical ideas with rationalistic methods to help magic "re-enter the realm of the possible."[3] That the cosmic nihilism of Lovecraft's gothic science fiction stories has become a mainstay of occultural phenomena like Chaos Magic is testament to the creative ways in which magicians, like fans, draw their own meanings from their chosen texts and make them applicable to their situations and purposes.

Occultural Fandom: Sacralizing Media from the Margins

The turn toward popular media for sources of the sacred is widespread, and not just in science fiction and fantasy fandoms. For instance, seeing a film may be a kind of religious experience for many.[4] However, science fiction (sf) and fantasy media are particularly good at delivering material for religious-like attachment because they provide (semi-)rational structures around symbols meant to evoke a "sense of wonder."[5] Science fiction is also a great source for imaginative enchantment because slippages between real and fantastic are intentional. As Farah Mendelson notes "[l]anguage is not trustworthy in sf: metaphor becomes literal."[6] Invented words, technobabble, and hypothetical situations are—or can be—made real in a fantasy or a sf text. That is important because it increases the ability of the respondent to, as Henry Jenkins says, "blur the boundaries between fact and fiction" when desired.[7]

The need to supplement the waning influence of traditional religion with alternative sources of speculation and enchantment makes clear that religious impulses remain despite increasing secularization. Fan devotion provides a crucial site for the study of religious or religious-like behaviors in supposedly secular contexts. David Chidester has pointed out that everything from baseball to Coca-Cola seems religious, and that fans "participate in similar kinds of sacred solidarity" that make of their fandoms a kind of religion.[8] Michael Jindra has famously demonstrated that *Star Trek* satisfies many religious impulses.[9] Additionally, fans insist that media narratives and symbols offer what religion does not. As one fan, Andy Balkus, explains, *Star Trek* "spoke to me and really shaped my outlook on life. It lead [*sic*] me into a life of public service…. Sure, they got a little preachy from time to time … but it's way simpler and a lot more forgiving than any established religion."[10]

To better understand the correlations between fandoms and religions, we may look, as Chidester does, to classic substantive definitions of religion such as that supplied by Clifford Geertz of religion as a "system of symbols."[11] There are issues with Geertz's model, and he is vague about how symbols work,[12] but the symbolic significance of media texts is essential to its magical, and therefore religious, application, especially in Chaos Magic. Symbol systems provide a structure for the shared and participatory experience necessary for building a sense of belonging and community, reinforced through rituals. As Randall Collins has argued, ritual actions of all sorts create emotional energy by bolstering group solidarity. These ritual actions "generate a variable level of emotional energy (EE) in each individual over time" and that energy allows practitioners a more satisfying range of choices and actions as well as a shared experience which leads to the strengthening of community.[13] Ritual, in Collins' model, serves to build up long-lasting emotional energy. For the emotional response to be generated and shared, the group must have "charged" symbols they can use in the ritual.

Popular media texts offer a range of symbols for such purposes, from more abstract visual and narrative motifs, to clearly identifiable characters, aesthetics, and lexicons. Fandoms generate their sense of community and emotional energy by means of deep investment, exploration, and artistic creation related to, or focused on, popular media. According to Jenkins, fan engagement is "playful, speculative, subjective…. They create strong parallels between their own lives and the events of the series … they construct a metatext that is larger, richer, more complex and interesting than the original series."[14] They live their lives with references to their favorite media in mind, or go to conventions and festivals where they can more fully enter their chosen media through cosplay, group performances, and shared experiences of viewing or discussion. They use that inspiration to create their desired realities around them, either in a community or alone. Similarly, the systems of symbols proffered by texts are used by Chaos magicians and other postmodern occultists to extend, explain, and even create their reality. Wouter Hanegraaff has defined occultism as "all attempts by esotericists to come to terms with a disenchanted world,"[15] and like fans who use texts to make sense of their own lives, magicians can use texts to generate new "occultural" worldviews, values, and systems of belief.

Christopher Partridge has put forward the term "occulture" to describe the mediated milieu in which Chaos Magic and other esoteric means of magic dwell. He explains that "occulture includes those often *hidden, rejected* and *oppositional* beliefs and practices associated with esotericism, theosophy, mysticism, New Age, Paganism, and a range of other subcultural beliefs and practices."[16] Examples of occulture are radically divergent. For example, some lay claims to historical antecedents, while others make use of esoteric methods independent of their heritage. All, however, intend to resist cultural narratives associated with dogmatic truth-claims of "patriarchal monotheisms."[17] Instead, occultural belief systems encourage one to "create one's own occultic dish according to one's own occultic tastes,"[18] picking and choosing from existing religious and non-religious systems to create their own personalized set of beliefs and practices.

While occulture may contain ideas that are contrary to or outside of mainstream religious and materialist worldviews, it does not exist separately from popular culture: occulture and popular culture have a cyclical relationship. Partridge's consequent theory of "popular occulture" posits three central points:

> (1) that occultural worldviews have been an important source of inspiration for popular culture, (2) that popular culture has in turn been an important source of inspiration for the formation of occultural worldviews, and, consequently, (3) that popular culture is beginning to have a shaping effect on Western plausibility structures.[19]

The ways in which Chaos magicians and other postmodern occultists and occultural fans engage with media sources are counter to and excluded from both the dominant rational and materialist and wider religious discourses. They are fitting examples of popular occulture in action. Similarly, fans, in their devotion to fictional texts, exhibit attachments, form ideologies, and create communities in ways that can be counter to and excluded from the dominant cultural discourse. As Jenkins points out: "the fan still constitutes a scandalous category in contemporary culture, one alternately the target of ridicule and anxiety, of dread and desire."[20] They worry people with their energetic consumption and creation, and function as the butts of jokes or perceived sources of discomfort. For instance, the "psychopathic fan" is still a common stock character in films.[21] Likewise, the taboo placed upon "alternative" forms of religion means they are taken less seriously and subject to more scrutiny than traditional forms, as Thomas Alberts explains: "the problem of authenticity arises when profane things do not keep their distance and instead approach or seek admission to the bounded space of the sacred."[22] Chaos Magic, in its anarchic understanding of truth, reality, and fiction, quintessentially resists the dominant paradigms in culture and religion. Erik Davis comments that the "desire to rebel against the tyranny of reason and its ordered objective universe is one of the underlying goals of Chaos Magic."[23]

Subcultural communities have radically different values "from those embedded within the formal economy" based on "loyalty and a sense of "identity" or "belonging" as opposed to the principle of forming ties on the basis of calculation, monetary or otherwise."[24] Political "opposition may be constituted by living, even momentarily, within alternative practices, structures and spaces to be filled with something, presumedly something one cares for passionately."[25] Fandom space can be "defined by its refusal of mundane values and practices, its celebration of deeply held emotions and passionately embraced pleasures."[26] Rather than find inspiration in either traditionally rationalist or religious contexts, fans, like occultists, look to the postmodern sacred, where the metaphysical meets the media, for sources. In Davis's words, "both fans and witches share a very concrete sense of the power of the imagination, seen not as an elite realm restricted to "artists" (or TV producers) but as a vital phantasmic faculty that links the realms of fantasy with the here and now."[27] In short, fandoms, like occultures, are communities based around shared ideas that are often countercultural and resist some element(s) of mainstream cultural discourse, but nonetheless allow for the production of meaningful shared and personal identities.

A Chaos of Ideas: Fandom, Occulture and Chaos Magic

Chaos Magic is particularly useful in understanding fandom because it demonstrates a self-conscious method for using fiction and art as sacred inspiration. It is also a kind of fandom of its own. As practitioner Phil Hine wrote "Chaos Magic borrowed freely from Science Fiction.... Chaos Magic is an approach that enables the individual to use anything that s/he thinks is suitable as a temporary belief or symbol system."[28] Since subjective reality alteration is the goal of the Chaos magician, rather than adherence to a scripturally-enshrined theological outlook, any source is useful for articulating a worldview so long as it provides the structure and the symbols desired. It is significant that Hine uses the phrase "temporary belief or symbol system." Chaos magicians may switch between multiple convenient symbol-systems depending on their needs at any one time. This is broadly comparable to a fan's movement through fandoms, across media formats, and between the lines of discussion or narration provided in fan-fiction, given their mood and needs. The following brief overview of the aspects of "belief," "symbols," and "rituals" in Chaos Magic will highlight the relationship between this system and the magico-religious use of fiction, It will also provide specific examples and a case study in the shape of H.P. Lovecraft's impact on Chaos magic.

Belief

The ideas of occultist Aleister Crowley have exerted a strong influence on Chaos Magic. Crowley's definition of magic, that "Magick is the Science and Art of causing Change to occur in conformity with Will,"[29] and his contention that "it is immaterial whether these [spirits, gods etc.] exist or not"[30] as long as magical operations work, have been especially influential on postmodern occulture. For example, Hine writes, "[t]he question of how much of it is "True" in the absolute sense is irrelevant, at least from a Chaos perspective, since it is the investment of belief in a concept which makes it viable, rather than its coherence."[31] Chaos Magic is indebted to this philosophy of utility by attempting to free the operator from inhibitions and is, in effect, a "continuous deconstruction of all dogmas and ideologies, including the premises of magic itself."[32]

Chaos Magic can be defined—insofar as it can be defined at this point at all—as a part of occulture specifically dedicated to resisting the culture and the cultural training the operator finds themselves embroiled in. Chaos Magic, "[w]ith its central principle of "nothing is true, everything is permitted" and its rejection of all fixed models of reality" is almost ideally suited to handle the anxieties and upheavals of the postmodern era.[33] Chaos Magic does not require something to be "real" to be powerful. Dave Evans says it "removes the absolute reality of any gods from the equation … any deity invoked is seen not as an objectively "real" entity but as a metaphorical construct with which to work."[34] As Carole Cusack puts it, "[i]n both contemporary religion and contemporary magic there are a significant percentage of practitioners who are uninterested in the ontological status of the gods and entities invoked or evoked in rituals."[35] A Chaos magician, like many religious people in the postmodern era, does not care if a god exists, only whether invocations of that god create measurable effects.

Because Chaos magicians decide that the reality of a deity or fictional character does not matter, they are able to induce effects in themselves and create their preferred experience of reality. Like fans who write and rewrite the destinies of their favorite characters and universes, Chaotes recontextualize popular or secular texts for their magical work. The result from both practices is a multiplicity of "traditions"; there is no longer a single or correct reading of a text, and anyone, any fan or magician, can adapt and personalize the symbols derived from the source. This multiplicity does not threaten to disrupt any sense of consistency. Fans and Chaos magicians both use fiction because it is malleable and re-interpretable, not linear and doctrinal, and in doing so create immersive and wondrous worlds in which elements from fantasy are made real.

Symbols

Chaote Peter Carroll, who along with Ray Sherwin is generally considered a founder of Chaos Magic theory, observes that Chaos magicians use magical symbols in a way similar to the symbols used in algebraic equations—they stand in for complex thought processes and intentions.[36] The use of generated symbols via sigilization (a subconscious artistic process popularized by Austin Osman Spare) is a common practice for Chaos magicians, but elements of culture, stories, media forms, and so forth can also be extrapolated as symbols. This requires, says Jaq Hawkins in *Understanding Chaos Magic*, "an independent thinking process leading to personal interpretation of what one will find."[37] Thus, innovation and creativity are more important than any particular tradition, as the point of Chaos Magic is to get results and support the user's individualism.[38] Whether the traditions they draw on are extremely old, venerated, or even "real" does not matter.

Crowley's injunction is particularly useful in understanding fandom's use of fiction as sacred material, as he opened the door to the use of fiction as an occult symbol system by claiming that it is the action, not the symbol, that matters. Some of Crowley's fellow practitioners agreed. Occultist A.E. Waite, famous now for his influence on the tradition of modern tarot, theorized that popular fiction had a "*mystical* function" that could "induce a spontaneous and epiphanic encounter with the divine in readers" even if they did not seek out that encounter.[39] Inheritors of this idea in the Chaos Magic milieu today like Carroll and Hine have promoted the use of a variety of types of popular culture products for spellcraft.

Chaos Magic prioritizes experimentation and idiosyncratic magical symbols and systems. Hine calls this idea "Theory-in-Use" and says that for an operator, these theories-in-use "cannot be taught: they are personal and tend to operate at the level of unconscious assumptions."[40] These unconscious assumptions come from the symbol-system the magician uses. They originate in culture, in reading, in what Hine calls "Theories-of-Action" learned from other magicians or fiction. Internalizing symbols, investing them with belief, and allowing them to affect one's day-to-day actions—the acts of a Chaos magician—could also describe loving a piece of art. Hine claims that magic "is not something which one merely "does." It's personal, up-close. It twists you and skews your perception of the world, tipping you into a world of signs and portents."[41] The magician is a well-trained reader, ready to synthesize significance from anything and everything.

Rituals

Hine compares attending a good ritual with attending "a good movie or play."[42] A magical ritual or event is supposed to plant in the participant particularly powerful thoughts and feelings.[43] The magic has been successful if the participant integrates the new concepts and ideas into his or her daily life, if they become part of the participant's "Theories-of-Action" or "Theories-in-Use." So, according to a Chaos magician, magic is successful insofar as it affects the way the participant perceives or thinks of their everyday reality. However, as Chaote Gordon White notes, "Chaos Magic is not "doing whatever you want," it is "trialling a lot of things and retaining those that work."[44] Utility is always the first priority to a Chaos magician, and experimentation and innovation are essential approaches.

Chaos magicians make "personal religions" from their individual symbol systems. They maintain the emotional energy they glean from religion, mythology, and even fiction, holding everything suspended through their manipulation of belief and ritual. What a religion does on a large-scale level, Chaos magicians do to themselves with whatever symbol-systems they choose. These symbol systems are "charged," as in Collins's model, with the belief and emotional energy of the practitioner. This helps to prolong the energy beyond the bounds of the ritual itself—watching a film, reading a book, or even wearing a t-shirt with a logo can remind the fan or the magician of the ritual and its symbols, imbuing their day-to-day life with some of that emotional energy.

The Magical Use of Fiction

In a way, Chaos Magic is simply an esoteric version of the way all readers read, especially fans whose engagement with the text is typified by its depth and intensity. However, Chaos Magic reveals something about fandoms that may not be immediately obvious. Fandoms are structures for fans to create meaning for themselves. The ways in which many fans use their favorite media are like the ways magicians, and particularly Chaos magicians, use magico-religious methods to invest symbols and stories with deeply personal, and magically powerful, meaning. That allows them to change their circumstances or behavior if desired. Both groups create their own realities with their chosen media as central symbol-systems.

That art, fiction, and magic share epistemological and ontological qualities is an idea shared by many contemporary occultists. Graphic novelist and occultist Alan Moore—who wrote fan favorites like *Watchmen* and *V for Vendetta*—posits that magic and art are the same. Moore argues that magic should be defined as "purposeful engagement with the phenomena and possibilities of consciousness."[45] He further proposes that "art and magic should be more closely connected" because magic "offers us a coherent and sensibly integrated world with which to relate."

Chaos Magic blurs the lines between art and magic even further by adopting fictional signs, symbols, and gods into its religious operations. Both Chaos Magic and certain fandom practices involve the participant in creating meaning through symbol-relationships usually reserved for religion. Creating this meaning in this way is a countercultural act and a partial rejection of the dominant meaning-making discourses of the operator's culture. It allows members of both groups to create a kind of personal reality, a conceptual space in which to live. This space is the rebellious place, the marginal town, created by pushing back against the dominant visions of reality with selected and sacralized symbol-systems.

A wide variety of fictional works have been used by Chaos magicians to create these sacred second worlds. Carroll devoted an entire book to magic based on Terry Pratchett's Discworld novels.[46] He points out that Chaos magicians borrowed Octarine (an invisible, magical color) from Discworld and regularly comb through the books for more images to use.[47] Grant Morrison, well-known comic book creator and editor, and a vocal Chaos magician, has written about using Ganesh, Superman, and John Lennon as sacred figures.[48] Michael Moorcock and H.P. Lovecraft have been perennial sources for Chaos magicians since the practice's inception. Examining how Chaos magicians have used fiction will reveal methods commonly used by both magicians and fans to sacralize fiction and create emotional energy akin to that made in rituals.

The use of Moorcock by early Chaos magicians is recorded by Dave Evans, who points out that the eight-pointed Chaos star comes straight from Moorcock's iconography.[49] Michael Moorcock (b. 1939) is a British fantasy author, perhaps most famous for his Elric of Melniboné stories. Moorcock weaves his

The "Symbol of Chaos" from Michael Moorcock's Eternal Champion series, adopted for use by Chaos magicians (Wikipedia).

dozens of disparate novel series into a multiverse in which characters can meet their doubles, heroes can meet themselves suffering under Nazi rule, and the powers of law and chaos squabble over who should rule the universe. Many themes in Moorcock's work make it appealing to Chaos magicians, such as the use of postmodern intertextuality, but the underpinning cosmological battle is the primary reason for Moorcock's adoption by Chaos magicians. Law and chaos are divorced from "good" and "evil." This means a hero could serve Chaos while a villain serves law. In fact, Gary Gygax, creator of *Dungeons & Dragons*, stated that the game's separation of the character binaries of Lawful/Chaotic and Good/Evil was inspired by Moorcock's work.[50] Given Chaos Magic's status as "a reaction against the moribund state of occultism in general"[51] it makes sense that it would adopt fictional symbols of fruitful chaos pushing back against old, decaying laws.

Moorcock spearheaded the promotion of New Wave science fiction as editor of *New Worlds* magazine in the 1960s. The themes of the *New Worlds* group of authors included "ontological insecurity, alienation, the hidden and hostile dimensions of media and machines, the disintegration of objectivity into subjective worlds of inner space, the dangerously exhilarating multiplication of "possibilities" (at the expense of certainty and absolute authority of all kinds)."[52] These themes were adopted by Chaos Magic, as it privileges personal experimentation and subjective perception. Just before acknowledging Moorcock's influence on Chaos Magic, Carroll writes, "[n]ow reality imitates art, because art explores the imagination, and we create reality mainly through imagination (or lack of it)."[53] The "disintegration of objectivity into subjective worlds of inner space" that characterizes Moorcock's work is not a crisis for Chaos magicians; it is the root of their practice.

Chaos Magic is also particularly indebted to science fiction and fantasy, and Chaos magicians who use fiction in their magico-religious practices are fans, and must be fans, for the practices to work. The confluence of the two can be seen not only in the uses of fiction by individual magicians, but in their own fans. For example, a visitor to Grant Morrison's convention in 2012 remarks on this effect on Morrison's followers, "I ran into a well-dressed kid from Kansas who earnestly explained to me that magic was real, and Morrison's pop magic advice not only worked but changed his life ... 'It's like hacking your mind,' he assured me."[54] Fans who are interested in magico-religious practices may be naturally drawn to Chaos magic, not only because popular figures like Morrison promote it, but because its sacralization of fiction provides an alternative source of re-enchantment. Meanwhile, Chaos magicians will be drawn to fandoms for raw materials. This mutually supportive relationship is additionally interesting because both groups use fiction to create emotionally charged symbols and resist dominant cultural discourses, while still drawing on widely available cultural products and techniques of cultural production.

Cosmic Chaos: Lovecraftian Magic

While contemporary fiction like Moorcock's repurposes the cultural anxieties in the postmodern fashion that so appeals to Chaotes, the existential horror novels of H.P. Lovecraft[55] are still some of the most widely used fictional resources. The running themes of the Lovecraftian "Mythos" are that malevolent and primordial extra-terrestrial creatures, the "Old Ones" and the "Elder Gods," are waiting for misguided humans to open a portal for them to re-enter our world and bring about its destruction. To know these beings is to know madness, and yet devotees revive their ancient cults and perform demonic rituals to call them back from the regions beyond. For Chaos magicians Lovecraft's fiction is, like other forms of fantasy, science fiction, and horror, laden with material for their religious activities, as Wouter Hanegraaff explains:

> the radical refusal to distinguish between fiction and reality makes it possible for Chaos magicians to invoke, and allow themselves to be possessed by, demons and deities that they know have been invented by Lovecraft: the objection "they don't exist, for Lovecraft made them up" has no power, for it presupposes the very distinction they reject.[56]

Lovecraft, who wrote most of his work in the opening decades of the twentieth century, was an ardent atheist and yet his work, with many arcane themes, has a long-running association with, and has been used by, many occultists. It featured in the early rituals of the Church of Satan.[57] Kenneth Grant, founder of the Typhonian O.T.O., claimed that "Lovecraft's writings, with their singular imagery and aesthetic of cosmic horror, have become popular totemic and meditative devices."[58] Groups such as the Cult of Cthulhu and the Esoteric Order of Dagon emerged in more recent decades to extend magical engagement with his texts, and many individual magicians continue to find use in Lovecraftian paradigms.[59] While much could be said of the use of Lovecraftian texts in occulture, here three aspects—worldview, symbols, and gnosis—will be touched on to demonstrate the religious derivations of the Mythos by Chaos magicians.

Worldview

John L. Steadman claims that for Lovecraftian magicians "Lovecraft's view of the cosmos is, in actuality, not at odds with the postmodernistic magickal view of the cosmos."[60] While Lovecraft's fictional universe is despairingly amoral, that does not mean Chaos magicians who use Lovecraft's work eschew concepts of right and wrong. Rather, most who work with Lovecraft's fiction in magic "adopt a balanced mode of gnostic existentialism that calls all constructs into question while refusing the cold comforts of skeptical reason or suicidal nihilism."[61] For example, Lovecraftian Chaos Magic practitioner Carl Oort says "[I] systematize my own form of Lovecraftian magick to work with on my own terms—a system which retains the dreadful sense of cosmic awe and allows for an encounter with them in a sorcerous context."[62] Another, Xenia, rereads Lovecraft's apathetic universe: "I reject Lovecraft's nihilism and prefer to take a more absurdist approach; a little disorder is often just what's needed." In his anthropological studies of Lovecraftian magicians, Justin Woodman concludes that the apparently horrifying gods of Lovecraft's alien pantheons can be "mobilised as a potent "apocalyptic" weapon in contesting the alienating consequences of modernity" and also emancipate the magician from the overarching moral binaries of his or her culture.[63]

System of Symbols

While Lovecraft's work allows operators to escape their familiar traditions and assumptions, it also provides a structure and mythology useful for spellcraft and building a system of symbols. According to Lovecraft himself, the weird tale is "coeval with the religious feeling and closely related to many aspects of it."[64] Not unlike the ways fans open up texts for their own reinterpretations, Lovecraftian magic is "an imaginative and coherent "reading" set in motion by the dynamics of Lovecraft's own texts, a set of thematic, stylistic, and intertextual strategies" according to Davis.[65] As Hine explains in his book on Lovecraftian Chaos magic, *The Pseudonomicon* (1999), Lovecraft's Mythos has

> all the key elements of magical exploration … a sense of sacred landscape; the power of dreams; participation in the sabbat; scrying; shape-shifting, and more. From the bare bones of the Mythos, a magician can weave himself a uniquely personal "system" based on experience with these entities.[66]

The entities in Lovecraft's cosmos have been particularly productive for Chaos magic. Oort comments, "one may work with the beings of Lovecraft's [M]ythos and be able to expect the same level of efficacy as one might imagine are found in deities of other, more historical pantheons."[67]

These fictional gods are rich in symbolism, and beget even more complex symbolic readings. Oort aligns them with both "internal aspects of our psyche" and "external cosmic forces." Frater Tenebrous attaches to Lovecraft's alien creatures various qualities designed to aid the magician in calling them forth in ritual: "The elemental nature of Shub-Niggurath is that of Earth, symbolized by the sign of Taurus. His station is the North.… On earth, the station of Hastur is the East, and his sign is Aquarius."[68] In using Lovecraftian themes in magic, Chaotes, Hine explains, create a religious system that reflects the inner motivations of the individuals, and connects this to a greater, cosmic plane: "Lovecraftian magic is *elemental*, it has an *immediate* presence, and resonates with buried fears, longings, aspirations and dreams."[69]

Gnosis

Finally, Lovecraft and his work have been attributed mystical qualities. That engagement with the Mythos leads to a kind of gnosis-madness, in the texts as well as the fandom. Hawkins claims Chaos Magic allows the operator to go "to the outermost reaches of imagination."[70] Lovecraft provides an ideal medium for imaginative experimentation. Venger Satanis, founder of the Cthulhu Cult, confirms this, saying embracing "cosmic horror" pushes the practitioner into enlightenment, where they can see what Lovecraft called in his fiction the "terrifying vistas of reality."[71] Madness itself gets re-written by Chaotes. Xenia, for instance, sees magical qualities in her own "mental illness," which are enhanced when attuned to the Lovecraftian gods she invokes in rituals: "These beings encourage madness, that is to say they value unusual ideas and atypical ways of thinking. I find I work with them best when I allow my brain to function as it wants to function and trust my own unique perspective."[72] That Lovecraft had a unique vision of the arcane layers of reality has been of interest to many fans and occultists. Lovecraft was an atheist and rationalist, but his fiction undoubtedly evinces a fascination with the liminal, magical, and fantastic.

Scott Cutler Shershow and Scott Michaelsen use the word "psychonaut" to describe Lovecraft, saying he was "constantly plumbing his unconscious via techniques of lucid dreaming."[73] Peter J. Carroll uses "psychonaut" to refer to himself and other Chaos magicians.[74] Again, that Lovecraft may not have considered his "truths" to be "true" at all is made unimportant, as esotericist Frater Tenebrous states: "Lovecraft is a particularly interesting case of the transmission of 'occult knowledge' via dream, in that he was one of the few authors to write effectively on the supernatural without conscious belief in the material which he was conveying."[75] Accidental mystic or not, Lovecraft and his multilayered Mythos have provided inspirational fodder in the shape of worldviews, symbols, systems, and gnostic modes for occultists. As not just magicians but also fans, Lovecraftian magicians open up the text to reinterpretation and repurpose its content to fit their personal and religious requirements.

Conclusion

This essay contains the underlying premise that there are important similarities, even shared methods and motivations, in the ways that fans and occultists use and sacralize texts. As a demonstration of the latter, the use of H.P. Lovecraft by Chaos magicians was explored with respect to how the rituals, symbols, belief of magical practice can draw on the worldview, symbols, and gnosticism of his Mythos. It is argued here that Chaos magicians engage in a kind of occultural fandom in their consumption of texts like Lovecraft's. As in other fandoms, their reading and appropriations of texts are counter to and excluded from dominant rational materialist and religious discourses. Fans do not (always) seek overtly magical symbolism and ritual in their media and fandom activities, but they often focus on properties and stories that provide such material Fans have used many other fictions as sources of sacred emotional energy; for example, Tië eldaliéva is based on the work of J.R.R. Tolkien and Otherkin believe they are non-human and often draw their other selves from fantasy fiction.[76] However, the horror fiction of Lovecraft has demonstrable appeal to those whose wish to "seize the methods of perception" by exposing themselves to the mysteries of the void and the existentially-challenging creatures that lurk within.

NOTES

1. Erik Davis, *Nomad Codes: Adventures in Modern Esoterica* (Portland, OR: YETI Books, 2010), 24.
2. Emily McAvan, *The Postmodern Sacred. The Postmodern Sacred: Popular Culture Spirituality in the Science Fiction, Fantasy and Urban Fantasy Genres* (Jefferson, NC: McFarland, 2012), 22.
3. McAvan, *The Postmodern Sacred*, 23.
4. Clive Marsh, quoted in Christopher Deacy, "Why Study Religion and Popular Culture?" in *Exploring Religion and the Sacred in a Media Age*, ed. Christopher Deacy and Elisabeth Arweck (Farnham and Burlington, VT: Ashgate, 2009), 3. See also the contributions from Marc Joly-Corcoran and Jyrki Korpua et al. in this volume.
5. Farah Mendlesohn, "Introduction: Reading Science Fiction" in *The Cambridge Companion to Science Fiction*, ed. Edward James and Farah Mendlesohn (New York: Cambridge University Press, 2009), 3.
6. Mendlesohn, "Introduction," 5.
7. Henry Jenkins, *Textual Poachers: Television Fans and Participatory Culture* (New York: Routledge, 2005), 18.
8. David Chidester, *Authentic Fakes: Religion and American Popular Culture* (Berkeley: University of California Press, 2005), 33.
9. Michael Jindra, "Star Trek Fandom as a Religious Phenomenon," *Sociology of Religion* 55, no. 1 (1994): 28.
10. Andy Balkus, quoted in Bethan Jones, "Fannish Tattooing and Sacred Identity," *Transformative Works and Cultures* 18 (2015), n.p.
11. Clifford Geertz, *The Interpretation of Cultures* (New York: Basic Books, 1973), 90; Chidester, *Authentic Fakes*, 16.
12. Nancy K. Frankenberry and Hans H. Penner, "Clifford Geertz's Long-Lasting Moods, Motivations, and Metaphysical Conceptions," *The Journal of Religion* 79, no. 4 (1999): 619.
13. Randall Collins, *Interaction Ritual Chains* (New Jersey: Princeton University Press, 2004), 126.
14. Jenkins, *Textual Poachers*, 284.
15. Wouter Hanegraaff, quoted in Colin Duggan, "Perennialism and Iconoclasm. Chaos

Magick and the Legitimacy of Innovation," in *Contemporary Esotericism*, ed. Egil Asprem and Kennet Granholm (New York: Routledge, 2014), 92.

16. Christopher Partridge, *The Re-Enchantment of the West*, Vol. 1 (London: T&T Clark International, 2004), 67–8. Emphasis in original.

17. Partridge, *The Re-Enchantment of the West*, 83–4.

18. Partridge, *The Re-Enchantment of the West*, 71.

19. Partridge, *The Re-Enchantment of the West*, 126.

20. Jenkins, *Textual Poachers*, 15.

21. Jenkins, *Textual Poachers*, 14.

22. Thomas Alberts, "Virtually Real: Fake Religions and Problems of Authenticity in Religion," *Culture and Religion* 9, no. 2 (2008): 136.

23. Davis, *Nomad Codes*, 128.

24. Jeff Bishop and Paul Hoggett, quoted in Davis, *Nomad Codes*, 286.

25. Lawrence Grossberg, "Putting the Pop Back into Postmodernism," in *Universal Abandon: The Politics of Postmodernism*, ed. Andrew Ross (Minneapolis: University of Minnesota Press, 1989), 170.

26. Davis, *Nomad Codes*, 289.

27. Davis, *Nomad Codes*, 108.

28. Phil Hine, quoted in Carole M. Cusack. "Discordian Magic: Paganism, the Chaos Paradigm and the Power of Imagination," *International Journal for the Study of New Religions* 2, no. 1 (2011): 138.

29. Aleister Crowley, *Magick in Theory and Practice* (New York: Dover Publications, 1976), xii.

30. Aleister Crowley, *Magick: Liber ABA* (Boston: Weiser Books, 2004), 375.

31. Phil Hine, *The Pseudonomicon* (Tempe, AZ: New Falcon Publications, 2007), 20.

32. Hugh B. Urban, *Magia Sexualis: Sex, Magic, and Liberation in Modern Western Esotericism* (Berkeley: University of California Press, 2006), 223.

33. Urban, *Magia Sexualis*, 240.

34. Dave Evans, *History of British Magic After Crowley* (London, UK: Hidden Design Ltd., 2007), 200–1.

35. Cusack, "Discordian Magic," 135.

36. Peter Carroll, *The Octavo: A Sorcerer-Scientist's Grimoire* (Oxford, UK: Mandrake Press, Ltd., 2010), e-book.

37. Jaq D. Hawkins, *Understanding Chaos Magic* (Chieveley: Capall Bann Publishing, 1996), 22.

38. Duggan, "Perennialism and Iconoclasm," 94–5.

39. Christine Ferguson, "Reading with the Occultists: Arthur Machen, A.E. Waite, and the Ecstasies of Popular Fiction," *Journal of Victorian Culture* 21, no. 1 (2016): 43. Emphasis in original.

40. Phil Hine, *Pseudonomicon* (Tempe, AZ: New Falcon Publications, 2007): 20–1.

41. Hine, *Pseudonomicon*, 7.

42. Hine, *Pseudonomicon*, 25.

43. Hine, *Pseudonomicon*, 25.

44. Gordon White, *Pieces of Eight: Chaos Magic Essays and Enchantments* (Amazon Digital Services LLC, 2016), e-book.

45. Alan Moore, quoted in Sam Proctor, "Alan Moore: The Art of Magic," *Pagan Dawn*, February 12 (2016), http://www.pagandawnmag.org/alan-moore-the-art-of-magic/.

46. Carroll, *The Octavo*.

47. Carroll, *The Octavo*.

48. Grant Morrison, "Pop Magic!" in *Book of Lies: The Disinformation Guide to Magick and the Occult*, ed. Richard Metzger (New York: Disinformation Company Ltd., 2003), 23.

49. Dave Evans, *History of British Magic*, 356–357.

50. John O'Neill, "Andre Norton, Michael Moorcock and Appendix N: Advanced Readings in *D&D*," *Black Gate: Adventures in Fantasy Literature*, September 9 (2013), https://www.blackgate.com/2013/09/09/andre-norton-michael-moorcock-and-appendix-n-advanced-readings-in-dd/.

51. White, *Pieces of Eight*.

52. Colin Greenland, *Entropy Exhibition* (London, UK: Gollancz, 2013), e-book.

53. Carroll, *The Octavo*, 31.

54. Josie Campbell. "Morrisoncon Wrap-Up: Fans Experience Magic, Religion, Comics, and Grant Morrison." ComicBookResources.com, October 5 (2012), https://www.cbr.com/morrisoncon-wrap-up-fans-experience-magic-religion-comics-and-grant-morrison/.

55. The Lovecraftian or Cthulhu Mythos was initiated by Lovecraft, but continued by other authors such as August Derleth.

56. Wouter Hanegraaff, "Fiction in the Desert of the Real: Lovecraft's Cthulhu Mythos," *Aries* 7 (2007): 103.

57. Daniel Harms and John Wisdom Gonce III, *The Necronomicon Files* (Boston: Red Wheel/Weiser Books, 2003), 111.

58. John Engle, "Cults of Lovecraft: The Impact of H.P. Lovecraft's Fiction on Contemporary Occult Practices," *Mythlore: A Journal of J.R.R. Tolkien, C.S. Lewis, Charles Williams, and Mythopoeic Literature* 33, no. 1 (2014): 87.

59. See John L. Steadman, *H.P. Lovecraft and the Black Magickal Tradition* (San Francisco: Weiser Books, 2015); Hanegraaff, "Fiction in the Desert of the Real"; Engle, "Cults of Lovecraft" for more on this.

60. Steadman, *H.P. Lovecraft and the Black Magickal Tradition*, 41.

61. Davis, *Nomad Codes*, 122.

62. Carl Oort, *Chthon: An Approach to Lovecraftian Chaos Magick* (self published, 2015), e-book.

63. Justin Woodman. "Alien Selves: Modernity and the Social Diagnostics of the Demonic in 'Lovecraftian Magick,'" in *Religion, the Occult, and the Paranormal*, Volume 4, ed. Carole M. Cusack and Helen Farley (London and New York: Routledge, 2016), 258.

64. Lovecraft in Scott Cutler Shershow and Scott Michaelsen, *The Love of Ruins: Letters on Lovecraft* (Albany: State University of New York Press, 2017), 136.

65. Davis, *Nomad Codes*, 116.

66. Hine, *Pseudonomicon*, 14.

67. Oort, *Chthon*, n.p.

68. Frater Tenebrous, *Cults of Cthulhu: H.P. Lovecraft and the Occult Tradition* (1998), https://archive.org/stream/MSS2014/Tenebrous%20-%20Cults%20of%20Cthulhu_djvu.txt.

69. Hine, *Pseudonomicon*, 11.

70. Hawkins, *Understanding Chaos Magic*, 5.

71. Lovecraft, "The Call of Cthulhu," in *The Call of Cthulhu and Other Weird Stories*, ed. S.T. Joshi (New York: Penguin Books, 1999), 139.

72. Xenia, "Working with the Cthulhu Mythos: A Practical Guide to Lovecraft's Lore," *Spiral Nature Magazine* (March 29, 2017), http://www.spiralnature.com/magick/cthulhu-mythos-practical/.

73. Shershow and Michaelsen, *Love of Ruins*, 7.

74. For example, in the dedication in Peter J. Carroll, *Liber Null & Psychonaut* (San Francisco: Weiser Books, 1987).

75. Tenebrous, *Cults of Cthulhu*.

76. Danielle Kirby, "From Pulp Fiction to Revealed Text: A Study of the Role of the Text in the Otherkin Community," in *Exploring Religion and the Sacred in a Media Age*, ed. Christopher Deacy and Elisabeth Arweck (Farnham and Burlington, VT: Ashgate, 2009), 145.

Bibliography

Alberts, Thomas. "Virtually Real: Fake Religions and Problems of Authenticity in Religion." *Culture and Religion* 9, no. 2 (2008): 125–139.

Campbell, Josie. "Morrisoncon Wrap-Up: Fans Experience Magic, Religion, Comics, and Grant Morrison." ComicBookResources.com, October 5, 2012. https://www.cbr.com/morrisoncon-wrap-up-fans-experience-magic-religion-comics-and-grant-morrison/ (accessed May 9, 2018).

Carroll, Peter J. *Liber Null & Psychonaut*. San Francisco: Weiser Books, 1987.
_____. *The Octavo: A Sorcerer-Scientist's Grimoire*. Oxford, UK: Mandrake Press, Ltd., 2010.
Chidester, David. *Authentic Fakes: Religion and American Popular Culture*. Berkeley: University of California Press, 2005.
Collins, Randall. *Interaction Ritual Chains*. Princeton, NJ: Princeton University Press, 2004.
Crowley, Aleister. *Magick: Liber ABA*. Boston: Weiser Books, 2004.
_____. *Magick in Theory and Practice*. New York: Dover Publications, 1976.
Cusack, Carole M. "Discordian Magic: Paganism, the Chaos Paradigm and the Power of Imagination." *International Journal for the Study of New Religions* 2, no. 1 (2011): 125–145.
Davis, Erik. *Nomad Codes: Adventures in Modern Esoterica*. Portland: YETI Books, 2010.
Deacy, Christopher. "Why Study Religion and Popular Culture?" In *Exploring Religion and the Sacred in a Media Age*, edited by Christopher Deacy and Elisabeth Arweck, 1–22. Farnham and Burlington, VT: Ashgate, 2009.
Duggan, Colin. "Perennialism and Iconoclasm. Chaos Magick and the Legitimacy of Innovation." In *Contemporary Esotericism*, edited by Egil Asprem and Kennet Granholm, 91–112. New York: Routledge, 2014.
Engle, John. "Cults of Lovecraft: The Impact of H.P. Lovecraft's Fiction on Contemporary Occult Practices." *Mythlore: A Journal of J.R.R. Tolkien, C.S. Lewis, Charles Williams, and Mythopoeic Literature* 33, no. 1 (2014): 85–98.
Evans, Dave. *History of British Magic After Crowley*. London, UK: Hidden Design Ltd., 2007.
Ferguson, Christine. "Reading with the Occultists: Arthur Machen, A.E. Waite, and the Ecstasies of Popular Fiction." *Journal of Victorian Culture* 21, no. 1 (2016): 40–55.
Frankenberry, Nancy K. and Hans H. Penner. "Clifford Geertz's Long-Lasting Moods, Motivations, and Metaphysical Conceptions." *The Journal of Religion* 79, no. 4 (1999): 617–40.
Geertz, Clifford. *The Interpretation of Cultures*. New York: Basic Books, 1973.
Greenland, Colin. *The Entropy Exhibition*. London: Gollancz, 2013. E-book.
Grossberg, Lawrence. "Putting the Pop Back into Postmodernism." In *Universal Abandon: The Politics of Postmodernism*, edited by Andrew Ross, 167–190. Minneapolis: University of Minnesota Press, 1989.
Hanegraaff, Wouter. "Fiction in the Desert of the Real: Lovecraft's Cthulhu Mythos." *Aries* 7 (2007): 85–109.
Harms, Daniel and John Wisdom Gonce III. *The Necronomicon Files*. Boston: Red Wheel/Weiser Books, 2003.
Hawkins, Jaq D. *Understanding Chaos Magic*. Chieveley: Capall Bann Publishing, 1996.
Hine, Phil. *The Pseudonomicon*. Tempe, AZ: New Falcon Publications, 2007.
Jenkins, Henry. *Textual Poachers: Television Fans and Participatory Culture*. New York: Routledge, 2005.
Jindra, Michael. "Star Trek Fandom as a Religious Phenomenon." *Sociology of Religion* 55, no. 1 (1994): 27–51.
Jones, Bethan. "Fannish Tattooing and Sacred Identity." *Transformative Works and Cultures* 18 (2015). DOI: doi.org/10.3983/twc.2015.0626.
Kirby, Danielle. "From Pulp Fiction to Revealed Text: A Study of the Role of the Text in the Otherkin Community." In *Exploring Religion and the Sacred in a Media Age*, edited by Christopher Deacy and Elisabeth Arweck, 141–54. Farnham and Burlington, VT: Ashgate, 2009.
Lovecraft, H.P. *The Call of Cthulhu and Other Weird Stories*. Edited by S.T. Joshi. New York: Penguin Books, 1999.
McAvan, Emily. *The Postmodern Sacred: Popular Culture Spirituality in the Science Fiction, Fantasy and Urban Fantasy Genres*. Jefferson, NC: McFarland, 2012.
Mendlesohn, Farah. "Introduction: Reading Science Fiction." In *The Cambridge Companion to Science Fiction*, edited by Edward James and Farah Mendlesohn, 1–14. New York: Cambridge University Press, 2009.
Moore, Alan. "Fossil Angels Part 2." *Glycon*, October 20 (2010). http://glycon.livejournal.com/14307.html (accessed May 9, 2018).

Morrison, Grant. "Pop Magic!" In *Book of Lies: The Disinformation Guide to Magick and the Occult*, edited by Richard Metzger, 16–25. New York: Disinformation Company Ltd., 2003.

O'Neill, John. "Andre Norton, Michael Moorcock and Appendix N: Advanced Readings in *D&D.*" *Black Gate: Adventures in Fantasy Literature*, September 9 (2013). https://www.blackgate.com/2013/09/09/andre-norton-michael-moorcock-and-appendix-n-advanced-readings-in-dd/ (accessed May 9, 2018).

Oort, Carl. *Chthon: An Approach to Lovecraftian Chaos Magick*. Self published, 2015. E-book.

Partridge, Christopher. *The Re-Enchantment of the West*. Volume 1. London: T&T Clark International, 2004.

Proctor, Sam. "Alan Moore: The Art of Magic." *Pagan Dawn*, February 12 (2016). http://www.pagandawnmag.org/alan-moore-the-art-of-magic/ (accessed May 9, 2018).

Shershow, Scott Cutler and Scott Michaelsen. *The Love of Ruins: Letters on Lovecraft*. Albany: State University of New York Press, 2017.

Steadman, John L. *H.P. Lovecraft and the Black Magickal Tradition*. San Francisco: Weiser Books, 2015.

Tenebrous, Frater. *Cults of Cthulhu: H.P. Lovecraft and the Occult Tradition* (1998). https://archive.org/stream/MSS2014/Tenebrous%20-%20Cults%20of%20Cthulhu_djvu.txt (accessed May 9, 2018).

Urban, Hugh B. *Magia Sexualis: Sex, Magic, and Liberation in Modern Western Esotericism*. Berkeley: University of California Press, 2006.

White, Gordon. *Pieces of Eight: Chaos Magic Essays and Enchantments*. Amazon Digital Services LLC, 2016. E-book.

Woodman, Justin. "Alien Selves: Modernity and the Social Diagnostics of the Demonic in 'Lovecraftian Magick.'" In *Religion, the Occult, and the Paranormal*, Volume 4, edited by Carole M. Cusack and Helen Farley, 258–284 (London and New York: Routledge, 2016).

Xenia. "Working with the Cthulhu Mythos: A Practical Guide to Lovecraft's Lore." *Spiral Nature Magazine*, March 29 (2017). http://www.spiralnature.com/magick/cthulhu-mythos-practical/ (accessed May 9, 2018).

PART 2

Sacred Viewing
Watching the Text

Cinephany, the Affective Experience of the Fan

A Typology

MARC JOLY-CORCORAN

Introduction

This essay proposes to fill a gap in fan studies concerning the absence of a theoretical framework that explains, or at least helps to understand, how the fan-object affective relationship works. In 2006, pioneer fan studies scholar Henry Jenkins lamented this dearth in *Fans, Bloggers, and Gamers*: "I would say that my entire work has been about intensity and emotional engagement, but what I lack, and still do ... is an adequate language to describe emotion or affect in theoretical terms that would be acceptable within academic discourse."[1] My first objective is to offer a heuristic approach to better understand fan affect and cultural reappropriation. This essay uses a transdisciplinary approach at the crossroads of three academic fields—Film Studies, Religious Studies, and Fan Studies—and my terminology is etymologically inspired by French theorists.[2] My second objective is to illustrate how the behaviors of the fan are similar in many ways to those of the figure Mircea Eliade calls *homo religiosus*, making the fan a sort of *homo religiosus* in a modern world. Eliade writes in the *Sacred and the Profane*: "the man who has made his choice in favor of a profane life never succeeds in completely doing away with religious behavior ... even the most desacralized existence still preserves traces of a religious valorization of the world."[3] It is in this sense that even our contemporaries who describe themselves as agnostic or non-religious are *homo religiosus*. The sacred has incarnated itself in the sphere of profane activities.

As a film director and an academic with a background in Religious and

Film studies, fanfilm-making has been of great interest to me. To engage further with this phenomenon, I have made a focused study of *Star Wars* (*SW*) fanfilms, eagerly made by those fans who have spent the time learning or employing the technical skills necessary to produce a film, not to mention the visual effects programs needed to recreate George Lucas' imaginary world as faithfully as possible. My efforts were concentrated on fanfilms from 1997 to 2005, the period that Clive Young calls the Golden Age of *SW* fanfilms.[4] I contacted sixteen fanfilm directors using email and Facebook and selected the most important and widely recognized fanfilms according to the *SW* fandom, including *TROOPS* (1997) and *George Lucas in Love* (1999). The directors were sent a thirty-three item questionnaire, in four parts: (a) personal information and their first contact with *SW*; (b) *SW* in their childhood; (c) their fanfilm; and (d) explanations and expectations of their filmmaking. Besides accumulating data about the directors' intentions, the goal was to identify a common thread, a shared emotional trigger factor present in their first viewing that would have motivated them, later in their lives, to produce a *Star Wars* fanfilm.

Fans and Affect

A significant number of people invest a considerable amount of time and money in certain types of artistic forms of expressions derived from popular culture; typically they are called fans. Some like to make fanfilms, engage in cosplay, write fanfic or create fanart, others like to buy and collect merchandise, while others will enjoy repeated viewings of their favorite films or television series. This essay does not aim to describe the various types of fans, be they enthusiasts, cultists, aficionados, or geeks,[5] but rather suggests a typology of possible triggers that evoke such an intense affective experience that sparks the consumer's desire to revisit the work several times after initial consumption.[6]

Matt Hills highlights an instructive distinction for our current discussion: he explains that a "cult fan" is defined by the "enduring form" of affective relationship the individual has to a cultural product such as a television series, film, or videogame, long after its release or the production of new content.[7] Kurt Lancaster, who wrote about *Babylon 5* and its fandom, speaks of an "original cathartic moment felt during the first viewing of the story."[8] This emotion, or affect, is what fans desire to relive again and again. However, "affect" has always been a difficult subject to tackle in academic terms. Laurence Grossberg explains the challenges associated with defining emotional response: "Affect is perhaps the most difficult plane of our lives to define.... You can understand another person's life: you can share the meaning and pleasures, but you cannot know how it feels."[9] For example, a religious person could say that he senses the presence of God, but cannot exactly explain how it feels, let alone prove it.

The intangible nature of the subject may be why it is difficult to find a theoretical framework that is acceptable in an academic context. About Lancaster's book, Hills goes on to say that there is a problematic absence of "a theoretical framework which might explicate how or why such an emotional "holding" or "reliving" could become important for fans."[10] I offer the term "cinephany" to describe the intense affective experience felt when encountering an artistic or media object. Elsewhere, I have developed and defined this concept as: Any affective arousal of any emotion, either punctual or spread over short periods of time, that creates a high degree of satisfaction (both powerful and meaningful) and gratification when consuming a specific film, television show and/or videogame."[11] There are different kinds of cinephany: each can be triggered by different components or parts of the artistic production; and the emergence of a cinephany is highly dependent on the viewer's competence and mental state. This essay describes a typology to illustrate various types of cinephany that motivate the viewer and the fan to engage in subsequent acts of cultural reappropriation (alone or within a fandom) with the intention of keeping their cinephanic experience alive.

The notion of cinephany draws heavily from religious experience as described by the historian of religion Mircea Eliade in his book *The Sacred and the Profane* (1961). Eliade utilizes the term *hierophany*, which means the "manifestation of the sacred,"[12] to refer to the manifestation of the sacred in a profane world. If Eliade's *homo religiosus* constantly aspires to periodically reactualize hierophany with the help of mythological stories told and enacted through rituals managed by a religious institution, the fan proceeds, more or less, in the same manner in their fan activities, often within an organized fandom. Thus, it may be possible to associate certain types of cinephany with specific fan creations, and to determine which types of cinephany are be more likely than others to motivate the production of fan labor.

Analogy and Etymology

The relationship of fandom to religion is an uneasy one. Jenkins expresses a certain reluctance about the analogy between religion and fandom: "people use religion as a metaphor to refer to the social practices of fandom.... I don't see why the metaphor should be a religion any more than it could be a union or a political party ... any number of which serve that same social function of being a community that articulates values and shared affect."[13] To this, Hills replies by distinguishing between religiosity and religion. The former is about "meaning and affect," whereas the latter is about the institution as "an organized social group."[14] Indeed, fandom scholars often find that fans lack words to describe their experiences, and that religious vocabulary is apt to describe an intense affective relationship with a cultural object. For example, we will see later how the fans in my research do not hesitate to choose the terms "epiphany" and "revelation" to describe their first emotional experience with *Star Wars*.[15]

Nevertheless, words like "religion," "religious," "sacred," and even "religiosity" remain, for the atheist, agnostic, or strictly secular context, problematic. For that reason, the terms Eliade uses, "hieros," "hierophany," and "sacred" have been abandoned in favor of "cinephany" to affiliate intense experiences of media with a profundity that is not institutionally religious. The term "cinephany" is derived from the prefix *cine-* from the Greek *kinema* meaning "movement," and the suffix—*phany* from the Greek *phainein*, meaning "to show."[16] Cinephany is experiencing the movement that manifests or is revealed to one. In cinephany, movement takes the meaning given to the term "emotion," the etymology of which is from the word French *émouvoir*, in Latin *emovere*, meaning to "to stir up."[17] For example, in English, we could say: "I was moved by this scene." Cinephany is an impulse: a direction that takes root in the human psyche, an impulse that forces the affective movement to slip out of the body to emancipate and express itself.

As such, Paul Willemen points to this idea when speaking of the cinephilia of early critics writing for the influential French film magazine *Cahiers du Cinéma*. In a conversation with Noel King,[18] Willemen expresses this thought in reaction to the word *epiphanic* used by King: "I'm glad you used the word 'epiphanic' … These are moments which, when encountered in a film, spark something which then produces the energy and the desire to write, to find formulations to convey something about the intensity of that spark."[19] However, for my typology, the term "epiphany," which is now commonly used to refer to a moment of revelation (mystical or personal, a revelation about something, a sudden passion), is also unsuitable because the term is historically connected to a Christian holiday (6 January, which commemorates the homage of the Three Kings to the Christ child). Nonetheless, the notion of the "spark" Willemen mentions, is key. Willemen notes that central figures in French New Wave cinema such as François Truffaut and Jean-Luc Godard, among others, wrote about these films in order to keep the spark alive as long as possible, and that, while they were indeed critics, they were responding to the film more than criticizing it. What Willemen calls the "spark" I call cinephany: a moment of revelation we seek to reappropriate *ad infinitum*, like Eliade's hierophany, in which people perform "re-mis-en-scène" through myths and religious rituals to sustain faith. Later, Willemen adds: "[w]hat you are reconsuming is the moment of revelation experienced in an encounter between you and cinema, which may be different from the person sitting next to you."[20] The cinephilic French school is not that different to the *Star Wars* fandom. The way in which a viewer reappropriates their cinephany might not be the same in both groups, yet all involve experiencing the spark that provokes an intense—and participatory—attachment to a cultural object.[21]

Cinephany

It should be kept in mind that the prefix *cine-* does not mean that a cinephany is experienced only with film. A cinephany can emerge during the viewing of a television show, or while playing a videogame. On that account, it is important to distinguish different types of screening conditions, depending on the technological apparatus used. To that end, I use a set of terms derived from the filmology wave during the 1950s. Filmology adopted a transdisciplinary approach so as to analyze the art of cinema from psychological and sociological perspectives. French scholar Etienne Souriau established a vocabulary that is appropriate for the discussion of cinephany. Souriau distinguished between objective and subjective manifestations. The former refers to the on-screen aspect only, the filmophany, that is, what appears on the screen, while the latter corresponds to what Souriau calls in French "les faits spectatoriels" (the spectator's psychic activities during the viewing).[22] So, if Souriau's filmophany is the on-screen manifestation of the film in a theater, then, *telephany*[23] would be the manifestation on a television screen, videophany would describe a screening on any other devices (like smart phones or tablets), and videoludophany would apply to videogames (console, PC, phone and tablet, and so on). Hence, we would say a filmophanic, telephanic, videophanic or videoludophanic cinephany,[24] depending on the apparatus used during the experience. In this essay cinephanies according to six types that are not mutually exclusive will be discussed. They are: (1) primordial; (2) energetic; (3) diegetic; (4) narrative; (5) aesthetic; and (6) cinephilic.[25]

Primordial Cinephany:
Conscious and Subconscious

I distinguish between two sub-categories for this first type: subconscious cinephany and conscious cinephany. The *subconscious primordial cinephany* is experienced during childhood, but forgotten, all the while having had an effect on the activities and development of the child. The child will not remember the precise moment they saw the film or television show. Later on though they will have concrete memories of activities (drawing, playing with toys, etc.) inspired by their forgotten experience. The second sub-category, *conscious primordial cinephany*, is the experience that a child will remember. They will be able to remember the film, as well as the context, the people with them at the time and the effect the experience had on them. This type may seem rather speculative at this point, I admit. That is why I will refer to my own experiences as a child, now that the auto-ethnographical approach is widely accepted in fan studies thanks to Henry Jenkins' seminal book *Textual Poacher*.[26] I saw *Star Wars* with my parents in 1977. Even though I do not remember it clearly, mainly because I was three years old, I can remember drawing spaceships and robots for months after the screening. This would be the subconscious cinephany. A few years later my father brought me to see Steven Spielberg's *E.T. The Extra-Terrestrial* (1982). I still to this day remember it plainly. And I knew, when I saw *E.T.*, that I wanted to become a filmmaker. That is an example of conscious cinephany.

This primordial experience will be one the child will be unknowingly trying to reproduce over the course of their life in order to rediscover the affective state initially created by the cultural object that affected them. Freud wrote of a similar reaction when speaking of games children play, claiming "that children repeat in their play everything that has made a great impression on them in actual life."[27] By repeating an experience, adult fans also perpetuate a behavior we thought deeply buried in childhood, and they do so within their respective fandom.[28]

Energetic Cinephany

Energetic cinephany is based on the film's potential to create immediate psycho-physiological reactions. The term *energetic* is borrowed from Roger Odin[29] who uses energetic attunement (*mise-en-phase* in French) to describe when the spectator sways to the rhythm of the images and sounds on the screen. Energetic cinephany is an affective experience that creates reactions like jump scare, excitement, wonder, etc. This is often the case in action films, but also science fiction and horror, or in every film that relies on spectacular effects. In other words, an energetic cinephany could occur when a film uses those spectacular effects, presents irrevocable intentions to arouse a spontaneous affective response (in horror films, for example), or succeeds in provoking in the viewer a strong affective and neuropsychomotor response (goose bumps, startle or jump scare, disgust, pity, relief, and so on), thus being conducive to the emergence of a precise mood.[30] It can be pleasant or unpleasant, but occurs over a short period of time. It is through the accumulation of these micro-cinephanies, carefully planned by the creators, that one can witness the emergence of a state favorable to the diegetic, narrative and aesthetic cinephanies.

Thus energetic cinephany ultimately represents the immediate effect that content producers attempt to create in viewers. Instantaneous effects are, shocks which that leave imprints that are perceivable in a viewer's reactions. However, the affective repercussions of these imprints quickly fade away if the energetic cinephany is not followed by another cinephany, one or more of the other cinephanies described here. For example, if a viewer returns to see the same film a second time because he felt strong emotions the first time, there is a good chance that he will not get the same sensorial impact as the first initial experience in a cinema, even less more so of during later viewings occurring at home on a small television. The meaning of the event becomes minor.

Diegetic Cinephany

Being captivated and absorbed by a fictional universe can lead to a unique type of cinephany that can grasp the viewer's attention, which I call a diegetic cinephany.[31] This cinephanic type provokes long-term effects. Many factors contribute to its emergence. Firstly, simple interest constitutes a pre-cinephanic determinant to the experience and plays an important role in the type of affective relationship that a fan can entertain with a fictional universe. When discussing the notion of interest, Greg M. Smith refers to Ed S. Tan, as both scholars' research focuses on emotion and affect in relation to cinema: "Tan asserts that the central emotional mechanism in film viewing is "interest." Interest induces us to investigate the film and discover more about the diegetic world it presents."[32] This is also what Jean-Marie Schaeffer explains in *Pourquoi la fiction?* about fictional immersion: "[i]n order for processes of immersion to work, it is essential that characters and their fates interest us. To do so they must resonate with our personal affective investments."[33] Characters are what first draw us in a diegesis; but the world the characters live in is what essentially charms and conquers fans. For many of them, for example, it is the universe of *Star Wars* that first attracts them, that motivates them to explore the narration within, not the other way around. The story is simple and mostly serves the wonder of the diegesis. Cosplay demonstrates the desire of certain fans to immerse themselves in a character, to adopt its attitude for a time, during a convention, in order to project themselves into a universe they care deeply about.

Narrative Cinephany

This type of cinephany invites the viewer to what I call a game of interpretation. Narrative cinephany encourages the viewer to seek and to reappropriate the cultural object and engage in textual and transtextual interpretative activities, which are, according to Gérard Genette, "all that sets the text in relationship, whether obvious or concealed with other texts."[34] The idea is always to prolong their experience as long as possible. Narrative cinephany is a type of cinephany that most engages the fan. The fan will willingly explore transmedia works,[35] and could even participate in the creation, individually and collectively, of fan works by using the original cultural object either to change its message or to pay homage to it. It is also a narrative cinephany because the spectator moves to the "rhythm of narrated events," what Odin also calls a narrative attunement.[36]

Despite the fact that being moved to the rhythm of narrated events is a good prerequisite, it is not the only criterion for experiencing narrative cinephany. One must also adhere to the values promoted by the story. These values must be in sync with those of the viewer. Being captivated by the intrigue of a story, animated by curiosity or interest for an actor are insufficient for the emergence of narrative cinephany; the story has to move you. Beyond the narrative attunement proposed by Odin, the values promoted by the story must resonate within the viewer.

Aesthetic Cinephany

The importance of another aesthetic emotion, the sublime is defined as follows:

> The one who contemplates … gains access to the highest of spiritual sentiments that humans can endure. And one thus reaches … this definition of the sublime: "*The sublime is the allegory, visible and perceptible, of a superior state accessible to the one who senses its impression.*"[37]

Thus, aesthetic cinephany is the affective experience that is born from contemplation and intensive immersion in an artistic work as a representational object. The experience of aesthetic cinephany is distinct from diegetic cinephany since it is born from contemplative immersion, not fictional immersion. The emotion of the sublime approaches the experience of the sacred. Indeed, the feeling of fulfillment when observing an image, and the impression of living an important moment, one in which an ontologically different state of being is revealed, is similar to the feeling described by Rudolf Otto: "[b]ut in neither the sublime nor the magical [intangible], effective as they are, has art more than an indirect means of representing the numinous."[38] It is also the feeling of the grandiose as Otto describes it while speaking of the sacred: "the bare feeling for solemn and imposing magnitude and for the pomp of sublime pose and gesture."[39] This feeling is provoked by the contemplation of existence and "profound things."[40]

Cinephilic Cinephany

The cinephile is fascinated by cinema itself, as its etymology suggests. Cinephilia is described by Antoine de Baecque as "a love of cinema, a ceremony of affections and passions called forth by viewing films."[41] Cinephilia is for them a manner of approaching the cinematographic experience, but especially to share it, to communicate its emotions, and to "practice its memory."[42] And yet, the practices of the cinephile can be compared to those of fans, and particularly cult fans. In the same way as a fan of popular culture operates, acts of reappropriation of the cinephile, such as group discussions, critical writing, participation in cine-clubs, are first motivated by important individual experiences, as Christian Keathley highlights:

> [C]inephilia begins with the individual who has a passionate love for cinema, and extends from him or her to other like-minded individuals; for the recounting of privileged moments in such details is a key feature of the dialogue about movies carried out among cinephiles.[43]

Like the modern fan who seeks to perpetuate the cinephanic experience through participatory culture, the young critics from the *Cahiers du Cinéma*, for example, reactualized their own cinephanies through the act of writing. They wrote about films, highlighting specific moments, meaningful fragments through which cinephilic pleasure emerges, what Willemen calls the "cinephiliac moment."[44] Keathley summarizes the paradox surrounding Willemen's term by underlining how the cinephile's passion is found most strongly in precise cinematographic moments: "[T]he cinephiliac moment may be understood as a kind of *mise-en-abyme* wherein each cinephile's obsessive relationship to the cinema is embodied in its most dense, concentrated form."[45] It could be the long shot in *Summer with Monika* (dir. Ingmar Bergman 1955) or even the charge led by Wagner's "Ride of the Valkyries" in *Apocalypse Now* (dir. Francis Ford Coppola 1979): "[C]inephiliac discourse tends to work on scenes, on moments of gesture, on looks."[46]

These fragments of instantaneity fall within a logic that de Baecque considers to be an act of fetishization of knowledge "gained through multiple viewings of films."[47] As de Baecque mentions, the fetishistic relationship associated with the accumulation of objects derived from films transforms itself in a sort of traffic, one that even a young Truffaut participated in. In this, we find in Truffaut the behavior of any modern fan that seeks to reactualize his cinephanic experience through reappropriation.

Fans and Their Cinephanies

This essay seeks to define different types of cinephanies all the while being aware that a series of pre-cinephanic determinants might predispose the fans to live an intense affective experience with a film, a television series or a videogame. There are as many combinations of determinants as there are individuals. In the same way, a cinephany shared by fans of a same group towards a common cultural object is the result of as many combinations of determinants as there are members within the group. In this sense, the difficulties in studying the fan come in part from the fact that being a fan represents an emotional posture that creates a deeply personal relationship to a cultural object. For that reason, it remains difficult to determine with certainty which type(s) of cinephany the fan has experienced; one can only speculate.

I conducted interviews with fans between 2011 and 2017, including fanfilm directors and cosplayers. Fanfilms, defined by Clive Young as "an unauthorized amateur or semi-pro film, based on pop culture characters or situations, created for noncommercial viewing,"[48] are frequently labors of love, as are many expressive forms of fan appreciation. For example, one of my respondents, the well-known Italian cosplayer Nadia SK, explained eloquently why she dedicates herself to cosplay: "I want to become the character, to be a part of this world." Immersion is an essential part of cosplay, because the participant wants to "play" in the world they fell in love with. Moreover, the attraction of the narrative also plays a big part to facilitate her immersion: "I always fall in love with the story and the character, always. When I choose a cosplay, there is always a feeling between me and the character."[49] The cinephanies in play with Nadia SK would be the narrative and the diegetic types, which suggest a strong and affective experience towards the story and the characters.

I also interviewed sixteen *Star Wars* fanfilmmakers like Kevin Rubio who made the famous fanfilm *TROOPS* (1997), and Joe Nussbaum who directed *George Lucas in Love* (1999). Their answers indicate that my theory about fanfilmmakers having experienced an energetic cinephany during their first screening is not to be overlooked. I used the traditional ethnographical approach with a thirty-three item questionnaire from which two are of special interest: "Question 4: How would you describe the feeling you had when you saw your first *Star Wars* movie ever?" and "Question 5: In what order would you rearrange these words (choose only five of them) to describe your "love at first sight" experience with *Star Wars*, starting with the most important word (for you)—curiosity, excitement, revelation, epiphany, affection, devotion, simple enjoyment and indifference?"

The words they use to describe their experience to Question 4 included: "exhilarating," "I sat on the edge of my seat," "excited," "elated," "inspired," "mesmerized," "amazement," "euphoria," "in awe," "enthralled," "thoroughly entertained." Nick Hallam, director of the fanfilm *Broken Allegiance* (2002), sums it up this way: "I remember being awestruck when the Star Destroyer flies over the camera in the opening shot of the film, and probably grasping my Mum for security."[50] Hallam's young age may be a contributing factor to this type of cinephany. As children we are more subject to be excited by fast-paced action and quick movements on screen, exactly what the first film in 1977 induced for a whole generation of toy consumers. But before the Internet and videogame era, children were quite imaginative when it came to reliving their favorite parts or scenes from their first viewing experience. As a child, Jon Sall directed what could be the first *Star Wars* fanfilm (early 1978) known to date (before *Hardware Wars*, directed by Ernie Fosselius in late 1978), shot with an 8mm camera and homemade costumes. He explains how he was playing with his friends in the streets recreating and reliving one of the most iconic and exciting scene in *New Hope*: "My friends and I would play a *Star Wars* Trench Run game on our bicycles: We would ride fast on the sidewalk in the cul-de-sac where we lived and try to drop a plastic bowling pin into a bucket, replicating the Proton Torpedo into the Death Star runs in the film!"[51]

For Question 5, participants were asked to select and place in order of importance five words out of nine suggested. Their answers support my assumption: out of sixteen fanfilmmakers, seven chose "excitement" first; "epiphany" was chosen by four; two chose "revelation," two chose "simple enjoyment" and one did not answer. It is worth mentioning that those who chose "simple enjoyment" are the youngest fans interviewed, and that they did not see *Star Wars* first hand when it was released in 1977, since they were not yet born. This raises a few questions: Is the younger generation less incline or susceptible to be as excited as the older generation who saw *Star Wars* in theater in 1977? Has the younger generation even had a cinephany at all? Most of the former mostly chose the word "excitement" which clearly hints at an energetic cinephany. Now, the *SW* universe is so rich that the younger generation seems more likely to have experienced a diegetic and/or a narrative cinephany through the comics and the novels from the Expanded Universe (now categorized as "legend" by Disney, ergo non-canon). Whereas we cannot confirm whether the fans (from the older generation) who chose the words "epiphany" and "revelation" first have experienced an energetic cinephany or not, we could assume they have. For instance, the fanfilmmaker Peter Mether (*The Dark Redemption*, 1999) also describes his first experience watching *SW* with these words: "Elated, inspired, excited—I wanted to be a filmmaker like George Lucas."[52]

We can also assume that the fanfilmmakers surely experienced a diegetic cinephany at one point. The activities that the fans are invested in suggest that they are also looking for various ways to get immersed again and again in their favorite film diegesis. As Adam Bertocci (*Run Leia Run*, 2003) puts it about his cinephany:

> You know the line "You have taken your first step into a larger world?" Yeah, like that. It was like I was being inducted into this special, secret club, this strange universe made just for me … seeing the movie was like getting the keys to the kingdom.

> When Obi-Wan discussed Vader's origins, it was like I was in the room with them, hearing something nobody had ever heard before.[53]

However, it might not be the first cinephany they have had, but rather and more likely the energetic type, the kind of cinephany fanfilmmakers want to recreate by reproducing the fast-paced action and well-choreographed lightsaber duels seen in the films.[54] In the end, the result and the intentions are still the same: contributing and recreating as closely as possible that fabulous universe that is *Star Wars.*

Patrick Read Johnson, director of *Spaced Invaders* (1990) and credited as a writer for *DragonHeart* (1996), started shooting ten years ago and released his long-awaited love letter the exact day of the fortieth anniversary of the saga. The movie *5-25-77* is a personal biopic drama inspired by his passion for *Star Wars* during his teen years. It may not be a fanfilm according to the definition given by Young, but it is certainly close in spirit. So much so that I am tempted to suggest the word "pro'fan'sionnal" to identify this category of fans who are working in the industry while being fans and directing films that reflect their passion for established universes and characters. J.J. Abrams (*The Force Awakens*, 2015), Joss Whedon (*The Avengers*, 2012), Peter Jackson (*Lord of the Rings* trilogy, 2001–03), and Paul W.S. Anderson (*Resident Evil* franchise, 2002–16), would fit in that category.

As for Patrick Read Johnson, he is considered by many as the "#1 fan" of *Star Wars*, as he puts it himself: "I may not be the world's biggest *Star Wars* fan, but, apparently, according to Gary Kurtz—producer of *Star Wars*, I am the FIRST!"[55] He was indeed the first non-crew member to have watched an early cut of *Star Wars* a few months before the initial release. He was fifteen years old and had an "epiphany" upon the first viewing in the theater, a feeling so intense that he went back twenty-eight times during the first month to watch it. According to him, the universe proposed by Lucas is what triggered his passion. As a teenager he felt understood: "I felt as though George had somehow heard ME, teenage Pat Johnson, standing in his backyard in Wadsworth, Illinois, Population 750, staring up at the night sky and wishing for a place I could go that would be very much like the *Star Wars* universe."[56] The epiphany he had was, in line with the typology I am proposing in this essay, clearly a diegetic cinephany.

Conclusion

There is, in the scholarship and in my own ethnographic findings, no cinephany unique to the fan. All ordinary fans and viewers can experience one or more of the cinephanies described in this essay. The difference resides in the various subsequent practices of reappropriation the two groups will devote themselves to. The fan can also be a cinephile, meaning that as well as being a fan of a specific content, they can also, in a larger sense, be fans of cinema. The ordinary viewer, without being a fan of a particular production, can also be a cinephile, a fan of cinematic content as a whole. The distinction made earlier by designating a cinephany as cinephilic, is that this type of cinephany leans on a body of historical and cultural practices linked to interaction with cinema in general, and not with a collection of works by a single director or emanating from a single genre. This does not prevent certain fans from adopting practices that are linked to cinephilia, like writing on their favorite films, criticizing them on a blog, or participating in public viewings in a festival or cine-club. Individuals who experience a cinephilic cinephany derive great pleasure in recognizing their own transtextual competence. They live to the rhythm of the cinematographic fragments that they know and are able to link them to one another. There is not one specific cinephany for fans, because they can experience one, or even all of the cinephanies described here. The cinephile is a form of fan, but since they care about cinema as a whole and not only a few precise films or a specific genre, my typology requires a distinct category to address this difference.

All fans have at one point or another experienced a cinephany. All activities undertaken by fans are aimed at maintaining themselves in their chosen universe for as long as possible, since this universe is generally what first attracted them. Is this to say that diegetic cinephany is the most commonly experienced form? An anime fan was asked what, precisely, he was a fan of (a television series or a specific film)? His answer was surprising: "In the end.... I'm not sure if I'm a fan of something. I'm more of a person that is a fan of wanting to present to the world an element of Japanese culture."[57] Thus, the fan can be enchanted by the story (narrative cinephany), seduced and hypnotized by the beauty of a film (aesthetic cinephany), or gratified through their personal knowledge of the cinematographic object (cinephilic cinephany). But it is essentially the energetic, narrative and especially diegetic attraction, the promise of living in a world that they love which, in the end, will captivate them and compel them to reactualize their experience through, among other thing, fanfics, fanfilms, or cosplay. Energetic, diegetic and narrative cinephanies would, consequently and in a larger sense, be the most common experiences lived by all fans of participatory culture. This is a sacred experience now secularized, an intense emotion, searching for a home out of the traditional religious institutions in order to exist and emancipate itself.

NOTES

1. Henry Jenkins, *Fans, Bloggers, and Gamers, Exploring Participatory Culture* (New York: New York University Press, 2006a), 26.

2. Such as Étienne Souriau and Anne Souriau (eds), *Vocabulaire d'Esthétique* (Paris: PUF, 1990), and Roger Odin, *De la Fiction* (Bruxelles: De Boeck Université, 2000).

3. Mircea Eliade, *The Sacred and the Profane: The Nature of Religion* (New York: Harper, 1961), 23.

4. Clive Young wrote the first book about the history of fanfilms, *Homemade Hollywood, Fans Behind the Camera* (London: Continuum, 2008).

5. Nicholas Abercrombie and Brian Longhurst, *Audiences* (London: Sage Publications, 1998); Matt Hills, *Fan Cultures* (New York: Routledge, 2002).

6. Greg M. Smith explains: "This is a book that examines the ways that particular films cue emotion, not a book about actual human emotional responses." See Smith, *Film Structure and the Emotion System* (Cambridge: Cambridge University Press, 2003), 12.

7. Hills, *Fan Cultures*, xi.

8. Kurt Lancaster, *Fan Performances in a Media Universe: Interacting with Babylon 5* (Austin: University of Texas Press, 2001), 155–156.

9. Lawrence Grossberg, "Is There a Fan in the House? The Affective Sensibility of Fandom," in *The Adoring Audience, Fan Culture and Popular Media*, ed. Lisa A. Lewis (London: Routledge, 1992), 56.

10. Hills, *Fan Cultures*, 42.

11. Further research might explore other works of art, such as literature, painting, and music.

12. Eliade, *The Sacred and the Profane*, 11, 14.

13. Jenkins, *Fans, Bloggers, and Gamers*, 19.

14. Hills, *Fan Cultures*, 20.

15. See Korpua et al.'s chapter in this volume on "sacred viewing" and *The Hobbit* for interesting comparative yet similar results.

16. "-phany," *Merriam Webster Dictionary*, https://www.merriam-webster.com/dictionary/-phany.

17. "emotion," *Merriam Webster Dictionary*, https://www.merriam-webster.com/dictionary/emotion.

18. Paul Willemen, *Looks and Frictions* (Bloomington: Indiana University Press, 1994).

19. Willemen, *Looks and Frictions*, 235.

20. Willemen, *Looks and Frictions*, 237.

21. The cosplayers from the group 501st Legion are good examples of dedicated *SW* fans. See: https://www.501st.com/.

22. Étienne Souriau, "La Structure de l'univers Filmique et le Vocabulaire de la Filmologie," *Revue Internationale de Filmologie* 7–8 (1951), 240.

23. The term *telephany* comes from Henry Sutton, the inventor of television. "Le Problème de la Téléphanie," *Journal Universel de l'Électricité* 50 (Décembre 13, 1890).

24. For more on *cinephany* see Marc Joly-Corcoran, "La Cinéphanie et sa Réappropriation: 'l'Affect Originel' et sa Réactualisation par le Fan, un Spectateur Néoreligieux" (Ph.D. thesis, Université de Montréal, 2014), 44.

25. Another type could be added, videoludic: triggered by an intense investment in the act of playing a videogame. The affects associated with a videoludic cinephany would be induced by a cognitive (understanding the rules of gameplay) and psychomotor (manipulating the remote controller) immersion.

26. Henry Jenkins, *Textual Poachers, Television Fans & Participatory Culture* (New York: Routledge, 1992).

27. Sigmund Freud, *Beyond the Pleasure Principle*, trans. C.J.M. Hubback (London and Vienna: International Psycho-Analytical, 1922), 17.

28. Percy H. Tannebaum, "'Play It Again Sam': Repeated Exposure to Television Programs," in *Selective Exposure to Communication*, ed. Dolph Zillmann and Jennings Bryant (Mahwah, NJ: Lawrence Erlbaum Associates, 1985), 225–241.

29. Roger Odin, *De la fiction* (Bruxelles: De Boeck Université, 2000), 160.

30. Grossberg, "Is There a Fan in the House?"

31. The term "diegetic" was popularized in film studies by Souriau in "La Structure de l'Univers Filmique," 231–240.

32. Smith, *Film Structure and the Emotion System*, 71.

33. Jean-Marie Schaeffer, *Pourquoi la Fiction* (Paris: Seuil, 1999), 186, my translation.

34. Gérard Genette, *The Architect: An Introduction*, trans. Jane E. Lewin (Berkeley: University of California Press, 1992), 83–84.

35. Henry Jenkins defines *transmedia storytelling* as follows: "Stories that unfold across multiple media platforms, with each medium making distinctive contributions to our understanding of the world." See Jenkins, *Convergence Culture, Where Old and New Media Collide* (New York: New York University Press, 2006b), 293.

36. Called *mise-en-phase* in French. See Odin, *De la fiction*, 39.

37. Souriau and Souriau, *Vocabulaire d'esthétique*, 1399. Emphasis in the original. In this explanation of the sublime, Anne Souriau cites Étienne Souriau in *Revue d'Esthétique* (July–December 1966).

38. Rudolf Otto, *The Idea of the Holy* (Oxford University Press, 1958 [1923]), 68.

39. Otto, *The Idea of the Holy*, 66.

40. Edgar Morin recently noted that the aesthetic emotion was, until the Renaissance, tightly tied to religion, but has since become autonomous. See Morin, *Sur l'esthétique* (Paris: Robert Laffont, 2016), 22. He also calls it "a poetic state," *Sur l'esthétique*, 19.

41. Antoine de Baecque, *La Cinéphilie: Invention d'un Regard, Histoire d'une Culture (1948–1966)* (Paris: Fayard, 2003), 365.

42. de Baecque, *La Cinéphilie*, 11.

43. Christian Keathley, *Cinephilia and History, or The Wind in the Trees* (Bloomington: Indiana University Press, 2006), 83.

44. Willemen, *Looks and Frictions*.

45. Keathley, *Cinephilia and History*, 32.

46. Willemen, *Looks and Frictions*, 235.

47. de Baecque, *La Cinéphilie*, 21.

48. Young, *Homemade Hollywood*, 4.

49. In an interview conducted by the author during *Montreal Otakuthon*. See Joly-Corcoran, "OTAKUTHON 2013—Panels and Cosplay," *Kinephanos*, August 18, 2013, http://www.kinephanos.ca/2013/otakuthon-2013-panels-et-cosplay/.

50. Respondent: Hallam, Questionnaire, November 2013.

51. Respondent: Sall, Questionnaire, January 2016.

52. Respondent: Mether, Questionnaire, February 2017.

53. Respondent: Bertocci, Questionnaire, October 2013.

54. There are different kinds of fanfilm directors. See Marc Joly-Corcoran and Sarah Ludlow: "Fans, Fics, and Films: 'Thanks the Maker(s),'" in *Fan Phenomena: Star Wars*, ed. Mika Elovaara (Bristol, UK: Intellect Publishing, 2013), 27–37.

55. Respondent: Read Johnson, Questionnaire, June 2017.

56. Respondent: Read Johnson, Questionnaire, June 2017.

57. Personal correspondence with author, October 21, 2013.

Bibliography

"emotion." *Merriam Webster Dictionary*. https://www.merriam-webster.com/dictionary/emotion (accessed 9 May, 2018).

"-phany." *Merriam Webster Dictionary*. https://www.merriam-webster.com/dictionary/-phany (accessed 9 May, 2018).

Abercrombie, Nicholas and Brian Longhurst. *Audiences*. London: Sage Publications, 1998.

Aumont, Jacques, and Michel Marie. *Dictionnaire théorique et critique du cinéma*. Second edition. Paris: Armand Colin, 2008.

Brooker, Will. *Using the Force, Creativity, Community and Star Wars Fans*. New York: Continuum, 2002.

de Baecque, Antoine. *La Cinéphilie: Invention d'un Regard, Histoire d'une Culture (1948–1966)*. Paris: Fayard, 2003.

Eliade, Mircea. *The Sacred and the Profane: The Nature of Religion*. New York: Harper, 1961.

Freud, Sigmund. *Beyond the Pleasure Principle*. Translated by C.J.M. Hubback. London and Vienna: International Psycho-Analytical, 1922.

Genette, Gérard. *The Architect: An Introduction.* Translated by Jane E. Lewin. Berkeley: University of California Press, 1992.

_____. *Palimpsestes, la Littérature au Second Degré.* Paris: Seuil, 1982.

Grossberg, Lawrence. "Is There a Fan in the House? The Affective Sensibility of Fandom." In *The Adoring Audience, Fan Culture and Popular Media*, edited by Lisa A. Lewis, 50–65. London: Routledge, 1992.

Hills, Matt. *Fan Cultures.* New York: Routledge, 2002.

_____. *The Pleasures of Horror.* New York and London: Continuum, 2005.

Jenkins, Henry. *Convergence Culture, Where Old and New Media Collide.* New York: New York University Press, 2006b.

_____. *Fans, Bloggers, and Gamers, Exploring Participatory Culture.* New York: New York University Press, 2006a.

_____. *Textual Poachers, Television Fans and Participatory Culture.* New York: Routledge, 1992.

Joly-Corcoran, Marc. *La Cinéphanie et sa Réappropriation: 'l'Affect Originel' et sa Réactualisation par le Fan, un Spectateur Néoreligieux.* Ph.D. dissertation, Université de Montréal, 2014.

_____. "OTAKUTHON 2013—Panels and Cosplay." *Kinephanos*, August 18 (2013). http://www.kinephanos.ca/2013/otakuthon-2013-panels-et-cosplay/ (accessed May 9, 2018).

Joly-Corcoran, Marc, and Sarah Ludlow. "Fans, Fics, and Films: 'Thank the Maker(s)." In *Fan Phenomena: Star Wars*, edited by Mika Elovaara, 27–37. Bristol, UK: Intellect Publishing, 2013.

Keathley, Christian. *Cinephilia and History, or The Wind in the Trees.* Bloomington: Indiana University Press, 2006.

Lancaster, Kurt. *Fan Performances in a Media Universe: Interacting with Babylon 5.* Austin: University of Texas Press, 2001.

Morin, Edgar. *Sur l'Esthétique.* Paris: Robert Laffont, 2016.

Odin, Roger. *De la Fiction.* Bruxelles: De Boeck Université, 2000.

Otto, Rudolf. *The Idea of the Holy.* Oxford: Oxford University Press, 1958 [1923].

Schaeffer, Jean-Marie. *Pourquoi la Fiction.* Paris: Seuil, 1999.

Smith, Greg M. *Film Structure and the Emotion System.* Cambridge: Cambridge University Press, 2003.

Souriau, Étienne. "La Structure de l'Univers Filmique et le Vocabulaire de la Filmologie." *Revue Internationale de Filmologie* 7–8 (1951): 231–240.

Souriau, Étienne, and Anne Souriau (eds). *Vocabulaire d'Esthétique.* Paris: PUF, 1990.

Sutton, Henry. "Le Problème de la Téléphanie." *Journal Universel de l'Électricité* 50 (December 13, 1890).

Tan, Ed S. *Emotion and the Structure of Narrative Film, Film as an Emotion Machine.* New Jersey: Routledge, 2009 [1996].

Tannenbaum, Percy H. "'Play It Again Sam': Repeated Exposure to Television Programs." In *Selective Exposure to Communication*, edited by Dolph Zillmann and Jennings Bryant, 225–241. Mahwah, NJ: Lawrence Erlbaum Associates, 1985.

Turner, Victor. *The Anthropology of Performance.* New York: PAJ Publications, 1987.

Willemen, Paul. *Looks and Frictions.* Bloomington: Indiana University Press, 1994.

Young, Clive. *Homemade Hollywood, Fans Behind the Camera.* London: Continuum, 2008.

Experiencing the Sacred
The Hobbit *as a Holy Text*

Jyrki Korpua, Maria Ruotsalainen,
Minna Siikilä-Laitila, Tanja Välisalo
and Irma Hirsjärvi

"The films are great and in some mystical way help me get through life."—Respondent #3191, *The World Hobbit Project*[1]

Introduction

As statements like the above indicate, we can experience something so mysterious yet profound that it is aligned with the sacred, even when doing something seemingly profane like watching a film or reading a book. The above quotation, from a large international survey about the reception of the *Hobbit* trilogy (2012; 2013; 2014) directed by Peter Jackson, demonstrates well how touched some of the viewers were by the films, to the extent that they assigned religious qualities to them and to the experience of viewing and consuming them. A growing number of studies on media audiences and fandom show that elements of sacredness and holiness can be part of audience beliefs, experiences, and practices.[2] This essay focuses on the fan responses to Jackson's cinematic adaptation of J.R.R. Tolkien's high fantasy classic *The Hobbit* (originally published in 1937),[3] and the ways in which the vocabulary of the sacred is utilized. We will first examine the ways religion and fandom have been argued to be similar, as well as the counter-arguments to these claims. We will then proceed to ask if the concept of sacred can be helpful while attempting to understand the experiences of the viewers, fans and non-fans alike, of *The Hobbit* films. In doing this, we the position of sacred in contemporary culture will also be examined.

102

A key primary source for this study will be the data gathered from a global survey of viewers of *The Hobbit* films, supplemented by the subsequent discussions on online forums and to online news articles and opinion pieces surrounding the release and reception of the trilogy. The survey responses were collected as part of *The World Hobbit Project*[4] which produced over 36,000 responses from more than 50 countries. In 2008, Martin Barker, Emeritus Professor of Film and Television Studies at Aberystwyth University, Matt Hills, also from Aberystwyth University, and Ernest Mathijs from the University of British Columbia, Vancouver, launched a program for international comparative research on Peter Jackson's *The Lord of the Rings* film trilogy, and in 2014 the new international study about the *The Hobbit* film trilogy commenced in more than fifty countries with an online survey (Barker et al. 2014–15). The data collected via the survey was expected to open up new research questions about the global reception of the adaptations, and the production, activity and meaning-making processes of the members of the audience. In this essay, our focus is on the Finnish responses (N=1,614) to the survey. The majority of the Finnish respondents answered the survey in Finnish, here translated into English. The survey included both closed and open-ended questions, but here we concentrate on the qualitative data that can be gleaned through analysis.

Another dataset utilized in this essay consists of online discussions. The online discussions addressed here are from two lengthy conversation threads connected to articles written about *The Hobbit* films. The first article is Ethan Gilsdorf's "Peter Jackson Must Be Stopped," published on the *Wired* magazine website.[5] The tone of the article is generally critical towards Jackson's films. This article accumulated, in just a couple of days, 941 comments, 761 Twitter shares, 12,500 Facebook shares and 281 Google+ shares (as of September 1, 2015, when the data was gathered). The other article, Christopher Orr's "*The Hobbit 2* Is Bad Fan Fiction"[6] from *The Atlantic* magazine website, was also critical of *The Hobbit* films. This article received 388 comments in total. The accumulated 1,323 comments between them, not to mention the shares, included a variety of opinions and nuances and demonstrate the provocativeness of the debate over Jackson's adaptation. They also demonstrate the premise of this study, that religious language and concepts related to sacredness have been valuable for fan articulation of their attachments to both Tolkien's and Jackson's narratives and the role of *The Hobbit* in their own lives.

To examine how Tolkien's story unfolds across different mediums and the reception of this among fans, we utilize the concepts of transmedia and transmedial worlds, as well as Anne Jerslev's idea of "sacred viewing," which allows us to analyze the emotional descriptions of the respondents in the framework of the sacred.[7] By "transmedia" we here refer to a story that is told via multiple mediated forms. An often-mentioned example of transmedia storytelling is the Marvel Universe, which consists of several narratives told originally through serialized comics, but today includes films, short films, animations, television series, action figures, games, and advertising campaigns. These narratives become connected and influential on one other in a way that makes the universe more comprehensive the more of its narratives are consumed—like a puzzle with an ever-increasing number of pieces, each expanding the overall image generated by their tessellation. As Rachel Wagner has noted, transmedial franchises are exercises in world-building. In this activity it is not only the creators who build the world, but also other participants: the fans or subcreators.[8] Moreover, the places built through this activity can quickly become sacred places, maintained through the repetition of rituals such as viewing and reviewing films, participating in conventions, contributing to multiply-authored fanfictions, and thus affirming and expanding the rules, coherence, and fate of the world. Transmedial worlds, in this way, function similarly to the communal efforts to create cohesion, meaning, and purpose in religious narratives by communities of believers.[9]

The transmedial body of Tolkien's works and world consists of not only the original novels by the author, but also the edited papers and posthumously published texts after his death, the fan products (fanfilms, fanfiction, fanart, handicrafts, poetry, and performances and so forth), as well as the commercial products: adaptations to different media, animations, films, theatrical and musical pieces, visual art, cartoons, dance performances, television programs, and so on. It is therefore, we argue, fruitful to include the concept of transmedia to our approach. The same holds true for the concept of the transmedial world, as it emphasizes the world as an abstract system, created through these different texts and products but existing also beyond them, as well as and how the world is experienced—something that is very prominent in the data we explored.[10] Finally, the notion of sacred viewing and implicit religion lends a way to interpret the respondent's spiritual engagement with the movies, even when the term sacred is not explicitly present in their answers.

"The Sacred" as an Interpretive Framework

There has been, as this volume demonstrates, a long-running interest in the academy in comparing the behaviors and motivations of fans to those of religious persons. Locating common elements between religion and fandom has sometimes led to fandom being framed as a form of secular religion, suggesting both fandom and religion share similar excessive and irrational involvement.[11] However, there has also been strong resistance to the comparison. For instance, Henry Jenkins has argued that there are more differences than similarities between fandom and religion, and we would be better off by comparing fandom to political parties or to other kind of organizational activities.[12] Jenkins makes a clear distinction between religion and fandom in a very practical way: the mythologies of the texts fans "worship" are not religious ones like myths which tend to give creation stories or etiologies of the things such as the world, humans, the stars, or animals.[13] With a focus on media rather than religious studies, Jenkins does not consider that fandom can be seen to represent what has been called "implicit religion," an idea that everyday experiences can be treated as "religious."[14] Nevertheless, there are some elements of religion that are indeed implicit in fandom activities.

Edward Bailey understands implicit religion as embedded in people's *commitment*, whether or not this commitment takes an explicitly religious form.[15] Originally implicit religion was defined by "any quest for meaning in life, poetic insight, artistic vision" and so on. To this Bailey has added that there are "occasions within the life of individuals and of groups, which fall outside the sphere of what is conventionally called religion, which look very much like religion."[16] Even common and civic activities can be seen having implicitly religious elements.[17] This is evident in fandom movements. For example, *Star Trek* fandom had been described as having "commonalities with broader definitions of religion," such as having an organization, dogmas, a recruitment system and a "canon," that is, a foundational history and cosmology for the world of *Star Trek*, determined by its creators.[18] However, while there may be a shared status of being untouchable for both dogma and canon in some spheres, this is not a constant: many fans see the mythologies of science fiction universes as open, and contribute to them their own "fanon" (fan-made canon).[19] In its contribution to the conversation of religion/fandom interrelations, this essay will not use a specific definition of what a religion is or is not to understand fan activities, but will be using the concept of "the sacred" to highlight the religious-like ways in which *Hobbit* fans respond to the text.

Originally the word "sacred," from Latin word *sacer* and Old English *sacre*, means to set apart or to consecrate something dedicated to a deity, to worship, and/or to religion or religious uses.[20] While the concept of sacred is usually linked to religion of some kind, the *Cambridge Dictionary* definition gives three qualifiers of the sacred: (1) something considered to be holy and deserving respect; (2) something connected with religion (for example sacred music or writings); and (3) something considered too important to be changed.[21] This last qualifier is of especial significance to the way in which Tolkien's work has been regarded as sacred in the context of this study. For our study, it is also interesting to note that originally in the Finnish language the concept of "sacred" means something protected, bordered, and segregated.[22]

The untouchability of the sacred recalls for many in the social sciences the classic reading of the sacred/profane divide by anthropologist Émile Durkheim. Durkheim, in addition to contrasting the sacred with the profane, stressed how the sacred is both socially constructed and accompanied by strong emotions.[23] An additional quality of the sacred, or what Rudolf Otto referred to as the "holy," is that it is beyond the common realm of human understanding.[24] This contributes to the ineffable emotional response that is triggered by an encounter with the sacred. In her examination of the intense emotional involvement among the viewers of the *Lord of the Ring*s films, Anne Jerslev utilizes this understanding of sacred by coining the term "sacred viewing,"[25] a framework we will return to in our own analysis of viewers of *The Hobbit*.

As part of its unknowable quality, the sacred is also veiled in mystery. The French author Stéphane Mallarmé wrote in the poem *Art Is for All*: "Whatever is sacred, whatever is to remain sacred, must be clothed in mystery. All religions take shelter behind arcana which they unveil only to the predestined. Art has its own mysteries."[26] The terminology of mystery, the sacred, and the holy are, in many ways and discourses, intermingled. For example when Otto is discussing his classic views on the concept of the "holy" in his *Das Heilige: Über das Irrationale in der Idee des Göttlichen und sein Verhältnis zum Rationalen* (1917), the German word *heilige* that he uses can be translated as either "holy" or "sacred," and he refers to this spiritual "feeling" as "numinous."[27] As Mallarmé writes, mystery and the sacred are often connected to art and such expressive forms, a notion that has interesting analogs to both Tolkien's fiction and to the fan cultures that celebrate, even worship, Tolkien's fiction as an artform through which one can either experience the sacred, or commit hubris by deigning to re/interpret its mysteries.

Northrop Frye famously plays with the notions of literary sacredness and religious sacredness. When discussing the so-called sacred and secular structures of literature, Frye regards romance and other later mundane genres of writing as "secular scriptures" that provide an integrated vision of the world wherein the hero is human: a parallel to the former holy and sacred scriptures wherein the mythic hero is a god.[28] Yet, as the title "scripture" intends, a sacred quality can be maintained even in non-religious narratives. In offering his take on this debate Jacques Derrida comments "[s]ecularization in literature doesn't mean anything to me. I think literature remains to us, a sort of sacred space, and we have to interrogate what this sacredness, this secularized sacredness may mean."[29] In the same vein, Terry Eagleton comments "[l]ike religion, literature works primarily by emotion and experience, and so was admirably well-fitted to carry through the ideological task which religion left off."[30] As this study argues, the overlap of the sacred and secular in the contemporary world is fascinatingly manifested in the emotive and mystical responses to works of literature that have mythic attributes, such as Tolkien's tomes.

There have been multiple studies of the concept of "secular sacredness" in contemporary social contexts.[31] Emily McAvan, for example, has coined the term "postmodern sacred" to bring together the array of examples from popular culture of nonreligious elements taking on spiritual importance. As the name suggests, McAvan's construction of the postmodern sacred relies heavily on the theories of postmodernism.[32] Following Bruno Latour and Jean Baudrillard, McAvan contends that what is at stake in postmodern society is the status of the real or the original: it has been eroded through the collapse of the grand narratives and taken over by the hyperreal—simulacra that have become more real than the originals themselves. Adam Possamai has used the concept of the hyperreal to speak of emerging postmodern religions which similarly combine elements of religion and popular culture into eclectic, sometimes irreverent, pastiche belief systems.[33] The collapse of grand narratives, as well as the ongoing process of secularization, produces the kind of sacred which is no longer firmly rooted in traditions of the past (as they would if they had remained connected and framed by the grand narratives), but rather the sacred is now spread and scattered, encountered in spheres where formerly it rarely manifested.

Today, the sacred can regularly be found in the works of popular culture and entertainment. One example that is both clearly religious in content but also in its re-packaging as a product is Mel Gibson's film *The Passion of the Christ* (2004). Such texts involve a multilayered sacrality by using religion not just as subject matter but by producing, through narrative, sound design, and potent imagery, the sensation of awe in the audience affiliated with encountering holiness. This, thus, incorporates into a profane and quotidian activity like watching a film the emotive experiences of religion, pushing viewing into the sacred realm. As a consequence, there is constant negotiation among the different individuals and socials groups as to what actually is sacred and what is not. As texts like *The Hobbit* get continuously reworked and re-told through different media, debate surrounding their sacrality and impact on audiences are likewise ongoing.

The Sacrality of Tolkien and His Texts

This essay discusses the perceptions and experiences of the sacred in relation to *The Hobbit* trilogy, consisting of the films directed by Peter Jackson and based on Tolkien's book. In fantasy fandom, Tolkien is not just "a Godfather of Fantasy,"[34] but his major works *The Hobbit, or There and Back Again* (1937), *The Lord of the Rings* (three parts, 1954–1955), and *The Silmarillion*

(1977, posthumously) have achieved an almost sacred status inside the genre. Works of fantasy are usually compared to these books and Tolkien himself is sometimes discussed with religious devotion. As Mark P.J. Wolf notes, Tolkien's fiction has a strong influence over "fantasy novels, fantasy art, role-playing games, and videogames of the adventure genre, and collectively an effect on the culture in general."[35] The so-called "post–Tolkien fantasy" has heavily relied on the Tolkien-esque kind of myth-making[36] and *The Oxford Companion to English Literature* has called him "the greatest influence within the fantasy genre."[37]

Serious fan commitment to Tolkien's books that enables comparisons with religion has been visible since the 1960s.[38] This devotion has grown among many generations and today members of Tolkien fandom—which includes fans of adaptations such as Peter Jackson's—are known as "Ringers."[39] On some occasions, Tolkien's texts are even considered sacred texts.[40] It seems as if adapting them, or even commenting on them is inappropriate and is even considered forbidden within some fan communities. This is quite clear when researching the comments made by audiences on adaptations of *The Hobbit* by Peter Jackson and his team.

In online conversations about Jackson's *The Hobbit* films, it is easy to find comments that refer to Tolkien's texts as more or less sacred, or at least highly valued and therefore untouchable. Christopher Orr's review article in *The Atlantic* magazine about Jackson's second *Hobbit* film, *The Desolation of Smaug* (2013), made some very blunt criticisms of its quality. Many commenters agreed with Orr, stating that Jackson was not faithful to the "spirit" of the original, and that the films were "complete betrayal of Tolkien's original novel."[41] For example, one wrote: "Well, you can argue like the author does that Jackson doesn't keep with the spirit of the book which is the greater sin." To this another commentator answered: "Agreed. In the very first 5 minutes, he violates the spirit of the book." Commentators also stated repeatedly that "Tolkien must be rolling in his grave."[42]

This "spirit of the book" the commentators referred to can be read through Walter Benjamin's conceptualization of the "aura" of an artwork or text. Writing in 1936, Benjamin argued that in modernity, the age of mechanical production and reproduction, art has lost its unique spirit, or "aura" of authenticity. For Benjamin, original works of art, adhering to the classic standards of beauty, presented a coherent whole, but with each iteration this aura was eroded. Reproduction, as in the case of photographs and films, meant these works are no longer unique and situational, but rather repeatable and in case of the film made out of multiple different parts (such as different scenes).[43] The "spirit" and its loss then, can be understood as the lost coherence of the original and its creator's embedded intentions. Clearly, for some critics of Jackson's *Hobbit*, reproducing Tolkien's work is in and of itself problematic in that it dilutes the beautiful whole of the original. Furthermore, in Benjamin's model any reproduction is not only an insult to the perfection of the first but affects its very aura; thus Jackson's work will automatically be inferior in spirit. It both commits hubris and produces an ersatz sacrality as an adaptation of Tolkien's *Hobbit*.

Evidently, religious language was deemed suitably powerful and emotive for the criticism some commenters wanted to level at Jackson. For example, one commentator wrote, "And I was irritated when I read that he left out the whole 'Scouring of the Shire' section because he 'just didn't like it' (Blasphemy!!) In the case of Tolkien, 'over-fidelity' would have been a plus."[44] Another commentator also used religious phrases when commenting: "Jackson has committed an egregious sin, he's created fanfic and, my God, how unentertaining it all is!" Yet another wrote,

> I really hope Jackson doesn't take on *The Silmarillion*. The reason being is because this is not a story that should be tampered with by anyone but Master Tolkien himself. Don't get me wrong I loved *LoTR* and *The Hobbit* series so far, with the creative twists and all, but the Silmarillion is way too precious to be askewed. That book is like the Bible of Tolkienism, and it is meant for taking in an abundance of information of "what really happened."[45]

The terms "blasphemy," "egregious sin," and "the Bible of Tolkienism" demonstrate very clearly how fans use religious vocabulary in describing their feelings toward interpretations of their favored texts.[46] Not only is the terminology religious (in this case drawing on Christianity generally), the sentiment being imparted in these statements suggests further that, despite the context being secular—anonymous comments posted on an online article—a strong sense of sacredness surrounds Tolkien's legendarium.

In contrast, irritation with the existence of hardcore Tolkien fans, who highly value the original book, was also easy to see in comments such as, "More moaning from purists," "I don't share the Tolkien aficionados [*sic*] mad outrage," "Why all this exegesis here of this children's book and it's movie versions? [*sic*]" and, sarcastically, "I welcome a correction from the Tolkien faithful."[47] Hence, concepts of the sacred are also connected to stereotypes of Tolkien fans. When considering our other dataset, this trend becomes more obvious. Some members of *The Hobbit* audience describe themselves as distinct from other viewers who they describe using terms such as *fanatic* and *fanaticism*. The words of one respondent displays this alleged division:

> I am one of moderate but faithful old fan audiences, who usually don't get excited but still watch several times and buy the films. Of course, many old fans have totally condemned *The Hobbit* films, while newcomers might not know their Tolkien and only get hyped about the new films.[48]

Another juxtaposed the strict attitude of some viewers with their own moderate approach by describing their own as "healthy," invoking a pathological depiction of the fan as one who is defined by their excessiveness "bordering on deranged."[49]

Sacred Experiences with The Hobbit

> We are people who love Tolkien's world and find inspiration and motivation from it in the middle of our ordinary lives. We are spiritually all connected to each other and are grateful for being allowed to experiences these larger-than-life experiences as a one big community.[50]

We have so far discussed elevating a text to the position of the sacred, in this case the original text of *The Hobbit*. Nevertheless, when we examined the data, there was also another way that the sacred made its appearance: this was the experience of viewing the films as sacred. Here we encounter the kind of sacred, which, for the viewers, is not exclusively related to original text of *The Hobbit* and its "aura of authenticity," but is more tolerant towards changes and disruptions to the original text, such as new events and characters, and altered characterizations.[51] When examining the process of viewing the films as a sacred experience, those viewers (in this case, the respondents of the survey) who experienced watching the films in this register did not find discomfort with the fact that the original text was changed, or in some cases did not acknowledge the existence of an original text at all. In addition, viewing was not an isolated event, but connected to larger contexts: if not to the respondents' expectations of the film as an adaptation of the book, then to *The Lord of the Rings* films, the broader frame of Tolkien's legendarium, the fantasy genre, or film as a medium.

The responses to *The Hobbit* trilogy in the survey were from varied audiences, including many viewers who reacted to the films similarly to the online commentators discussed above. It is also worth noting that the respondents who had read the book multiple times were likely to give the film a lower rating than those respondents who had not read the book, or had read it once.[52] Yet there were a number of respondents who found *The Hobbit* films emotionally engaging and found viewing them a profound experience—those responses are of interest here. One respondent when asked what most surprized him/her while watching the films, noted: "How great the scale of emotions they evoked in me was. I never thought I would be crying so much during the last movie. I had tears in my eyes almost throughout the movie."[53] This kind of intense emotional engagement is at the center of Jerslev's "sacred viewing."

In "Sacred Viewing: Emotional Responses to *The Lord of the Rings*" Jerslev examines the data gathered in Denmark during the precursor to the *Hobbit Research Project*, the *Lord of the Rings Research Project*. In her reading of the data, she focuses on those aspects of the responses which can be read as "neo-sacred."[54] Jerslev approaches the neo-sacred or modern sacred as something which no longer is constituted in a distinct, religious sphere of its own, but is part of the everyday life and appears in contexts that can be considered mundane, while the experience itself is far from mundane. Jerslev furthermore draws upon Matt Hills' concept of "neoreligiosity" which refers to the way sacred elements become part of profane spaces in modern society. In sacred viewing then these elements are part of the reception of the *Lord of the Ring* films. As a starting point for sacred viewing, Jerslev takes the kind of descriptions by the respondents where the experience of seeing the films is described through emotional and quasi-religious expressions such as "awe," "spell-binding," and "magnificent," and where the respondents indicate that they have been touched and emotionally engaged by the films while viewing them.[55]

In a similar manner, we examine these types of responses in connection to the sacred experience of viewing *The Hobbit* films. When assessing how the respondents to *The Hobbit* survey explained and conceptualized their experience of viewing the films, the descriptions laden with emotion fell roughly into two categories. There were the viewers who were awestruck by the films (indeed, some even said they could not find the words to explain how the films affected them and how they feel about them) and who experienced the films, borrowing the religious vocabulary we have used here so far, as original and important works of their own. One respondent wrote: "Simply excellent! Well-made quality movies I myself at least greatly enjoyed watching. The last movie left me speechless, it was that glorious."[56] Another, quoted at the start of this essay, stated clearly that the films were so impressive as to have a "mystical" quality that helped the viewer "get through life."[57]

Then there were the viewers who also discussed related aspects of Tolkien's world while describing their feelings about the films, such as Jacksons' *Lord of the Rings* movies (which for some of the respondents were the original works) or Tolkien's original novels. For these respondents, it was the sense of nostalgia that often triggered a sense of the sacred. Some respondents, for instance, remembered having had *The Hobbit* book read them to as a child, and when watching the films recalled this and experienced nostalgia. As one respondent said:

> Tolkien and the world of Middle-Earth have been important to me since I was young, ever since I read the *LoTR* books and watched the films made of them. Because of this, *Hobbit* films have been some kind of continuations for this and created nostalgia and I have returned to the feelings I have felt with Tolkien's world. I went to see *The Hobbit* films in the same town, on the same screen where I have been to see all the

LoTR films. It became a three-year-tradition with friends. And in that way an experience. The films as films have been from mediocre to okay, but for me the experience is why I have liked them. I was emotional when watching the last film, it felt like an end of an era.[58]

This sense of nostalgia and ritual was also present in the responses that referred to *The Lord of the Rings* films (or *LoTR*) as a return to the fictional world itself, a sort of "coming home":

I have personally experienced a loss at the time when *LoTR* films came out. Then I wanted to lean on to something and these films were my salvation. The films made me deal with my grief. And when I heard that films would be made about *The Hobbit* I was very excited, because it was like returning home. The book was important for me as a child and ever since I was young I have had a clear image in my mind of the moment when Bilbo rises above the tree tops of Mirkwood and takes the first breath of fresh air. This was the scene that has stayed in my mind ever since I was a child.[59]

Lisbeth Klastrup has observed that affection for transmedial worlds can be connected to a nostalgic desire to return to the first encounter with that particular world.[60] Here, returning and repetition function both as marking the space and separating it from the everyday. In religions, rituals fulfill this function as Durkheim notes, and revisiting transmedial worlds can be considered a ritualistic activity and they enable sacred space to be born.

Transmedial worlds can be seen ideal for establishing sacred spaces of returning. Wagner argues that they enable world-building practices which in turn are in her words religious practices: they help to construct meanings and uphold believes. Transmedial world are ideal for this not only because they allow world-building through inviting participation of fan activities, but also exactly because they are transmedial: the stories they told are not confined to one sphere but can be found in multitude of places.[61] Thus, in the case of transmedial worlds the sacred space is never fully confined, or its borders fully established: instead they are porous. This is because the products in question consistently refer outside of themselves or sometimes even unfold across multiple mediums. Accordingly, there can then also be great debates which elements of it should be included to it and to what degree it should be altered—a complex and potentially controversial discussion if the text has, as Tolkien's work does, the status of sacred among its devotees.

Conclusion

This essay discusses the perceptions and experiences of the sacred among the audiences of *The Hobbit* film trilogy. We started our examination by defining what is actually meant by the concept of sacred and offered two different, albeit intertwined ways of understanding sacred: one in which what is sacred is perceived through its originality and uniqueness itself, and another, postmodern sacred or neo-sacred, where sacred is no longer set apart or bordered, but where it, or what is perceived as sacred, borrows, changes, and is open to modification. We furthermore explored how Tolkien, his works and especially *The Hobbit* and its film adaptations appear in this framework, from the perspective of reception and audiences.

To examine the audiences' views on the films, we used two sources of data: online discussions and data gathered through a survey. With our reading of the research material, we identified three different positions to understanding sacred in the audience reception of *The Hobbit* films. First, there were the audiences who regarded the original work of Tolkien as sacred and considered the films based on it almost as blasphemy. Second, there were the audiences who fell into the category of sacred viewing and who focused on the viewing experience of the films, not referring beyond them when describing their experience. Third, there were those for whom the sense of nostalgia and returning to the story of *The Hobbit* or to Tolkien's world were the markers of the sacred. For both of these latter two occurrences of the sacred, the emotional, affective experiences were essential.

While comparisons between fandom and religion have been widely rejected by fandom research, we argue that the concept of sacred can be useful in understanding the experiences of contemporary audiences and especially their engagement with vast transmedial worlds. Even though the experiences of all *Hobbit* audiences cannot be described as sacred, for some the sense of sacredness plays part of this experience. Moreover, while some viewers connect the sacred strictly with the original text and reject the variations from it, for some the sacred experiences can be understood in part as resulting from an affordance created by the transmedial nature of Tolkien's world. Furthermore, these respondents are committed to this experience and they bring in into their accounts of their reception of *The Hobbit* films resources having to do with prior experiences with other cultural texts. In a usually implicit way, this brings elements of "religion" and "the sacred" into their reading, understanding, and experience of *The Hobbit* as a transmedial holy text.

NOTES

1. Respondent #3191, Martin Barker, Matt Hills, and Ernest Mathijs, *The World Hobbit Project Survey*, 2014–2015.

2. Key studies include Michael Jindra, "*Star Trek* Fandom as a Religious Phenomenon," *Sociology of Religion* 55 (1994): 27–51; Daniel Cavicchi, *Tramps Like Us: Music and Meaning Among Springsteen Fans* (New York: Oxford University Press, 1998); and Jennifer Porter, "Implicit Religion in Popular Culture: The Religious Dimensions of Fan Communities," *Implicit Religion* 12, no. 3 (November 2009): 271–280.

3. J.R.R. Tolkien, *The Hobbit, or There and Back Again* (London: George Allen & Unwin, 1937); Peter Jackson's adaptation of *The Hobbit* comes in three parts: *An Unexpected Journey* (NZ/U.S.: Warner Bros Pictures, 2012); *The Desolation of Smaug* (NZ/U.S.: Warner Bros Pictures, 2013); and *The Battle of the Five Armies* (NZ/U.S.: Warner Bros Pictures, 2014).

    4. Barker et al., *The World Hobbit Project Survey*.
    5. Ethan Gilsdorf, "Peter Jackson Must Be Stopped," *Wired*, December 19 (2014). http://www.wired.com/2014/12/hobbit-peter-jackson-must-be-stopped/#disqus_thread.
    6. Christopher Orr, "*The Hobbit 2* Is Bad Fan Fiction," *The Atlantic*, December 13 (2013), https://www.theatlantic.com/entertainment/archive/2013/12/-em-the-hobbit-2-em-is-bad-fan-fiction/282316/.
    7. Henry Jenkins, *Fans, Bloggers, and Gamers. Exploring Participatory Culture* (New York: New York University Press, 2006); Lisbeth Klastrup and Susana Tosca, "The Networked Reception of Transmedial Universes, an Experience-Centered Approach," *MedieKultur: Journal of Media and Communication Research* 32, no. 60 (2016): 107–122; Anne Jerslev, "Sacred Viewing: Emotional Responses to *The Lord of the Rings*," in *The Lord of the Rings Popular Culture in Global Context*, ed. Ernest Mathjis (London: Wallflower Press, 2006), 206–221.
    8. For more about subcreation and subcreators, see: Mark J.P. Wolf, *Building Imaginary Worlds: The Theory and History of Subcreation* (New York: Routledge, 2012).
    9. Rachel Wagner, *Religion, Ritual and Virtual Reality* (New York: Routledge, 2012).
    10. See also Lisbeth Klastrup and Susana Tosca, "Transmedial Worlds: Rethinking Cyberworld Design," *Proceedings of the 2004 International Conference on Cyberworlds* (2004): 409–416.
    11. Andrew Crome, "Religion and the Pathologization of Fandom: Religion, Reason, and Controversy in *My Little Pony* Fandom," *Journal of Religion and Popular Culture* 27, no. 2 (2015): 130–147.
    12. Henry Jenkins, *Fans, Bloggers, and Gamers. Exploring Participatory Culture* (New York: New York University Press, 2006), 20.
    13. Matt Hills and Henry Jenkins, "Intensities interviews Henry Jenkins @Console-ing Passions, University of Bristol, July 7th," *Intensities* 2 (Autumn/Winter 2001), https://intensitiescultmedia.com/2012/12/11/intensities-the-journal-of-cult-media-2-autumnwinter-2001/.
    14. See for example Edward Bailey, *Implicit Religion: An Introduction* (London: Centre for the Study of Implicit Religion and Contemporary Spirituality, 1998).
    15. Bailey, *Implicit Religion*, 14–22.
    16. Edward Bailey, "The Notion of Implicit Religion: What It Means, and Does Not Mean," *The Secular Quest for Meaning in Life: Denton Papers in Implicit Religion*, ed. Edward Bailey (Lewiston, NY: Edwin Mellen Press, 2002), 1–2.
    17. John H. Evans, "Public Vocabularies of Religious Belief: Explicit and Implicit Religious Discourse in the American Public Sphere," in *The Blackwell Companion to the Sociology of Culture*, eds Mark D. Jacobs and Nancy Weiss Hanrahan (Malden, MA: Blackwell Publishing, 2005), 398–400.
    18. Jindra, "*Star Trek* Fandom as a Religious Phenomenon," 45, 48–49.
    19. Irma Hirsjärvi, *Faniuden Siirtymiä. SuomalaisenSscience Fiction Fandomin Verkostot* (Jyväskylä: Publications of the Research Centre for Contemporary Culture, 2009), 256–266. Hirsjärvi's study showed that this "irreverence" for sci-fi texts is due in part to the genre. Science fiction as a genre encourages its readers to use its hypothetical world as a critical and an analytical tool for analyzing the world around them. Themes of possible and impossible worlds in sci-fi are about play and imagination; nothing is sacred. Even when fans used religious terms were used in connection to the reading, they were distanced from their religious meanings.
    20. James Stormonth and Philip Henry Phelp, *Etymological and Pronouncing Dictionary of the English Language. Including a Various Copious Selection of Scientific Terms for Use in Schools and Colleges and as a Book of General Reference* (Edinburgh and London: William Blackwood and Sons, 1876), 544.
    21. "Sacred," in *The Cambridge Dictionary*, https://dictionary.cambridge.org/dictionary/english/sacred.
    22. See for example *Suomen Sanojen Alkuperä—Etymologinen Sanakirja 2 L-P* (Helsinki: Suomalaisen Kirjallisuuden Seura, 1995) and Veikko Anttonen, *Ihmisen Ja Maan Rajat. "Pyhä" Kulttuurisena Kategoriana* (Helsinki: Suomalaisen Kirjallisuuden Seura, 1996).
    23. Émile Durkheim, *The Elementary Forms of Religious Life*, trans. Joseph Sward Swain (Mineola, NY: Dover Publications, 2008 [1915]).

24. Rudolf Otto, *Das Heilige: Über das Irrationale in der Idee des Göttlichen und sein Verhältnis zum Rationalen* (Münich: Verlag C.H. Beck, 2004 [1917]).

25. Jerslev, "Sacred Viewing," 206–21.

26. Quoted in Garry Sherbert, "Frye's 'Pure Speech': Literature and the Sacred without the Sacred," in *Northrop Frye: New Directions from Old*, ed. David Rampton (Toronto, ON: University of Toronto Press, 2009), 143.

27. Otto, *Das Heilige*, 8–28.

28. Northrop Frye, *Anatomy of Criticism. Four Essays by Northrop Frye* (New York: Atheneum, 1967), 131–233, and Northrop Frye, *The Secular Scripture. A Study of the Structure of Romance* (Cambridge, MA: Harvard University Press, 1976), 159–190.

29. Sherbert, "Frye's 'Pure Speech,'" 144. Derrida's essay is available in English in Jacques Derrida, *The Gift of Death and Literature in Secret, Second Edition*, trans. David Wills (Chicago: University of Chicago Press, 2008).

30. Terry Eagleton, *Literary Theory: An Introduction. Anniversary Edition* (Oxford: Blackwell Publishing, 2008), 22.

31. See for example Robert Wuthnow, *Rediscovering the Sacred. Perspective on Religion in Contemporary Society* (Grand Rapids, MN: William B. Eerdmans Publishing Company, 1992).

32. Emily McAvan, *The Postmodern Sacred: Popular Culture Spirituality in the Science Fiction, Fantasy and Urban Genres* (Jefferson, NC: McFarland, 2012).

33. Adam Possamai and Murray Lee, "Hyper-Real Religions: Fear, Anxiety and Late-Modern Religious Innovation," *Journal of Sociology* 47, no. 3 (2011): 227–242.

34. Jyrki Korpua, *Constructive Mythopoetics in J.R.R. Tolkien's Legendarium* (Oulu: University of Oulu, 2015), 28.

35. Wolf, *Building Imaginary Worlds*, 5.

36. See Brian Attebery, *Stories About Stories. Fantasy and the Remaking of Myth* (Oxford: Oxford University Press, 2014).

37. "Fantasy Fiction," in *The Oxford Companion to English Literature*, 6th Edition, ed. Margaret Drabble (Oxford: Oxford University Press, 2000), 352.

38. Mike Foster, "America in the 1960s: Reception of Tolkien," in *J.R.R. Tolkien Encyclopedia. Scholarship and Critical Assessment*, ed. Michael C. Drout (New York: Routledge, 2007), 14.

39. See *Ringers: Lord of the Fans*, written by Cliff Broadway and Carlene Cordova, directed by Carlene Cordova (U.S.: Stormcrow Entertainment, 2005).

40. For a study of religious groups based on the texts and mythologies of Tolkien, see Markus Altena Davidsen, "The Elven Path and the Silver Ship of the Valar: Two Spiritual Groups Based on J.R.R. Tolkien's Legendarium," in *Fiction, Invention, and Hyper-reality*, eds. Carole M. Cusack and Pavol Kosnáč (New York: Routledge, 2017), 15–30.

41. Orr, "*The Hobbit 2* Is Bad Fan Fiction."

42. Orr, "*The Hobbit 2* Is Bad Fan Fiction."

43. Walter Benjamin, *The Work of Art in the Age of Mechanical Reproduction* (London: Penguin, 2008 [1936]).

44. Orr, "*The Hobbit 2* Is Bad Fan Fiction."

45. Orr, "*The Hobbit 2* Is Bad Fan Fiction."

46. For more on "secular" use of "religious" vocabulary, see Cavicchi, *Tramps Like Us*, 187.

47. Comments on Orr, "*The Hobbit 2* Is Bad Fan Fiction."

48. Respondent #34268, Martin Barker et al., *The World Hobbit Project Survey*, 2014–2015.

49. Joli Jensen, "Fandom as Pathology: The Consequences of Characterization," in *The Adoring Audience: Fan Culture and Popular Media*, ed. Lisa A. Lewis (London: Routledge 1992), 9–29.

50. Respondent #12763, Barker et al., *The World Hobbit Project Survey*.

51. For example, Jackson added the non-canonical character of Tauriel to his films, which received mixed reactions and criticism from fans. See Jyrki Korpua, "What About Tauriel? From Divine Mothers to Active Heroines: The Female Roles in J.R.R. Tolkien's

Legendarium and Peter Jackson's Movie Adaptation," in *Gender Identity and Sexuality in Current Fantasy and Science Fiction*, ed. Francesca T. Barbini (Edinburgh: Luna Press Publishing, 2017), 207–227.

52. For more on the subject, see Aino-Kaisa Koistinen, Maria Ruotsalainen, and Tanja Välisalo, "The World Hobbit Project in Finland: Audience Responses and Transmedial User Practises," *Participations* 13, no. 2 (November 2016): 356–379.

53. Respondent # 1025, Barker et al., *The World Hobbit Project Survey*.

54. Jerslev, "Sacred Viewing," 206–221.

55. Jerslev, "Sacred Viewing," 213.

56. Respondent # 34277, Barker et al., *The World Hobbit Project Survey*.

57. Respondent #3191, Barker et al., *The World Hobbit Project Survey*.

58. Respondent #1099, Barker et al., *The World Hobbit Project Survey*.

59. Respondent #32737, Barker et al., *The World Hobbit Project Survey*.

60. Lisbeth Klastrup, "Transmedial Worlds, Social Media and Networked Reception," Keynote presentation at the *Transmedia Use(r)s—20th International Summer School in Cultural Studies*, University of Jyväskylä, Finland (June 13, 2016).

61. Wagner, *Godwired*.

BIBLIOGRAPHY

Aamenesta öylättiin—kirkon sanasto. "Pyhä." Suomen evankelis-luterilainen kirkko. https:// evl.fi/sanasto/-/glossary/word/Pyh%C3%A4 (accessed May 9, 2018).

Anttonen, Veikko. *Ihmisen ja maan rajat. 'Pyhä' kulttuurisena kategoriana*. Helsinki: Suomalaisen Kirjallisuuden Seura, 1996.

Attebery, Brian. *Stories About Stories. Fantasy and the Remaking of Myth*. Oxford: Oxford University Press, 2014.

Bailey, Edward. *Implicit Religion: An Introduction*. London: Centre for the Study of Implicit Religion and Contemporary Spirituality, 1998.

_____. "The Notion of Implicit Religion: What It Means, and Does Not Mean." In *The Secular Quest for Meaning in Life: Denton Papers in Implicit Religion*, edited by Edward Bailey, 1–14. Lewiston, NY: The Edwin Mellen Press, 2002.

Barker, Martin, Matt Hills and Ernest Mathijs. *The World Hobbit Project Survey*. Aberystwyth, 2014–2015.

Benjamin, Walter. *The Work of Art in the Age of Mechanical Reproduction*. London: Penguin, 2008 [1936].

Cavicchi, Daniel. *Tramps Like Us: Music and Meaning Among Springsteen Fans*. New York: Oxford UP, 1998.

Cordova, Carlene, director. *Ringers: Lord of the Fans*. Written by Cliff Broadway and Carlene Cordova. USA: Stormcrow Entertainment, 2005.

Crome, Andrew. "Religion and the Pathologization of Fandom: Religion, Reason, and Controversy in *My Little Pony* Fandom." *Journal of Religion and Popular Culture* 27, no. 2 (2015): 130–147.

Davidsen, Markus Altena. "The Elven Path and the Silver Ship of the Valar: Two Spiritual Groups Based on J.R.R. Tolkien's Legendarium." In *Fiction, Invention, and Hyper-Reality*, edited by Carole M. Cusack and Pavol Kosnáč, 15–30. New York: Routledge, 2017.

Derrida, Jacques. *The Gift of Death and Literature in Secret. Second Edition*. Translated by David Wills. Chicago: University of Chicago Press, 2008.

Durkheim, Émile. *The Elementary Forms of Religious Life*. Translated by Joseph Sward Swain. Mineola: Dover Publications, Inc, 2008 [1915].

Eagleton, Terry. *Literary Theory: An Introduction. Anniversary Edition*. Oxford: Blackwell Publishing, 2008.

Evans, John H. "Public Vocabularies of Religious Belief: Explicit and Implicit Religious Discourse in the American Public Sphere." In *The Blackwell Companion to the Sociology of Culture*, edited by Mark D. Jacobs and Nancy Weiss Hanrahan, 398–411. Malden: Blackwell Publishing, 2005.

"Fantasy Fiction." In *The Oxford Companion to English Literature*, 6th Edition, edited by Margaret Drabble, 352. Oxford: Oxford University Press, 2000.

Foster, Mike. "America in the 1960s: Reception of Tolkien." In *J.R.R. Tolkien Encyclopedia. Scholarship and Critical Assessment*, edited by Michael C. Drout, 14. New York: Routledge, 2007.

Frye, Northrop. *Anatomy of Criticism. Four Essays by Northrop Frye*. New York: Atheneum, 1967 [1957].

_____. *The Secular Scripture. A Study of the Structure of Romance*. Cambridge: Harvard University Press, 1976.

Gilsdorf, Ethan. *Fantasy Freaks and Gaming Geeks. An Epic Quest for Reality Among Role Players, Online Gamers, and Other Dwellers of Imaginary Realms*. Guilford: The Lyons Press, 2009.

_____. "Peter Jackson Must Be Stopped." *Wired*. December 19 (2014). https://www.wired.com/2014/12/hobbit-peter-jackson-must-be-stopped/#disqus_thread (accessed May 9, 2018).

Hills, Matt, and Henry Jenkins. "*Intensities* Interviews Henry Jenkins @Console-ing Passions, University of Bristol, July 7th." *Intensities* 2 (Autumn/Winter 2001). https://intensitiescultmedia.com/2012/12/11/intensities-the-journal-of-cult-media-2-autumnwinter-2001/ (accessed May 9, 2018).

Hirsjärvi, Irma. *Faniuden siirtymiä. Suomalaisen science fiction fandomin verkostot*. Jyväskylä: Publications of the Research Centre for Contemporary Culture, 2009.

Jackson, Peter, director. *The Hobbit* (3 parts). NZ/U.S.: Warner Bros. Productions, 2012, 2013, 2014.

Jenkins, Henry. *Fans, Bloggers, and Gamers. Exploring Participatory Culture*. New York: New York University Press, 2006.

Jensen, Joli. "Fandom as Pathology: The Consequences of Characterization." In *The Adoring Audience: Fan Culture and Popular Media*, edited by Lisa A. Lewis, 9–29. London: Routledge, 1992.

Jerslev, Anne. "Sacred Viewing: Emotional Responses to *The Lord of the Rings*." In *The Lord of the Rings Popular Culture in Global Context*, edited by Ernest Mathjis, 206–221. London: Wallflower Press, 2006.

Jindra, Michael. "Star Trek Fandom as a Religious Phenomenon." *Sociology of Religion* 55 (1994): 27–51.

Klastrup, Lisbeth. "Transmedial Worlds, Social Media and Networked Reception." Keynote presentation at the *Transmedia Use(r)s—20th International Summer School in Cultural Studies*. University of Jyväskylä, Finland, June 13, 2016.

Klastrup, Lisbeth and Susana Tosca. "Transmedial Worlds—Rethinking Cyberworld Design." *Proceedings of the 2004 International Conference on Cyberworlds* (2004), 409–416.

_____. "The Networked Reception of Transmedialuniverses, an Experience-centered Approach." *MedieKultur: Journal of Media and Communication Research* 32, no. 60 (2016): 107–122.

Koistinen, Aino-Kaisa, Maria Ruotsalainen Maria, and Tanja Välisalo. "The World Hobbit Project in Finland: Audience Responses and Transmedial User Practices." *Participations* 13, no. 2 (November 2016): 356–379.

Korpua, Jyrki. *Constructive Mythopoetics in J.R.R. Tolkien's Legendarium*. Oulu: University of Oulu, 2015.

_____. "What About Tauriel? From Divine Mothers to Active Heroines: The Female Roles in J.R.R. Tolkien's Legendarium and Peter Jackson's Movie Adaptation." In *Gender Identity and Sexuality in Current Fantasy and Science Fiction*, edited by Francesca T. Barbini, 207–227. Edinburgh: Luna Press Publishing, 2017.

McAvan, Emily. *The Postmodern Sacred: Popular Culture Spirituality in the Science Fiction, Fantasy and Urban Fantasy Genres*. Jefferson, NC: McFarland, 2012.

McGrath, Alister E. *Christian Theology. An Introduction*. 5th Edition. Chichester: Wiley-Blackwell, 2011.

Orr, Christopher. "*The Hobbit 2* Is Bad Fan Fiction." *The Atlantic*. December 13 (2013). https://www.theatlantic.com/entertainment/archive/2013/12/-em-the-hobbit-2-em-is-bad-fan-fiction/282316/ (accessed May 9, 2018).

Otto, Rudolf. *Das Heilige: Über das Irrationale in der Idee des Göttlichen und sein Verhältnis zum Rationalen.* München: Verlag C.H. Beck, 2004 [1917].

The Oxford Companion to English Literature, 6th Edition. Edited by Margaret Drabble. Oxford: Oxford University Press, 2000.

Porter, Jennifer. "Implicit Religion in Popular Culture: The Religious Dimensions of Fan Communities." *Implicit Religion* 12, no. 3 (November 2009): 271–280.

Possamai, Adam and Murray Lee. "Hyper-Real Religions: Fear, Anxiety and Late-Modern Religious Innovation." *Journal of Sociology* 47, no. 3 (2011): 227–242.

Sherbert, Garry. "Frye's 'Pure Speech': Literature and the Sacred without the Sacred." In *Northrop Frye: New Directions from Old*, edited by David Rampton, 143–168. Toronto: University of Toronto Press, 2009.

Stormonth, James and Philip Henry Phelp. *Etymological and Pronouncing Dictionary of The English Language. Including a Various Copious Selection of Scientific Terms for Use in Schools and Colleges and as a Book of General Reference.* 3rd Edition. Edinburgh and London: William Blackwood and Sons, 1876.

Suomen Sanojen Alkuperä—Etymologinen Sanakirja 2 L-P. Helsinki: Suomalaisen Kirjallisuuden Seura, 1995.

Taira, Teemu. *Notkea Uskonto*. Turku: Eetos, 2006.

Tolkien, J.R R. *The Hobbit, or There and Back Again.* London: George Allen & Unwin, 1937.

Wagner, Rachel. *Religion, Ritual and Virtual Reality.* New York: Routledge, 2012.

Wolf, Mark J.P. *Building Imaginary Worlds: The Theory and History of Subcreation.* London: Routledge, 2012.

Wuthnow, Robert. *Rediscovering the Sacred. Perspective on Religion in Contemporary Society.* Grand Rapids, MI: William B. Eerdmans Publishing Company, 1992.

Transformative Souls and Transformed Selves

Buffy, Angel *and the Daimonic Tale*

JAMES REYNOLDS

Introduction

This essay explores one of the most significant factors in the continuing appeal of *Buffy* and *Angel*[1]—the features of the sacred they employ in narrative arcs of character development, and the ritualistic interaction this creates with fans of the television shows. I argue that *Buffy* and *Angel*'s deployment of the idea of the soul produces a distinctive approach to identity, and I here use the concept of the daimonic as a framework for textual analysis. Their distinctive approach to identity begins with the idea of the soul as an essential self that can be separated from the body and relocated. These transportable identities support particular types of narrative, and thus help in recognizing why these shows continue to appeal. These divisible and changeable selves also help us to understand the Buffy-verse's style of horror. In combination, these features help us appreciate not only the ritual of watching and re-watching, but also the ways in which *Buffy* and *Angel* bring the religious themes of ancient, spiritual traditions into popular culture and fandom—with vital contemporaneity.

The Millennium: A Transformative Moment

The first step in explaining the continued attraction of *Buffy the Vampire Slayer* (henceforth *BtVS*) is recognizing what it captured in its cultural moment. Launching *BtVS* on television in 1997, Joss Whedon and his creative team were looped into the re-circulation of the ancient idea of the soul, via their inversion of the vampire trope, reconfiguring the monster's soullessness through the character of Angel, the vampire *with* a soul. Stacey Abbott writes that Angel is but "one in a long line of sympathetic, reluctant vampires,"[2] but through him the makers of *BtVS* tapped into a wider resurgence of the soul in fantasy fiction. This dynamic is epitomized in the hugely successful Philip Pullman *His Dark Materials* novels (1995–2000)—with the animal daemons of its characters being external expressions of an inner self—and in the torn soul of Voldemort in J.K. Rowling's *Harry Potter* book series (1997–2007) and films (dirs. Columbus, Newell, and Yates, 2001–2011). Both these series showed similarly sustained creative play with the ancient idea of the soul as an emblem of essential self, separable from the physical body. Beyond these daemons, horcruxes, and ensouled vampires would lie an explosion of work that elided psychology to fold identity back into spirituality via the fundamental question posed by the existence of the soul—the nature and/or possibility of eternal life.

Speculations on immortality are appropriately millennial, given that such moments bridge past, present, and future. However, the September 11, 2001, attack upon New York's Twin Towers brought the apparition of soullessness front and center through its apocalyptic inhumanity. Millennial hope gave way to millennial terror. Yet the resurgence of the soul in fiction that *BtVS* and *Angel* both served and helped to produce seemed to receive extra momentum through the wars and revolutions that ensued. It is not surprizing that both *BtVS* and *Angel* ultimately end in apocalyptic battles against ancient evil, reflecting their relevance and helping pave the way for the return of religion in fiction, by acting as a gateway to narrative experiment with the sacred across multiple screen and print platforms.

It is important to note that this dynamic has continued and evolved elsewhere, and that the ensuring popularity of such apocalyptic and eschatological themes is one aspect of their extensive relevance. For example, like *BtVS* and *Angel*, *Battlestar Galactica* (Glen A. Larson and Ronald Moore, 2004–2009) would deploy a "coherent cultural backdrop" of religious tropes to amplify "the central conflict of the series"—the massacre of humanity by their cybernetic enemies, the Cylons—"to the level of a holy war."[3] Angel, the love interest of Buffy and protagonist of *Angel*, embodies a duality of divinity and monstrosity through his vampiric condition—an experiment that stimulated subsequent reconfigurations like Stephenie Meyer's "vampire-lite" *Twilight* novels (2005–2008) and films (dirs. Hardwicke, Weitz, Slade and Condon, 2008–2012).[4] Charlaine Harris's Southern vampire mysteries (the Sookie Stackhouse novels 2001–2013, and their television adaptation by Alan Ball as *True Blood* 2008–2014) would offer more culturally specific, even hyper–

American takes on the tropes of supernatural beings like vampires, werewolves, and faeries. Lauren Kate's *Fallen* series of novels (dir. Hicks: 2009–2012; film adaptation 2016–) would bring angels to the table, as would the television series *Dominion* (2014–2015), and Cassandra Clare's *Shadowhunter* novels would effectively return the dynamic to the pan-supernaturalism of the Buffy-verse, with teenage vampires, werewolves, angels, demons, faeries, and warlocks playing out their complicated romances and inter-dimensional conflicts against the New York City skyline (2007-; film adaptation dir. Zwart: 2013; television adaptation 2016–). While *BtVS* and *Angel* undoubtedly played their part in parenting these and other works, the key difference is that the soul is intrinsic to, and underpinning of, the narrative arcs and character transformations of *BtVS* and *Angel*. Indeed, it gives these shows form and style, not just content. It seems, then, that this aspect of the sacred is central to their ongoing appeal.

The continued attraction of *Buffy* and *Angel* remains very much in evidence. Josh Stenger cites Boyd Tonkin's survey of the situation when *Buffy*'s last episode aired in 2003; "1200 dedicated websites testify to the show's hold on near-obsessive fans," Tonkin wrote. In turn Stenger remarks that the show's "fiercely loyal and highly participatory fan base endowed the programme with a popular-cultural significance that far surpassed the size of [its television] audience."[5] Katherine Schwab, writing in 2015, looked back to this moment when Buffy "went off the air," remarking that in 2003 "its cult status was still very much nascent." However, she shows that this fan base was significant enough to subsequently support "novels, comics, videogames, and spinoffs, not to mention fan sites, fanfiction, conventions, and inclusion on scores of 'Best TV Shows of All Time' lists." Consequently, Schwab says, "hundreds of scholarly books and articles have been written about *Buffy*'s deeper themes."[6] Prominent and continued academic interest is shown through the journal *Slayage*, launched in 2001 by David Lavery and Rhonda V. Wilcox, and joined by yearly conferences since 2004.[7] But interest outside academia is also sustained. English journalist Lucy Mangan wrote in *The Guardian* that "Twenty years on, the brilliance of [*Buffy*] remains undimmed. It paid to watch and rewatch then and now, two decades later."[8] In 2018, Fox CEO Gary Newman admitted that the company discusses revivals of *Buffy* "frequently,"[9] and Joanna Robinson, writing in *Vanity Fair*, shows how its meaning continues to develop. The "entitled, misogynist rhetoric" of Season 6 villains Andrew, Warren and Jonathan importantly foreshadows the recent surfacing of rank sexism and abuse in multiple areas of society, around the world.[10] Understanding the use of the soul in these series is a key element in explaining this continuing appeal.

Souls and Soullessness

In Seasons 1–3 of *BtVS*, we can identify wide-ranging experiments with the portability of the soul, and the change of identity that its absence signifies. Neither *BtVS* nor *Angel* engage with the idea of the soul in any critical depth, but rather use it as an emblem for selfhood, as we shall see. Character transformation, consequently, can be achieved at the flick of a switch—something that occurs in the span of many discrete episodes[11]—because if you remove or replace the soul-self, you trigger another identity, or animate another body or object. This is perhaps most remarkable in the case of Angel, born Liam in 1727 and turned into a vampire at the age of 25. In his undead form, he takes the name "Angelus" and wreaks havoc on humankind until he is cursed with the return of his soul, and thus his conscience, and becomes "Angel."

The high stakes for the characters involved provides excitement for audiences, while the sheer variety of transformational strategies creates the pleasure of re-inventive storytelling. More importantly, the strategy of deletion, augmentation, switching or restoration of personality articulates and consolidates the vocabulary of a distinctive approach to identity by the show's writers, who deploy flick-of-a-switch transformations as a means to both expose character and build appealing narrative arcs culminating in the recuperation of self. Lynn Schofield Clark writes that "analyzing why certain stories in the media hold appeal" for teenagers requires that we separate "the obvious from the inferential meanings and pleasures that young people may draw from popular culture."[12] The pleasure of *BtVS* and *Angel* comes at least in part from their inferring a great deal regarding what Schofield Clark describes as "contemporary culture's unresolved conflicts over teenage life … as well as religion's role in society." These shows, she writes, express a "relativistic approach to belief" that is not limited by the tenets of "organized religion," but which nevertheless relies on "a romantic notion still central within Christianity: that of the individual's need for community and her capacity for transformation."[13] It is this particular capacity which requires our attention here.

From Season 4 of *BtVS* and Season 1 of *Angel* onwards, character transformations increasingly dominate larger narrative structures. Where a single-episode transformation entails the recuperation of identity by the end of that episode, later series would follow individual transformation across multiple episodes, and even entire seasons. We might say this approach was seeded by the appeal of Angel's transformation back into Angelus in *BtVS* Season 2—powering a step change in narrative quality from Season 1. Angel's overnight transformation gives ironic truth to the trope that that love changes everything as Buffy must change course to destroy Angelus, whom she realizes was unleashed the night they first have sex.[14]

Both *BtVS* and *Angel* would subsequently explore variations of such reversals—particularly their pacing—across season narrative arcs. Buffy dies (again),[15] and Season 6 contains the revelation that she—her soul—ascended to some kind of heaven. Her body remains behind, which we know because we see its decay reversed when her soul is called back to it through magic.[16] Seasons 2 and 3, and Seasons 5 and 6, end and begin with Buffy's most immediate transformations—death and rebirth—metaphorical and literal. Season 6 bravely probes the slower transformations of neglect, with Buffy multiply distracted and largely oblivious to the decay of her relationships, and particularly her best friend Willow's arc of transformation from a mild-mannered Wiccan into the murderous "Dark Willow," addicted to destructive magic.[17]

Buffy's other vampiric love interest, Spike, has his identity split by the insertion of a mind-control chip in Season 4 and undergoes another immediate transformation when he is re-ensouled.[18] But Spike continues to act unconsciously as a mind-controlled sleeper agent for the "First Evil" (Season 7), constituting his fourth identity split. Spike's fifth split—from his body—when he returns as a ghost in *Angel*.[19] positions him at the apogee of divided identity, and we can but lament that such complexity did not result in a *Spike* television series.[20]

These examples illustrate a certain level of device-saturation. This storytelling convention grows outward from Angel's capacity to switch identities but we should note that immediate transformation is reiterated visually in each episode via the computer-generated transmogrifications of each vampire's "doubled face" when they shift into their fearsome feeding (or perhaps their "natural") mode.[21] Crucially, the portability of the soul seems to underpin a veritable parade of fascinating character transformations, positioning this sacred trope, again, at the heart of these shows enduring appeal.

The Soul and the Trials of Selfhood

The soul may facilitate appealing creative play, but its centrality may also introduce critical problems. Scott McLaren describes its operations in the Buffy-verse as it switches between functions of metaphor, morality, and identity. His analysis first helps to explain how the soul—by acting as a "Platonic object that comprises human identity and will"[22]—creates the principle of portable identity which underlies the transformations described above. It is effectively a shorthand term for identity, which permits us to accept the idea of an instantaneous character switch or transformation. By the same token, the vacuum created by the absence of this soul-identity allows us to believe in the possession of the body by other entities. This connects these narratives to the idea of the possession of the body by alien souls, forces, even military machinators. McLaren argues further that the soul operates variously here as "a metaphor or a reified organ for moral choice."[23] Soulless or possessed characters are licensed to commit acts outside of the accepted morality, allowing swift reincorporation into the moral framework once the soul-self returns. As McLaren's analysis shows, *BtVS* and *Angel* use the soul as an index both of identity and of moral capability.

McLaren, in fact, argues that "Angel's quest for redemption" of crimes he cannot be held morally responsible for diminishes the credibility of his character.[24] This is particularly important because Angel's transformability is a crucial underpinning for the many other explorations of character transformation in the Buffy-verse. It is likely that the terms of Angel's separations in identity will permeate and shape other areas. Consequently, it is essential to further understand Angel's transformations, in detail: if they lack credibility, others might too. The problem McLaren outlines points the way; why do Angel and Spike experience traumatic guilt for the crimes of other entities? This trauma has much to do with the "psychological continuity"[25] of sharing memories, whether vampire or human. Additionally, even when the soul is restored, the vampire body still needs blood. Angel has an embodied experience of Angelus's legacy of violence, and he "is repelled by his own unquenchable thirst for blood,"[26] repeatedly demonstrated by his unwillingness to drink it openly. Angel does not bear moral responsibility for the crimes of Angelus; as Amy Kind argues, "identity alone is not what matters for moral responsibility,"[27] but, nevertheless, culpability is precisely what Angel experiences.

To appreciate this fully we must explore the origins of vampirism in the Buffy-verse, that is, the process of siring. A vampire entity enters and possesses the body of a human when that human—as they expire—drinks the siring vampire's blood. This vampire entity is not random, but assigned; whenever Angel's soul absents his body, it is always Angelus that comes to possess the flesh. The creation of a vampire, therefore, is an act connected with particularity to the human life that is destroyed. The same principle is seen in Darla's second coming. This intimate relationship, I suggest, comes about because the human victim must participate in siring by drinking blood; in other words, part of the process has an element of consent. A voluntary, participatory act is involved; in the same way "explicit permission" is required for Buffy-verse vampires to "enter a private home."[28] Even though Angel did not commit the crimes of Angelus, he knows on some level that by swallowing Darla's blood—an act of physical acquiescence and complicity—he enabled them. Siring in the Buffy-verse thus constitutes both murder and a contract of invitation to a demon—an act of surrender signalling abandonment of the soul. Retrospectively, this surrender will be interpreted as participation, producing intense remorse and feelings of culpability for the unleashing of the vampire, even if not for their crimes. Again, Angel is continuously reminded of this culpability "through the physical reality of his vampirism" and his continued "thirst for human blood."[29] Stacey Abbott's perspective summarizes the situation neatly: "*Angel* undermines the distinction between Angel and Angelus and presents the hybrid Angel/Angelus."[30]

Beyond the historical index the soul creates for the moral status of Buffy-verse characters, we also need to consider the conceptual index of identity it introduces. Taylor Boulware argues that the removal and replacement of identity in Whedon's *Dollhouse* "neatly embodies a rejection of essentialist identity."[31] In *Dollhouse*, Whedon disturbingly presented a gallery of prostitutes whose memories are wiped clean, and programed to order with new, fantasy personas. But in the case of vampire identity, the retention of the memories of the original human host acts as an antagonistic and deterministic form of essentialism. As Boulware writes, drawing on Judith Butler, "it is the very process of subordination that creates the subject."[32] These dynamics run in both directions, with human memories defining the trajectory of the newly installed vampire, and vampire memories defining the mission for the returning soul on ethical terms like redemption, and atonement: after all, "Regaining one's soul means regaining one's conscience."[33] The "core self" of human memories operates as a "social and structural violence" of limitation for Angelus; he is clearly repulsed by Angel's mental continuum and feelings.[34] By the same token, the memories Angel inherits of Angelus's atrocities are equally repulsive.

This causes both Angel and Angelus to experience the most intense duality, illustrated perhaps no better than in *Angel* where the two meet face-to-face in a drug-induced coma they share with Buffy's fellow vampire slayer, Faith.[35] With a soul that "doubly hybridizes his vampire existence,"[36] Angel/Angelus provides the supreme exemplar of separation not only from, but also within, identity. This gives significant amplification to the theme of split identity and hence the crucial importance of Angel's transformation narrative in establishing credibility for other character transformations. Indeed, this baseline of credibility sculpts the reality principle of the Buffy-verse so distinctly that we might ask whether or not what we are actually discussing here is the Angel-verse. The transformations of Buffy and Angel themselves are therefore of paramount importance, as it is through these more complex lenses that simpler character transformations appear less predictable. Willow going from good-witch-to-bad-witch or Giles descending from responsible-educator-to-dissipated-drunk may be straightforward character inversions on paper. But they do not feel perfunctory or contrived because *BtVS* and *Angel* set the terms of a mutable reality based on the idea of the soul, and its other transformations are filtered through those terms.

Schofield Clark, we may recall, notes that the religious backdrop of these shows is "relativistic,"[37] but we should also remember that fictional realities require sufficiently solid foundations if we are to recognize characters changing from one state to another. The soul cannot provide this coherent reality on its own, without reference to contextual terms. Therefore, from death in the hell mouth in Season 1's "Prophecy Girl," to the death of the hell mouth in Season 7's "Chosen"[38] these transformations are set against what Naomi Alderman and Annette Seidel-Arpaci call "a great deal of inspiration from Christianity"—angels, demons, crucifixes, holy water, prophecies, apocalypse, redemption, exorcism, hell, heaven, the chosen—with Willow bringing Judaism, Paganism, and Wicca to the table.[39] The soul sits among these fragments of religion, gluing them together and creating a relativistic but coherent horizon, while continuously offering the possibility of immediate character transformation.

Angel's transformation narrative defines him almost from the outset. Sired by Darla, Liam firstly turns into Angelus. When Liam's soul is returned to the same body, then Angel is created. With a vampire body, he can no longer be Liam, but with a soul, he can no longer be Angelus. Restored thus, Angel is effectively a "curious hybrid between human and vampire": retaining the vampiric, blood drinking body and memories of Angelus, tempered by the original soul of Liam.[40] These, then, are the three states through which we understand Angel in seasons 1–3 of *BtVS*. Although *Angel* rehearses these states in greater depth, in order for the character to progress the narrative arc must promise a further state. This is duly introduced at the end of *Angel* Season 1, with the promise of a return to a human existence if Angel fulfills the Shanshu prophecy.[41] Buffy's transformation narrative is initially structured by teenage realities—including love, and running away from home—until Angel leaves for Los Angeles at the end of *BtVS* Season 3. Buffy follows the education system up to graduation, and begins her transition into adulthood by starting university in Season 4, much as her compatriots do. But it is not until the end of Season 4 that Buffy begins to properly experience the same kind of forces that Angel does. Her mature transformational arc properly begins with her prophetic dream encounter with the primordial first slayer, Sineya.[42] Having taken the essences of Giles, Willow and Xander into her body to defeat Adam, Buffy unwittingly triggers a relationship with the hallowed source of the slayer's power. In Seasons 5–7, this leads to her greatest challenges: self-sacrificial death, unbridled lust, and ultimately a fight to the death with evil itself. Buffy's maturity narrative moves her from teenage transitions to her near-apotheosis, though coming ever closer to mythic status does not mean Buffy gains the abilities she needs to deal with her complex adult life.

Buffy and Angel seem to be headed in opposite directions, she towards the mythic, he towards the mundane. Their heroic trajectories seem to contrast, but the real-world obstacles they face—money, work, and caring for others—are shared. However, the crucial similarity in their transformational narratives is the soul. Angel is promised a human life, which he sacrifices for a greater good even at the risk of death and Buffy is offered an enhancement of power by the shaman who created Sineya, which she too rejects as it will strip her humanity, even though without that power she will likely die.[43]

Indeed, by the final episode of their final series, both Buffy and Angel have embraced self-sacrifice, and attain the identity of spiritual warrior by choosing to accept death rather than betray their cause. The transformation narratives of Buffy and Angel root their respective series in narratives depicting the epiphanies of spiritual ascent—narratives that trickle that credibility down towards a multitude of smaller transformations. Structurally speaking, these are rites of passage: the recuperation of self after facing tests, returning to normality at a higher level of being, or deeper understanding of the world.

The Daimonic Narrative

As tales of on-going transformations, these texts therefore take on the qualities of daimonic narratives, which is a vital point in appreciating the role of the sacred in the enduring popularity of *BtVS* and *Angel*. In exploring this, I here draw on Austrian critic and novelist Stefan Zweig's interpretation of the classical concept of the daimonic, as expressed in part two of his 1925 analysis of European culture, *Master Builders: A Typology of the Spirit*, which focuses on Friedrich Hölderlin, Heinrich von Kleist, and Friedrich Nietzsche. Titled *Der Kampf mit dem Dämon*, the German word *dämon* has been variously spelled by his translators as "daimon" and "daemon," but here I use "daimon" (as do Eden and Cedar Paul in their 1930 translation), a notion distinct from both the idea of the "demonic," and the aforementioned "daemons" of Pullman's work.[44] It is important to consider the term fully for, as Philipp Kneis shows, there are not only spelling discrepancies and homophonous confusions, but competing notions of the daimonic.[45] Bernhard Greiner usefully illustrates how, in classical Greece, the daimon was a "value-neutral" higher spirit, connecting the human subject to the divine on a path that could lead "to happiness or unhappiness." For Johann Wolfgang von Goethe, he writes, the daimon was laden with value, representing "the laws laid down for each human being at the moment of his birth." And for Zweig, the daimonic force is "aorgic," or the "drive towards boundlessness,"[46] which, for those most susceptible to it, can lead "into the abyss."[47] Its force, Zweig says, is as if "nature had left in each individual soul an inalienable, restless part of its own original chaos," which drives the individual "out of himself" and "into the infinite."[48] Carl Jung would later develop a special relationship with the concept.[49]

Multiple inflections of the daimonic can be read into Angel, Buffy, Cordelia and Spike as they march towards self-knowledge and destruction—with viewers accompanying them on a daimonic rite of passage through death and rebirth. Much like Zweig and his heroes, daimonic energy draws us "into the self-destructive poetic madness" of these characters.[50] Each subject of Zweig's analysis was "hounded" out of a "cosy existence" "by an overwhelming and in some sense supernatural power," and were thus "[d]isconnected from their times," and "misunderstood by their cohorts."[51] Additionally, they "themselves do not know their path, their meaning, because they are in transit from an infinite distance into infinity."[52] These culturally disconnected and socially isolated figures were driven by unknown forces into destruction but also towards self-discovery.

Cultural disconnection, misunderstanding and hounding into discomfort and isolation apply to many core characters at the onset of their transit "into infinity." Buffy's "valley girl" identity shatters when she is made the slayer, exacerbated by her parents' divorce, expulsion from school, and relocation from Los Angeles to Sunnydale. Liam is a drunken rake, uncaring that his debauchery breaches social acceptability, and leading to rejection by his father. William is rejected by the love of his life, and both his poetry and romantic aspirations ensure he is a laughing stock in society. Cordelia—mean-girl-cheerleader-snob—must leave Sunnydale to struggle as an actress in Los Angeles, where her riches-to-rags narrative reduces her social capital considerably. These stories follow the pattern of being driven into destruction and reinvention: an archetypal, religious narrative pattern of death and rebirth. Cordelia's burgeoning spirituality results in her ascent to a higher plane[53] before her rebirth in Season 4 and actual death in Season 5. Liam and William experience crises of rejection that drive them into the arms of their sires, the death of vampirism, and the rebirth of re-ensoulment. Buffy also dies and is reborn (twice). These features combine to make these character narratives daimonic.

Moreover, each of these characters' transformations is driven by an apparently external force which might be said to reflect their subconscious—the path they do not know they are on. Spike is driven by obsessive love, a force that accompanies him across incarnations, ultimately leading to a transformation resulting in spiritual ascent via self-sacrificial death.[54] He even describes himself as "Love's bitch."[55] As we have seen, Angel is driven by the consequences of Angelus's existence, which inspires continuous watchfulness against his re-emergence, and striving for atonement. Cordelia is driven towards spiritual ascendancy by visions sent by hidden powers, and also shows her willingness to die for the cause.[56] Buffy, of course, is driven by her relationship with slayer-ness—most obviously through her interactions with Sineya—and more broadly with the power, history and destiny this gift bestows upon her.

As for Zweig's poets, the essence of existence for them is "tension and stress,"[57] and a "catastrophic polarisation"[58] within the self. This is why Angel ultimately avoids being "too neatly split across polar oppositions," as Abbott suggests the character was initially on *BtVS*.[59] He exists between "two unattainable states of being: humanity and "vampirity."[60] Separations of self are crucial in generating this tension; indeed, "only one who has been ripped in pieces knows the longing for completeness"[61] at the heart of such tension, and the drive it produces. We can begin to see precisely how daimonic the Buffy-verse is by relating these ideas to these characters. Philipp Kneis briefly applies the notion of the daimon to Buffy and Angel, describing it as an "inner voice" offering "an alternative view of reality," or stirring up "situations" or "conscience."[62] However, we might also say it is forces of destiny, remorse, desire and prophecy that drive these characters to change. Alternatively, we could note that these characters experience or address these forces as Others—Sineya, Angelus, Eros, The Powers That Be—that impose upon them from without the challenges that stimulate their spiritual evolution.

It is also important to note why the daimonic rite of passage does not suffer from narrative fatigue. It uses the power underpinning one of the West's most sacred narratives—the resurrection—to generate television-viewing habits akin to a personal, religious tradition. It can do so because the principle of the narrative is similar enough to psychological frameworks of knowledge to be coherent to the secular mind, even where the power of archetypal religious narratives of death and rebirth, transformation and spiritual ascent, is clearly present. As Schofield Clark writes, while these morally relativist shows may seem distant from "organized religion," they also allow audiences to "interpret the intersection of traditional religion and … popular beliefs about good and evil,"[63] and this helps us to understand their enduring appeal in the secular sphere.

Split Selves and Monstrous Duality: A Reason to Watch?

The split identities of the Buffy-verse display just such complex and contradictory psychologies, but more pertinently, they facilitate daimonic narratives which involve audiences in characters' journeys. This is crucial in understanding not only the Buffy-verse's style of horror, but also its aforementioned continuing charm. We can stand to watch these characters go through these processes—again and again and again and again—because of the daimonic tale's intrinsic structural relationship with the idea of separation from, and within, self. This has a different appeal to abjection in horror; these stories use psychic division more than bodily expulsions to create affect. The daimonic tale provides pleasure because of the intricate interactions split-identity narratives can create. Angel goes to hell; Buffy goes to heaven. Both come back. Willow, Cordelia and other characters transform into, or host, deities and demons, but only Willow survives. For these characters the stakes of self-realization are high. They live at the level of epiphany—unsustainable in the real world—so that their daimonic journeys can offer a unique process of individual transformation to fans willing to travel along: as you grow, the Buffy-verse grows with you. It cannot be exhausted because each time you re-watch you bring a new set of experiences to the table: new lessons to learn, a new self to recuperate. Indeed, Stacey Abbott describes the "intensive loyalty" engendered by cult television as due in part to fans being able to "write themselves into the centre" of narratives.[64] *BtVS* and/or *Angel* may even become your daimon, an almost ritualistic process of self-empowerment driven by television and, if that is the case, re-watching is a ritual, and this is sacred horror.

Indeed, a narrative of divided self makes the spectator the site of horror—probing our lacerations, triggering our own self-and-other-alienations, split psyches, irrationality, amoral and inexplicable drives. The etymology of the word daimon is "the verb *daiomai*, 'to divide, lacerate,'" so for Giorgio Agamben, the daimon correctly means "the lacerator, he who divides and fractures," and therefore its power to assign fate and destiny lies in its ability to divide. It is, he argues, an essential function; "Man is such that, to be himself, he must necessarily divide himself."[65] The daimonic tale—what we might legitimately call the narrative of divided self—has additional fascination because, in reality, the monster that I am to myself is more present, truthful, hated, dangerous, and abject than the monsters outside. Therefore, the divisions of self that saturate the Buffy-verse very much help to create its particular sense of the monstrous.

Dev Kumar Bose and Esther Liberman-Cuenca argue that, although *BtVS* launched with "binary qualities," its multiple uses of the "soul as a plot device" allowed "definitions of good and evil" "to become more complicated" in parallel to the show's evolving character relationships.[66] These stories remind us that (after Foucault) the self is a discourse. Even the soul, rather than constituting an essential and stable identity, is coherent only in growth. By using this sanctified trope of essential self to instead demonstrate that identity is dynamic and that we lack stability of identity, *BtVS* and *Angel* reboot horror as *us*. Our compensation is that they also show us how to live as a dynamic—in a state of tension—and not as a stasis. As Boulware suggests, it is through such awareness that we "begin to form ourselves as subjects on our own terms."[67]

The shadow side of that empowerment is that it is achieved by reworking the sacred tropes of religion, loosening still further the last vestiges of "truth" imposed by grand narratives, and it is no coincidence that the golden age of television narrative coincides with the "post-truth" era. This is an age of massive reinvention, in both positive and negative terms, offering a special moment of narrative creativity as well as fake news and implausible denial. It may, then, be that the personal and emotional fulfillment of the daimonic narrative lacks a properly political basis, and this, in itself, may signpost an area of further creative potential for it, and for subsequent analysis.

Conclusion

Many of the most horrific atrocities in history have been committed blindly in honor or pursuit of religion. In the Buffy-verse, prophecy often lays down the future to be pursued. However this sacred horror does not impose blind obedience upon, but tests the moral framework of its protagonists. As Alderman and Seidel-Arpaci argue, the many prophecies in the Buffy-verse are "evoked to tell us that they can be overcome," sending "a powerful message of individual freedom" emphasizing "individual possibilities of moral choice and responsibility."[68] The daimon is essential in this choice and responsibility. It is not, as Kneis suggests, something to be emancipated from.[69] Rather, it is the presence of a "catastrophic" polarity within the self, and therefore the presence of meaningful choice and real free will.

It is ironic, therefore, that such work seems to signpost towards to a proliferation of possession narratives. Shows like *Dollhouse* (2009–2010), *Hand of God* (2014–), *South of Hell* (2015), and *iZombie* (2015–)—which (respectively) use brainwashing, visions from God, demonic hosting, and identity consumption as forms of daimon—have been cleverly reworking traditional notions of possession, splicing them with ideas of split-identity to be found in the Buffy-verse. The classic horror film *The Exorcist* (1973) has recently been reimagined as a television series (2016–). At the same time, in the U.S. "the number of official priest exorcists … more than quadrupled from 12 to 50" from 2006 to 2016, and there is reportedly "an ongoing struggle to keep up with the demand."[70]

If our millennial interest in the soul revealed some aspect of Western culture at that time, we may well ask what more recent interest in possession reveals. This is especially so as possession narratives seem to have little opportunity to place human choice, freedom and responsibility under the spotlight when possession ostensibly removes it. Perhaps a spate of possession narratives reveals a historical moment in the West characterized by a sense of lost control. Alternatively, it may be that the soul has simply been done to death, and other tropes from the realm of the sacred are rising to take its place. Either way, such fiction will continue to play an important role in circulating and raising the profile of the sacred within fandom, pop culture texts, and the world itself.

NOTES

1. *Buffy the Vampire Slayer* (hereafter *BtVS*) seasons 1–7, created by Joss Whedon (U.S.: 20th Television, 1997–2003); *Angel*, seasons 1–5, created by Joss Whedon and David Greenwalt (U.S.: 20th Television, 1999–2004).

2. Stacey Abbott, "Walking the Fine Line between Angel and Angelus," *Slayage* 3, no. 1 (August 2003), http://www.whedonstudies.tv/uploads/2/6/2/8/26288593/abbott_slayage_3.1.pdf.

3. A.M. Dellamonica, "Stripping the Bones," in *So Say We All*, ed. Richard Hatch (Dallas: Benbella Books, 2006), 164. The question of who is soulless would be posed here through regular scenes of torture and execution, while the visibility of cyborg immortality (through potentially unlimited digital resurrection) would be juxtaposed with humanity's definitive mortality—and indefinite post-mortem destination.

4. Whereas in *BtVS* the loss of the soul is intrinsic to vampirism, in *Twilight* this is open to debate. In *New Moon*, Carlisle tells Bella that Edward "thinks we've lost our souls." This belief underpins Edward's reluctance to turn Bella into a vampire. But it is a weak belief—and it gives way easily when Edward must make Bella a vampire to prevent her death. Stephenie Meyer, *New Moon* (London: Atom, 2006), 33.

5. Josh Stenger, "The Clothes Make the Fan: Fashion and Online Fandom When *Buffy the Vampire Slayer* Goes to eBay," *Cinema Journal* 45, no. 4 (Summer 2006): 28.

6. Katharine Schwab, "The Rise of Buffy Studies," *The Atlantic*, October 1 (2015), https://www.theatlantic.com/entertainment/archive/2015/10/the-rise-of-buffy-studies/407020/.

7. The Whedon Studies Association, *Slayage: The Journal of Whedon Studies* (2001–2017), http://www.whedonstudies.tv/slayage-the-journal-of-whedon-studies.html.

8. Lucy Mangan, "Buffy the Vampire Slayer at 20: The Thrilling, Brilliant Birth of TV as Art," *The Guardian*, 10 March (2017), https://www.theguardian.com/tv-and-radio/2017/mar/10/buffy-the-vampire-slayer-at-20-the-thrilling-brilliant-birth-of-tv-as-art.

9. Debra Birnbaum, "Fox Boss on *Buffy the Vampire Slayer* Revival: 'It's Something We Talk About Frequently,'" *Variety*, 13 March (2018), http://variety.com/2018/tv/news/fox-boss-gary-newman-buffy-the-vampire-slayer-revival-1202725161/.

10. Joanne Robinson, "How *Buffy the Vampire Slayer*'s Most Hated Season Became Its Most Important," *Vanity Fair Online*, 10 March (2017), https://www.vanityfair.com/hollywood/2017/03/buffy-season-6-anniversary-warren-jonathan-andrew.

11. A whistle-stop tour: Amy's witch mother forces her to swap bodies with her (Season 1: Episode 3); Xander becomes a human hyena (Season 1: Episode 6); Moloch's demonic identity is digitized and he is reborn a robot (Season 1, Episode 8); Sid seeks justice while cursed into a ventriloquist's doll (Season 1: Episode 9); human identities are called back to dead or reanimated bodies (Season 2: Episodes 2 and 3; Season 3: Episode 13); Ethan's Halloween costumes possess all who wear them (Season 2: Episode 6); Eyghon lays waste to Rupert Giles's acquaintance through possession (Season 2: Episode 8); Sunnydale falls under the mind-control of parasitical demon spawn (Season 2: Episode 12); Buffy and Angel have their bodies possessed by the spirits of dead lovers (Season 2: Episode 19); Joyce's Zombie God mask possesses all who wear it (Season 3: Episode 2); Buffy loses her mind when she absorbs demon telepathy via demon blood (Season 3: Episode 18), and, in possibly the grandest example of immediate, single-episode character transformation, Cordelia's vengeful wish (Season 3: Episode 9) transforms everybody in Sunnydale (except Anya) into a different version of themselves.

12. Lynn Schofield Clark, *From Angels to Aliens: Teenagers, the Media, and the Supernatural* (Oxford and New York: Oxford University Press, 2003), 47–48.

13. Schofield Clark, *From Angels to Aliens*, 48.

14. "Innocence," *BtVS*, Season 2: Episode 14, writer and dir. Joss Whedon (1998). The season finale sees Willow using magic to restore Angel's soul, bringing the flick-of-a-switch character change to its apotheosis, perhaps; Buffy thrusts her sword into Angel's body to save the world, and in doing so simultaneously destroys herself. The act causes her to reject both her secret slayer identity, and her public Buffy Summers identity, as she leaves town and recreates herself as "Anne."

15. "The Gift," *BtVS*, Season 5: Episode 22, writer and dir. Joss Whedon (2001).

16. "Bargaining—Part 1, *BtVS*, Season 6: Episode 1, writer Marti Noxon, dir. David Grossman (2001).

17. "Villains," *BtVS*, Season 6: Episode 20, writer Marti Noxon, dir. David Solomon (2002).

18. "Grave," *BtVS*, Season 6: Episode 22, writer David Fury, dir. James A. Contner (2002).

19. "Just Rewards," *Angel*, Season 5: Episode 2, writers David Fury and Ben Edlund, dir. James A. Contner (2003).

20. Unsurprisingly, *Angel* also builds series-level narrative arcs through removal, augmentation, swapping or reinstatement of identity. Absorbing Conan Doyle's connection to the-powers-that-be abruptly redirects Cordelia's path towards the spiritual (Season 1: Episode 9). Darla returns from death with a soul (Season 1: Episode 22)—which she loses when Drusilla re-turns her into a vampire (Season 2: Episode 9). In Season 4, Jasmine possesses Cordelia's body in order to give birth to herself (Episode 17), and Connor must have his identity removed and replaced in order to be saved from his death wish (Episode 22). In Season 5, Gunn is re-booted as a world-class attorney via psychic implants (Episode 1): the empath Lorne becomes a psychopath when his sleep is removed (Episode 5)—and Fred is hollowed out by the demon god Illyria (Episode 16)—which Wesley believes irreversibly destroys her immortal soul in the process.

21. Naomi Alderman and Annette Seidel-Arpaci, "Imaginary Para-Sites of the Soul: Vampires and Representations of 'Blackness' and 'Jewishness' in the *Buffy/Angel*verse," *Slayage* 3, no. 2 (November 2003), http://www.whedonstudies.tv/uploads/2/6/2/8/26288593/alderman_seidel-arpaci_slayage_3.2.pdf.

22. Scott McLaren, "The Evolution of Joss Whedon's Vampire Mythology and the Ontology of the Soul," *Slayage* 5, no. 2 (September 2005), http://www.whedonstudies.tv/uploads/2/6/2/8/26288593/mclaren_slayage_5.2.pdf.

23. McLaren, "The Evolution of Joss Whedon's Vampire Mythology."

24. McLaren, "The Evolution of Joss Whedon's Vampire Mythology."

25. Amy Kind, "The Vampire with a Soul: Angel and the Quest for Identity," in *The Philosophy of Horror*, ed. Thomas Fahy (Lexington: University Press of Kentucky, 2010), 95.

26. Kind, "The Vampire with a Soul," 86.

27. Kind, "The Vampire with a Soul," 98.

28. Philipp Kneis, *Emancipation of the Soul: Memes of Destiny in American Mythological Television* (Frankfurt: Peter Lang, 2011), 74.

29. Abbott, "Walking the Fine Line."

30. Abbott, "Walking the Fine Line."

31. Taylor Boulware, "'I Made Me': Queer Theory, Subjection, and Identity in *Dollhouse*," *Slayage* 10, no. 1 (Winter 2013), http://www.whedonstudies.tv/uploads/2/6/2/8/2628 8593/boulware_slayage_10.1.pdf.

32. Boulware, "'I Made Me.'"

33. Kind, "The Vampire with a Soul," 88.

34. Boulware, "'I Made Me.'" Boulware is discussing *BtVS/Angel* creator Joss Whedon's *Dollhouse* here, but the analysis translates.

35. "Orpheus," *Angel*, Season 4: Episode 15, writer Mere Smith, dir. Terrence O'Hara (2003).

36. Dev Kumar Bose and Esther Liberman-Cuenca, "Buffy, Angel, and the Complications of the Soul," in *Buffy Conquers the Academy*, eds Melissa U. Anyiwo and Karoline Szatek-Tudor (Newcastle on Tyne: Cambridge Scholars Publishing, 2013), 10.

37. Schofield Clark, *From Angels to Aliens*, 48.

38. "Prophecy Girl," *BtVS*, Season 1: Epsiode 12, writer and dir. Joss Whedon (1997); "Chosen," *BtVS*, Season 7: Episode 22, writer and dir. Joss Whedon (2003).

39. Alderman and Seidel-Arpaci, "Imaginary Para-Sites of the Soul."
40. Abbott, "Walking the Fine Line," *Slayage*. Liam's "drinking and whoring undermines any suggestion that [Angel] possessed a particularly good or altruistic soul" to start with.
41. "To Shanshu in L.A.," *Angel*, Season 1: Episode 22, writer and dir. David Greenwalt (2000).
42. "Restless," *BtVS*, Season 4: Episode 22, writer and dir. Joss Whedon (2000).
43. "The Gift," *BtVS*; "Get It Done," *BtVS*, Season 7, Episode 15, writer and dir. Doug Petrie (2003).
44. Stefan Zweig, *The Struggle with the Daimon: Hölderlin, Kleist, Nietzsche*, trans. Eden and Cedar Paul (New York: Viking Press, 1930[1925]).
45. Kneis, *Emancipation of the Soul*, 73.
46. Stefan Zweig cited in Bernhard Greiner, "At Kithaeron Mountain: Stefan Zweig's Approach to the Daemonic," in *Stefan Zweig Reconsidered*, ed. Mark H. Gelber (Berlin: De Gruyter, 2007), 144.
47. Zweig cited in Greiner, "At Kithaeron Mountain," 141–142.
48. Zweig cited in Greiner, "At Kithaeron Mountain," 142.
49. For a useful discussion of similarities and differences between Carl Jung's concept of the shadow and its role in individuation, and the notion of the daimonic, see Stephen A. Diamond, *Anger, Madness, and The Daimonic: The Psychological Genesis of Violence, Evil and Creativity* (Albany: State University of New York Press, 1996).
50. Greiner, "At Kithaeron Mountain," 144.
51. Zweig cited in Greiner, "At Kithaeron Mountain," 142.
52. Zweig cited in Greiner, "At Kithaeron Mountain," 142.
53. "Tomorrow," *Angel*, Season 3: Episode 22, writer and dir. David Greenwalt (2002).
54. "Chosen," *BtVS*.
55. "Lovers Walk," *BtVS*, Season 3: Episode 8, writer Dan Vebber, dir. David Semel (1998).
56. "Tomorrow," *Angel*.
57. Zweig cited in Greiner, "At Kithaeron Mountain," 140.
58. Zweig cited in Greiner, "At Kithaeron Mountain," 146.
59. Abbott, "Walking the Fine Line."
60. Bose and Liberman-Cuenca, "Buffy, Angel, and the Complications of the Soul," 10.
61. Zweig cited in Greiner, "At Kithaeron Mountain," 140.
62. Kneis, for example, uses the idea to characterize the behaviour of demons like Sweet ("Normal Again," *BtVS*, Season 6: Episode 17, writer Diego Gutierrez, dir. Rick Rosenthal [2002]), but this seems to me to corrupt the term too much. See Kneis, *Emancipation of the Soul*, 73.
63. Schofield Clark, *From Angels to Aliens*, 74
64. Stacey Abbott, "Case Study: Buffy The Vampire Slayer," in *The Cult TV Book*, ed. Stacey Abbott (London and New York: IB Tauris, 2010), 102.
65. Giorgio Agamben, *Potentialities: Collected Essays in Philosophy* (Stanford: Stanford University Press, 1999), 118.
66. Bose and Liberman-Cuenca, "Buffy, Angel, and the Complications of the Soul," 13.
67. Boulware, "'I Made Me.'"
68. Alderman and Seidel-Arpaci, "Imaginary Para-Sites of the Soul."
69. Kneis, *Emancipation of the Soul*, 70.
70. Rachel Ray, "Leading U.S. Exorcists Explain Huge Increase in Demand for the Rite—and Priests to Carry Them Out," *The Telegraph*, September 26 (2016), http://www.telegraph.co.uk/news/2016/09/26/leading-us-exorcists-explain-huge-increase-in-demand-for-the-rit/.

Bibliography

Abbott, Stacey. "Walking the Fine Line between Angel and Angelus." *Slayage* 3, no. 1 (August 2003). http://www.whedonstudies.tv/uploads/2/6/2/8/26288593/abbott_slayage_3.1.pdf.
Abbott, Stacey. "Case Study: *Buffy The Vampire Slayer*." In *The Cult TV Book*, edited by Stacey Abbott, 101–102. London and New York: IB Tauris, 2010.

Agamben, Giorgio. *Potentialities: Collected Essays in Philosophy*. Stanford, CA: Stanford University Press, 1999.

Alderman, Naomi and Annette Seidel-Arpaci. "Imaginary Para-Sites of the Soul: Vampires and Representations of 'Blackness' and 'Jewishness' in the *Buffy/Angel*verse." *Slayage* 3, no. 2 (November 2003). http://www.whedonstudies.tv/uploads/2/6/2/8/26288593/alderman_seidel-arpaci_slayage_3.2.pdf.

Angel. Seasons 1–5. Created by Joss Whedon and David Greenwalt. U.S.: 20th Television, 1999–2004.

Birnbaum, Debra. "Fox Boss on *Buffy the Vampire Slayer* Revival: 'It's Something We Talk About Frequently.'" *Variety*, March 13 (2018). http://variety.com/2018/tv/news/fox-boss-gary-newman-buffy-the-vampire-slayer-revival-1202725161/ (accessed May 6, 2018).

Bose, Dev Kumar, and Esther Liberman-Cuenca. "Buffy, Angel, and the Complications of the Soul." In *Buffy Conquers the Academy*, edited by Melissa U. Anyiwo and Karoline Szatek-Tudor, 6–18. Newcastle on Tyne: Cambridge Scholars Publishing, 2013.

Boulware, Taylor. "'I Made Me': Queer Theory, Subjection, and Identity in *Dollhouse*." *Slayage* 10, no. 1 (Winter 2013). http://www.whedonstudies.tv/uploads/2/6/2/8/26288593/boulware_slayage_10.1.pdf.

Buffy the Vampire Slayer. Seasons 1–7. Created by Joss Whedon. U.S.: 20th Television, 1997–2003.

Dellamonica, A.M. "Stripping the Bones." In *So Say We All*, edited by Richard Hatch, 161–180. Dallas: Benbella Books, 2006.

Diamond, Stephen A. *Anger, Madness, and the Daimonic: The Psychological Genesis of Violence, Evil and Creativity*. Albany: State University of New York Press, 1996.

Greiner, Bernhard. "At Kithaeron Mountain: Stefan Zweig's Approach to the Daemonic." In *Stefan Zweig Reconsidered*, edited by Mark H. Gelber, 139–150. Berlin: De Gruyter, 2007.

Kind, Amy. "The Vampire with a Soul: Angel and the Quest for Identity." In *The Philosophy of Horror*, edited by Thomas Fahy. Lexington: University Press of Kentucky, 2010.

Kneis, Philipp. *Emancipation of the Soul: Memes of Destiny in American Mythological Television*. Frankfurt: Peter Lang, 2011.

Mangan, Lucy. "*Buffy the Vampire Slayer* at 20: the thrilling, brilliant birth of TV as art." *The Guardian*, March 10, 2017. https://www.theguardian.com/tv-and-radio/2017/mar/10/buffy-the-vampire-slayer-at-20-the-thrilling-brilliant-birth-of-tv-as-art (accessed May 6, 2018).

McLaren, Scott. "The Evolution of Joss Whedon's Vampire Mythology and the Ontology of the Soul." *Slayage* 5, no. 2 (September 2005). http://www.whedonstudies.tv/uploads/2/6/2/8/26288593/mclaren_slayage_5.2.pdf.

Meyer, Stephenie. *New Moon*. London: Atom, 2006.

Ray, Rachel. "Leading US Exorcists Explain Huge Increase in Demand for the Rite—and Priests to Carry Them Out." *The Telegraph*, September 26 (2016). http://www.telegraph.co.uk/news/2016/09/26/leading-us-exorcists-explain-huge-increase-in-demand-for-the-rit/ (accessed May 6, 2018).

Robinson, Joanne. "How *Buffy the Vampire Slayer*'s Most Hated Season Became Its Most Important." *Vanity Fair*, 10 March (2017). https://www.vanityfair.com/hollywood/2017/03/buffy-season-6-anniversary-warren-jonathan-andrew (accessed May 6, 2018).

Schofield Clark, Lynn. *From Angel to Aliens: Teenagers, the Media, and the Supernatural*. Oxford: Oxford University Press, 2003.

Schwab, Katherine. "The Rise of Buffy Studies." *The Atlantic*, 1 October (2015). https://www.theatlantic.com/entertainment/archive/2015/10/the-rise-of-buffy-studies/407020/ (accessed May 6, 2018).

Stenger, Josh. "The Clothes Make the Fan: Fashion and Online Fandom When Buffy the Vampire Slayer Goes to eBay." *Cinema Journal* 45, no. 4 (Summer 2006): 26–44.

The Whedon Studies Association. *Slayage: The Journal of Whedon Studies*. 2001–2017. http://www.whedonstudies.tv/slayage-the-journal-of-whedon-studies.html.

Zweig, Stefan. *The Struggle with the Daimon: Hölderlin, Kleist, Nietzsche*. Translated by Eden and Cedar Paul. New York: Viking Press, 1930 [1925].

PART 3

Sacred Play
Performing the Text

Until the End of the World

Fans as Messianic Heroes
in World of Warcraft

JOVI L. GERACI

Introduction

Video games give rise to a new kind of mythology in popular culture, one that requires active participation and decision-making by players rather than passive consumption by viewers. By examining the places where religion and videogames intersect we can come to a better understanding of the appeal of videogames as a medium, and of the ways that fandom and religion combine to create a powerful in-game experience for players. In the study of videogames there is a debate between grounding the research in textual narratives or in game play; this essay focuses on the former. I will explore the ways that the Massively Multiplayer Online Role Playing Game (MMORPG) *World of Warcraft* (*WoW*) functions as a form of lived religious practice for its most devoted fans. In a deeply dualistic world grappling with the potential for its own destruction, players are cast in the role of the messianic hero, engage in a first-person narrative of apocalyptic catastrophe and salvation via gameplay, and emerge victorious in a world where their choices and actions have tangible moral results.

Videogames have become an "increasingly important form of digital culture" in the twenty-first century,[1] and through them, William Sims Bainbridge observes, "the user experiences a marvelous world ... frequently encountering religious symbolism."[2] The number of people who play immersive videogames is enormous, with current estimates placing the worldwide gaming population at 1.8 billion.[3] Some of the popularity of videogames stems from a characteristic they share with books, television series, and films: they tell exciting stories that lend meaning and adventure to what might otherwise be a routine, day-to-day existence. However, while these media are unidirectional, with the reader or viewer a more-or-less passive observer of a story that will unfold in exactly the same way every time, videogames are multidirectional, allowing players to actively participate in the narrative and, in some respects, even to change the outcome.[4] Additionally, the religious aspects of videogames like *WoW* "provide a measure of transcendence from the material world."[5]

In his sociological study, Bainbridge has noted that, "*World of Warcraft* is far more than a game,"[6] due to the immersive and wide-ranging nature of the experiences that it allows fans. This dynamic can be observed in the way that *WoW* reconfigures apocalyptic imagery, not only using it to authorize the storyline but also using it to produce a heroic messianic identity for players. By exploring the end-time themes and narratives in this game and the religious opportunities it affords players, this essay expands on the literature that argues that the situations, quests, and stories of *WoW*, the game designers of its parent company Blizzard, and its fans and players, together generate an experience steeped in religiosity for the participant.

The Immersive World of Warcraft

Within the genre of videogames, the immersive nature of MMORPGs is unique because it requires that the players become actively involved in the game world and narrative. Some players fully embrace this aspect of the experience, role-playing their character in speech and action; but even casual players are forced to create an in-game life that, minimally, includes business transactions and interactions with non-player characters (NPCs) and other gamers. *WoW* is the most popular subscription based MMORPG in the world. It was not the first such game to become popular (*Ultima Online, EverQuest,* and *Final Fantasy* are three of the more successful early MMORPGs in the Western world), but *WoW* outstripped the competition almost as soon as it was released in 2004. This overwhelmingly positive response from consumers proved a good indicator of the long-term appeal of the game.

WoW's popularity and longevity is dependent on various factors, including the aesthetic appeal of its virtual world, the "flow" experience of playing the game, and its large number of devoted fans. There is a long-standing debate within fan studies as to what, exactly, constitutes a fan. Many popular definitions across all genres define fans as people who actively engage with their fandom, particularly in creative ways.[7] This broad definition can be a useful tool for analysis, though scholars such as Garry Crawford have critiqued it as being sufficiently vague as to potentially apply to even casual videogamers, as even casual players are understood to be more active in their consumption of the medium than fans of other media.[8] Yet Crawford allows that players who engage with the text of their preferred game(s) in other contexts are legitimately classified as fans; therefore, I use this definition in this essay. Not all *WoW* players are fans, but those who are active outside the game, whether by watching other players engage in game runs on YouTube, by creating in-game mods or add-ons, by participating in *WoW* bulletin boards, by doing background reading on lore, attending conventions, and even encouraging other players to engage in such activities via in-game chat can be understood to be fans of the game.

Another reason for the game's great success and devoted fanbase is the level of attachment players are able to form to their avatars and their roles in game play and unfolding narratives Recent research indicates that our brains are limited in their capacity to meaningfully differentiate between events that we experience in the real world and those we experience in digital worlds of simulated virtual reality. For example, studies show that when people with a morbid fear of heights are shown great heights in a videogame or other digital virtual reality, they physically react in the same way that they do to heights in the real world: with sweaty palms, racing hearts, and dizziness.[9] In another study, when children watched a digital representation of themselves swim with whales in a virtual reality environment fully fifty percent of them later believed that they have had this experience in real (physical) life.[10] While the brains of children and adults are obviously rather different, these studies provide important insight into the ways that people experience events in virtual reality worlds such as immersive videogames, and what they appear to tell us is that our criteria for what constitutes "reality" are somewhat fluid. Virtual reality is, after all, a type of reality, even if it is generally understood to be less real, or less important, than physical reality. Our brains respond to this, as indicated by their lack of certainty in separating events that we experience in virtual from those of physical reality. Thus, it is possible that the religious work that fans perform in *WoW* can be viewed as religious in the "real world."

This crossover between players' in-game and out of game lives is also manifests in other ways. *WoW* has many devoted fans who attend conventions, dress in cosplay, read background literature and fanfiction, post on bulletin boards, create game add-ons, make and watch YouTube videos, and many more activities. All of these activities take place outside the gameworld, and are clear evidence of both the power of fandom and *WoW*'s enduring appeal. Further, they help to cement players' identities as fans by combining their in-game and out of game activities and identities. In fact, the game itself can be particularly compelling because of the tendency of fans to identify with their characters. Game designers are aware of the benefits of players identifying with their characters, and make concerted efforts to build such identification into game play.[11] When asked about the degree to which they identified with their characters, roughly 50 percent of *WoW* players indicated that they view their characters as either identical with themselves or reflecting aspects of themselves.[12] This extension of personhood into digital realms suggests that "virtual worlds and online games are not exotic environments dedicated to the "identity play" of a few, but instead spaces that users move in and out fluidly [*sic*], which in turn leads to the construction of a "synthetic" identity that remains fairly stable online and off."[13] The meshing of the synthetic identity and the physical identity allows fans to craft a self which is consistent both within the game and outside of it, which in turn reinforces both the religious experience of the gameplay and their status as fans. *World of Warcraft* uses the apocalyptic elements of dualism, tragedy and eschatology to imbue a sense of messianism in each individual player/character.

The Apocalypse in Azeroth

The multitude of religious ideas and traditions utilized by the game designers of *WoW* have garnered academic attention, not least of all because some of them bear out inaccuracies and stereotypes about certain races and religions.[14] David Chidester has defined religion as "the negotiation of what it means to be human with respect to the superhuman and the subhuman,"[15] and by applying this construct we can see that players in the *WoW* universe are regularly called upon to do religious work by negotiating their identities and choosing their actions with regard the super-humans and sub-humans who populate Azeroth. For example, Rachel Wagner points to the blue-skinned Trolls (who use Afro-Carribean idioms) and the minotaur-like Tauren (whose culture is based on that of Native Americans) as figures clearly performing religious work—magic in the first instance, protection of the sacred environment in the other—in the *WoW* narrative.[16] Sociologist and game scholar William Bainbridge has also noted that "religion is a quest for meaning, and gameworlds mirror this fact by being assemblies of quests."[17] This is another dimension of the religious work performed in *WoW*. This essay focuses specifically on the ways that the narrative and mythos of *WoW* are shaped by the biblical Book of Revelation, the most widely read and culturally influential apocalyptic text in the Western world.[18] No other apocalyptic book has been the focus of so many people's religious and creative energies, and as such it has left a unique imprint on Western culture. As a result of this, the apocalyptic expectations found in the Book of Revelation have become the default, or normative definition of apocalypse everywhere that Christianity is the dominant religion.

To determine if a narrative is apocalyptic in the biblical sense, or apocalyptic in a more general way (meaning something like "total destruction" or "the end of the world"), I have developed a four-part typology. The four criteria are: dualism, a tragic present, eschatological expectations, and the presence—either current or anticipated—of a messianic savior.[19] According to this typology, the narrative of *WoW* can be understood as biblically apocalyptic. Its cultural perspective is deeply dualistic, and the narrative takes place in a tragic present. Further, there are eschatological expectations for the future; and the potential salvation of the world rests in the hands of a messianic savior. Since the interactive nature of videogames creates a narrative construct wherein the player assumes an active role in the unfolding story, players are able to assume the messianic role themselves, and thus the apocalyptic narrative becomes a type of lived religious experience for players. Recently scholars of religion and media have increasingly observed that when people are encouraged to identify with the protagonist of a narrative, they are significantly more likely to accept the plausibility of the supernatural in that particular mythology,[20] and that the "appropriation of real world iconography and religious beliefs might affect the religious imagination of the players."[21] The experience of playing *WoW* as the messianic hero encourages the player to understand that game world, and their actions and choices within it, as having functionally real ethics and morals attached to them. In other words, the gameplay performs religious work and allows *WoW* fans to instigate religious experience.

As the phrase "lived religious experience" implies, the religion that players may experience in videogames does not necessarily remain confined to in-game lives. The interactivity of videogames means that "neither the gamer nor the game designer [has] complete control over the experience,"[22] and thus neither the outcomes nor the experience of the player can be predetermined, which makes for both a more exciting game experience, and potentially for a more meaningful religious experience, as players shape their actions in ways that are more important to them personally and see the in-game outcomes of their choices. This type of interaction, in which the game affects the player and the player affects the game, lends additional weight to the narrative experience for the player, because he or she is not just a viewer or consumer. It is not surprising, therefore, that "many videogames are structured around this powerful combination [of heroism and first-hand experience]."[23]

By enabling players to become heroes, videogames create potent incentives for people to play. After all, "not everyone lives in a community with rich traditions, faiths, and stories that put meaning into everyone's life, whereas in synthetic worlds, everyone is asked to complete quests, fight enemies, and become a hero."[24] In other words, for some fans videogames fill a void of meaning in their lives that religious people have traditionally filled with religion. Both religious traditions and videogames ask people to consider their morals, their communities, their place in the world, and then to act upon those understandings. *WoW* combines the visceral, first person subjectivity of videogames with a richly complex narrative; moreover, elements of the narrative and the landscape actually change based on individual player choices and accomplishments. *WoW* offers fans a wide-ranging and detailed mythology with a regularly evolving storyline that builds upon past events, and as we will see, this storyline is rife with apocalyptic elements that ultimately allow the player to take on the role of heroic messiah.

Defining Apocalypticism

The term "apocalyptic" has a broad range of meanings, and is often conflated with the related terms "eschatology" and "millenarianism." As a religious or literary genre, apocalyptic works are diverse, containing settings ranging from the mythological to the historical, revelations through prophecy, dreams, or direct contact with the divine (including tours of heaven or hell), marginalized communities, communities in crisis, communities in exile, and even communities that do not appear to display any particular sense of displacement or alienation.[25] Some texts envision a transcendent new order in the physical world, while others focus on the transcendence of judgment after death, and a heavenly reward for the righteous. This makes constructing a coherent definition difficult, but in this essay the terms "apocalypse" and "apocalyptic" rely on the characteristics mentioned above, that together constitute a working definition for these terms: (1) a dualistic world view; (2) large-scale or widespread tragedy; (3) eschatological expectations; and (4) messianic expectations.

Eschatology means "words about the end" (from the Greek *eschaton*, meaning "end"). Yet, even in a traditionally religious setting, the end is never really the end, and this is true in *WoW* as well. Generally speaking, eschatology first envisions a world that is systematically being destroyed by the forces of iniquity. Secondly, a "beast" plays an important role as the embodiment of evil, or of the opposing forces. Evil is literally conceptualized as a monster: ugly, deformed, cruel, and terrifying.[26] Thirdly, eschatology is marked by the belief that this current time is evil, that the people and forces who have allowed this evil to flourish will be judged, and this judgment will be followed by a war between the forces of good and evil. Notably, the actual eschatological event remains perpetually on the horizon, encouraging believers and players alike to remain steadfast in the pursuit of their goals. Narratives that display these characteristics, like that of *WoW*, can be said to be eschatological.

Another fundamental feature of apocalyptic works is that they describe an enormous tragedy, often of an environmental nature. The Book of Revelation, for example, speaks of earthquakes, a blackened sky, burned grass, and the devastation of crops. People and animals die as earth and water are poisoned, and in the end, only a remnant remains. This remnant will go on to inhabit the new earth that will be revealed after the messiah has thoroughly cleansed the old, setting right the wrongs, and removing the evil that has infected the world. The third characteristic of apocalypse is an insider/outsider dualism. In biblical apocalypses, there are those who are aligned with God, and those who are not. Those who are not are never neutral; instead they actively persecute and work against the people of God, thereby reinforcing the dualistic world view. An unlivable world (along with a host of other traumatic events) necessitates change, both in order to (re)create a life-sustaining environment, and in order to correct the behaviors that caused the situation in the first place, which is where messianism plays a role.

Apocalypticism in *World of Warcraft*

WoW displays all four of the characteristics of my apocalyptic typology, and all four are integral parts of the game's narrative.[27] Unlike the use of these strategies in literature or film, the apocalyptic elements of *WoW* encourage player immersion, working to ensure that players are involved and invested in the game. The identification of the player with the messianic hero, rather than situating him or her as a spectator at the apocalyptic finale, is a substantial departure from film and other narrative forms. Understanding the player's messianic role is impossible, however, without appreciating how the other three apocalyptic elements operate in the game. Dualism, eschatology, and tragedy are what make the presence of a messianic figure desirable, both as a narrative element and as a component of game play.

Players immediately encounter dualism when they begin playing *WoW* as they are forced to choose a side in the Alliance vs. Horde conflict when they create their character. They may not choose a particular race based on factional allegiance, but by dividing up the available races into two factions, the game makers ensure that everyone takes sides. Early research showed that new players overwhelmingly preferred the Alliance, the more visually appealing "good" races, while long-term players tended to gravitate towards the Horde.[28] Blizzard has been careful to develop a narrative in which neither side can be said to be right or wrong, good or evil, but the aesthetics of the game suggest that the Alliance is good (they tend to be attractive and human-like) and the Horde is evil (the Horde races tend to be monstrous in appearance, and nearly all have a hunched or stooped posture).[29] Players may initially rely on visual cues when choosing a faction or race, but it appears that over time these visual cues are, to some degree, sublimated by the narrative.

Once a player has chosen a faction, it is necessary to build up some type of factional allegiance, and many of the early quests a player is sent on serve to create this type of loyalty. Successfully completing quests that help particular factions builds a player's reputation with those factions, and increased factional reputation leads in turn to desirable rewards such as discounted merchandise and exclusive in-game pets and mounts. In addition, completing quests for one faction also deepens the sense of dualism in the game by highlighting the destructive actions of the other side, and asking the player to address and reverse some of that damage. This sort of straightforward dualism is engaging and creates clear insider/outsider boundaries that serve to maintain the community. This is the same type of dualism that is used in both the Books of Revelation and Daniel, in order to strengthen the sense of community, and therefore the player's or reader's commitment to that community.

However, the dualism in *WoW* is more complex than it appears at first glance. There is the ongoing conflict between the Alliance and the Horde, but there are always larger threats that loom over Azeroth. These threats require players to re-evaluate the original dualism that the game presents, and to subordinate or relinquish it in favor of other dualistic constructs that are continually revealed to be of greater importance. So, while the Alliance and the Horde appear, at first glance, to be opposing forces, the narrative trajectory of *WoW* is increasingly structured around a dualism that places them in the same community, working towards the same goals. In this way, the *WoW* narrative creates a dualistic dichotomy between those who would protect Azeroth and slow or stop the demonic threat to the cosmos, and those who—for love of power, or addiction or despair—seek to destroy all of creation. It is worth noting that not all fans approve of this narrative shift, and some have expressed a nostalgia for the Alliance/Horde conflict and dualistic worldview that the early game provided.[30]

The world of Azeroth is constantly on the brink of being destroyed and the primary role of the player is to work to prevent that destruction. As mentioned above, each of the game expansions has introduced a new, potentially eschatological event to the narrative. From the demons of the Burning Legion, to the Lich King's undead, to Deathwing and his allies, each of these threats forces a reconfiguration of group boundaries, showing a fluidity in the dualistic ordering of the world. For example, in "Wrath of the Lich King" the eschatological threat takes the form of a rapidly expanding undead plague on Azeroth. As is often the case with zombies, the undead in *WoW* grow their ranks by simply killing their enemies. The newly deceased enemy soldiers quickly rise again as undead, and the undead forces grow as their enemy's numbers shrink. Additionally, the Lich King's armies have poisons that can kill entire towns, turning all of the inhabitants into undead like themselves. In the fact of this threat, the inhabitants of Azeroth put aside the Horde/Alliance dualism that has pervaded the game up to this point, and work together in order to defeat the plague that threatens to engulf them all. However, despite this shift in previously impenetrable group boundaries, dualism remains a potent force in the narrative. Instead of the inhabitants of

Azeroth fighting each other, they now fight the undead together, and the dualism has become global: Azeroth vs the undead. This in no way lessens the apocalyptic feeling or sentiments in the game. As one fan noted, this shift "almost sounds like a prophetic gathering of grudgingly cooperating forces in preparation for the ultimate, apocalyptic battle."[31] Thus, enhanced cooperation between the Alliance and Horde actually contributes to the sense of apocalypticism, rather than detracting from it.

Because the eschatologies in *WoW* are never actually realized, the player's world is persistently tragic. The eschatological threats are unsuccessful in that they do not in fact destroy Azeroth, but they nevertheless wreak considerable havoc, and cause enormous amounts of death and destruction. Characters operate in a world that faces the ongoing possibility of a demonic alien invasion, while coping with a barely-contained undead plague, and which has just suffered global environmental catastrophes that include rising sea levels, floods, fires, and massive earthquakes as a corrupt dragon emerged to annihilate all of creation.[32] People have died, families have been torn apart, and resources are scarce. Yet despite all this, there is no time to dwell upon sorrows, for the next catastrophe always looms, and always contains the possibility that this time Sargeras' assault on creation will succeed and Azeroth will be obliterated. The narrative structure of *WoW* relies heavily on both new and ongoing eschatological threats to drive game play by ensuring that the world remains on the brink of disaster and destruction. At the same time, the game is perpetually hopeful, looking forward to a better, more peaceful future that can be brought about by the actions of fans. The moment of eschatology remains perpetually on the horizon.

The ongoing tragedies frame the player's role on Azeroth, especially regarding their community affiliations. The individual tragedies that plague Azeroth drive the Horde and Alliance apart, but the cosmic eschatological threats bring them together into one community. This is the same dualistic narrative structure that Revelation uses—a small community, beset by tragedy, becomes a larger community as creation is re-ordered. Initially Revelation presents a very strong dualism with closed group boundaries, with only the "saints," those who "have come out of the great ordeal" (Rev. 7:14), whose names have "been written from the foundation of the world in the book of life" (Rev. 13:8), and who are not "lukewarm" (Rev. 3:16) being viewed as a part of the community. However, by the end of Revelation the community boundaries have widened considerably and include "every nation and tribe and language and people" (Rev. 14:6), "everyone who hears ... everyone who is thirsty ... anyone who wishes" (Rev. 22:17). Revelation maintains a strong dualistic mentality however, insisting that "outside are the dogs and sorcerers and fornicators and murderers and idolaters and everyone who loves and practices falsehood" (Rev. 22:15). Likewise, the mythos of *WoW* maintains that Sargeras and his demons will forever be outsiders, never able to overcome the basic division between good and evil in the game.

Messianism and the Player as Savior

In the Book of Revelation, as in virtually all Jewish and Christian apocalypses, believers look forward to an eschatological future where both "rewards for the faithful and punishment for the wicked [are] enacted by God."[33] Yet in *WoW* players engage in an active, rather than passive, relationship with the both the medium and the story by consistently making choices that affect the outcome of the narrative. This means that in *WoW*, as in other immersive videogames, the messianic "agency is situated squarely with the player … who ultimately enacts salvation by him or herself."[34] By participating in and engaging in the quest narrative, players take up the messianic responsibilities of apocalyptic heroes, personally working to ensure that tragedy is overcome and the end of the world is prevented.

It is fundamental to MMORPGs that players are active participants, and the game narrative is structured in such a way so as to give the individual player a maximal sense of importance to that narrative. Quest givers in the game greet characters by name, class, or race (and sometimes by all three), often stating that they have heard good things about the character, or are in need of someone with that character's particular skills. *WoW* is a world constantly on the verge of destruction, and in need of salvation. By placing each individual player in the role of the savior/messiah/hero, Blizzard ensures that players have a vested interest in Azeroth, and that they are therefore likely to continue their involvement in the game. The experience of (virtually) meeting and overcoming challenges, as well as helping people and a planet desperately in need of one's assistance can be a heady combination. Indeed, some fans even explicitly note that the feeling of being needed to help avert an impending catastrophe is one of their motivations for playing the game, saying things like, "I want to feel like this is an apocalypse" and "I want the NPCs to show they are scared."[35] The lived religious experience of the *WoW* fan is strengthened by the intensity of the threats facing Azeroth.

Because there are multiple apocalyptic threats occurring at more or less the same time, the needs of Azeroth and its inhabitants are many, and therefore the messianic roles that players may engage are numerous and varied. In the beginning, they vary from faction to faction, race to race and class to class, but all of them situate the player as the savior who can resolve the community's crisis. For example, a novice Draenei character is asked to find and heal survivors of the crash landing with which their ship arrived on Azeroth, to find medicinal herbs for a wounded Night Elf, and to administer potions that reverse the magical corruption that is spreading among many of the native inhabitants of Azuremist Isle. Fledgling Night Elves are sent on quests to heal corrupted plant and animal life, and Dwarves battle against enemies trying to annex their land. Horde examples include new Taurens fighting against invasive species and learning to care for the earth or Orcs protecting their territory and seeking to eradicate the Shadow Council (a group of warlocks and demons who continue to serve the Burning Legion). In each case the new character is greeted by name, and garners increasing praise and renown as s/he successfully completes the quests that will help to ensure the salvation of his/her faction, race, or planet.

As characters progress the messianic overtones to the quests and narrative remain quite strong. At higher levels players are asked to perform feats that will benefit increasingly larger populations. On Outland, for instance, the quests focus on repairing the planet and driving back the Burning Legion. One of the high-level zones on Azeroth needs help cleansing and purifying the land and the people who have been corrupted by the demonic influences. These quests emphasize the increasing power and importance of the character, as well as his/her influence on the world at large. As the character becomes more powerful she is required to help ever greater numbers of people and beings, and to change corrupted bodies (of people, animals, and even planets) into new, pure bodies (cf. 1 Corinthians 15:51–54). The player's growing power and importance are even remarked upon by NPCs, who can be overheard saying things like, "I heard Highlord [player name] defeated Ragnaros the firelord. Twice!" and "Do you think that [player name] is a demigod?" These kinds of comments reinforce the player's identity as heroic messiah and serve to subtly remind the player that her actions and choices in the game have real and discernable outcomes. The work maybe slow and ongoing—the new heaven and new earth do not replace the old in one fell swoop—but it moves steadily forward, building towards the time when the old earth, with its eschatological threats, will be no more.

In studying what appeals to players, game designers have noted that, "fantasy is probably the most important feature of computer games,"[36] because the emotional engagement created by a good fantasy lends tremendous appeal to the game. Thus, a fantasy that casts the player as a "messianic character in a virtual world of secularized dualisms"[37] provides a powerful emotional hook for fans. In this way fantasy in videogames can fill emotional needs in players' real lives, or, through re-framing, encourage players to perform rote tasks that might otherwise be too boring to engage with.[38] The player-as-messiah aspect of *WoW* clearly fits into these categories, and the emotional engagement created by the fantasy of the player as messianic hero furthers both the storyline and player motivation to continue investing the game. As one fan noted: "You can't lose an apocalypse scenario and win again another day."[39]

Because the narrative is ongoing (as opposed to the completed descriptions of Revelation and other apocalyptic texts), the messianic role of the player is also ongoing, having not yet reached its final fulfillment in judgment day, or the ultimate triumph of good over evil. Crawford has suggested that "intrigue and suspense are key factors in holding a videogamer's attention and absorbing them in the videogame,"[40] indicating that *WoW*'s failure to actualize messianic and eschatological fulfillment is a feature, not a bug, as it keeps fans in a perpetual state of hope and uncertainty, which ensures that they remain both immersed in and engaged with the game.

Conclusion

Apocalyptic mythology and imagery have been enduring features of the religious landscape for millennia. Today they can be found in many different types of media, including Blizzard Entertainment's *World of Warcraft*, the most successful subscription based MMORPG in history. The presence of apocalypticism in *WoW* involves fans in the narrative through the first person experience of messianism, and incentivizes continued play through enhanced immersion by keeping the eschatological moment always on the virtual threshold. These things, in turn, help to create fans whose engagement with the game and the gameworld spills over into the worlds of YouTube, bulletin boards, and fan conventions.

The world of Azeroth itself is one of ongoing tragedy, and each time the world appears likely to be saved from destruction a new threat emerges. This tension reveals an apocalyptic mindset that fans are called upon to mitigate. The world will soon end thanks to demons, the undead, or dragons and the player must shoulder the burden of defeating such evil forces, moving Azeroth one step closer to its final redemption. While Blizzard may never take both fan and scholarly advice that the game come to an actual narrative close,[41] fans still see themselves as pressing on toward the new world in which orcs and humans "beat their swords into plowshares" (Isaiah 2:4) and demons are forever cast into the "bottomless pit" (Rev. 20:1).

NOTES

1. Hilde G. Corneliussen and Jill Walker Rettburg, "Introduction: 'Orc Professor LFG,' or Researching in Azeroth," in *Digital Culture, Play and Identity: A World of Warcraft Reader*, eds Hilde G. Corneliussen and Jill Walker Rettburg (Cambridge, MA: MIT Press, 2008), 4.

2. William Sims Bainbridge, *eGods: Faith versus Fantasy in Computer Gaming* (New York: Oxford University Press, 2013), 3.

3. "There are 1.8 Billion Gamers in the World and PC Gaming Dominates the Market," *Mygaming*, https://mygaming.co.za/news/features/89913-there-are-1–8-billion-gamers-in-the-world-and-pc-gaming-dominates-the-market.html.

4. Garry Crawford, *Video Gamers* (New York: Routledge, 2012), 67.

5. Bainbridge, *eGods*, 22.

6. William Sims Bainbridge, *The Warcraft Civilization: Social Science in a Virtual World* (Cambridge, MA: MIT Press, 2010), 9.

7. Henry Jenkins, *Textual Poachers: Television Fans and Participatory Culture* (London: Routledge, 1992); James Newman, *Videogames*. (London: Routledge, 2004); and Judith Dormans, "Understanding Fan Practices: A Study into Videos, Role-Play and Fanfiction Based on Pervasive Gameworlds," paper presented at *Under the Mask 3*, University of Bedfordshire, June 2, 2010, http://underthemask.wdfiles.com/local—files/papers-2010/Judith%20Dormans.pdf.

8. Crawford, *Video Gamers*, 104.

9. Jay David Bolter, "Digital Media and Cinematic Point of View," *Telepolis*, February 14, 1997, https://www.heise.de/tp/features/Digital-Media-and-Cinematic-Point-of-View-3445933.html.

10. Rachel Dretzin, "Life on the Virtual Frontier," *Digital Nation*, February 2, 2010, http://www.pbs.org/wgbh/frontline/film/digitalnation/.

11. Richard A. Bartle, *Designing Virtual Worlds* (Berkeley, CA: New Riders, 2004); Gary A. Fine, "Network and Meaning: An Interactionist Approach to Structure," *Symbolic Interaction* 6, no. 1 (Spring 1983): 97–110.

12. Robert M. Geraci and Jovi L. Geraci, "Virtual Gender: How Men and Women Use Video Game Bodies," *Journal of Gaming and Virtual Worlds* 5, no. 3 (2013): 329–248.

13. Nicholas Ducheneaut, "The Chorus of the Dead: Roles, Identity Formation and Ritual Process Inside a FPS Multiplayer Online Game," in *Utopic Dreams and Apocalyptic Fantasies: Critical Approaches to Researching Video Game Play*, eds J. Talmadge Wright, David G. Embrick, and Andras Lukacs, 199–222 (Lanham, MD: Lexington Books, 2010).

14. Julian Schaap and Stef Aupers, "'Gods in *World of Warcraft* Exist': Religious Reflexivity and the Quest for Meaning in Online Computer Games," *new media & society* 19, no. 11 (2017): 1750; Rachel Wagner, "God in the Game: Cosmopolitanism and Religious Conflict in Videogames," *Journal of the American Academy of Religion* 81, no. 1 (2013): 245–6; Lauren Bernauer, "'Elune be Praised!' *World of Warcraft*, its People and Religions, and Their Real World Inspiration," *Literature and Aesthetics* 19, no. 2 (2009): 307.

15. David Chidester, "Moralizing Noise," *Harvard Divinity Bulletin* 32 (2004): 17.

16. Rachel Wagner, *Godwired: Religion, Ritual and Virtual Reality* (London and New York: Routledge, 2012), 110.

17. Bainbridge, *eGods*, 264.

18. John Collins, *The Apocalyptic Imagination: An Introduction to the Jewish Matrix of Christianity* (New York: Crossroad, 1984); Richard K. Emmerson and Ronald B. Herzman, *The Apocalyptic Imagination in Medieval Literature* (University Park: University of Pennsylvania Press, 1992); Amy Frykholm, *Rapture Culture: Left Behind in Evangelical America* (New York: Oxford University Press, 2004); Paul D. Hanson, *The Dawn of Apocalyptic: The Historical and Sociological Roots of Jewish Apocalyptic Eschatology* (Philadelphia: Fortress Press, 1979); David Lawton, *Faith, Text and History: The Bible in English* (Charlottesville: University of Virginia Press, 1990); Bernard McGinn, John J. Collins, and Stephen J. Stein (eds), *The Encyclopedia of Apocalypticism* (New York: Continuum, 2000); and Eugen Weber, *Apocalypses: Prophecies, Cults and Millennial Beliefs Through the Ages* (Cambridge, MA: Harvard University Press, 1999). Other examples of apocalyptic texts include the Book of Daniel, Mark 13, 2 Ezra, 2 Baruch, and 3 Baruch.

19. Jovita L. Geraci, *Imagining the End: Apocalyptic Imagery in Visual Media* (Ph.D. thesis, University of California, Santa Barbara, 2012).

20. Markus Altena Davidson, "Fiction-Based Religion: Conceptualizing a New Category against History-based Religion and Fandom," *Culture and Religion: An Interdisciplinary Journal* 14, no. 4 (2013): 379.

21. Bernauer, "'Elune be Praised!'" 307.

22. Andreas Jahn-Sudmann and Ralf Stockmann (eds), *Computer Games as a Sociocultural Phenomenon* (New York: Palgrave MacMillan, 2008), 9.

23. Bonnie A. Nardi, *My Life as a Night Elf Priest: An Anthropological Account of World of Warcraft* (Ann Arbor: University of Michigan Press, 2010), 8.

24. Edward Castronova, *Exodus to the Virtual World: How Online Fun Is Changing Reality* (New York: Macmillan, 2007), 69.

25. Robert L. Webb, "'Apocalyptic': Observations on a Slippery Term," *Journal of Near Eastern Studies* 49, no. 2 (1990): 115–126.

26. David D. Gilmore, *Monsters: Evil Beings, Mythical Beasts, and All Manner of Imaginary Terrors* (University Park: University of Pennsylvania Press, 2003), 47, 52, 55, 178.

27. In fact, Blizzard itself describes aspects of the *World of Warcraft* narrative as apocalyptic, writing that "Azeroth has paid a terrible price to end the apocalyptic march of the Legion's crusade," in their publicity material for the upcoming expansion: https://worldof warcraft.com/en-us/battle-for-azeroth.

28. Nicholas Ducheneaut, Nick Yee, Eric Nickell, and Robert J. Moore, "Building an MMO with Mass Appeal: A Look at Gameplay in *World of Warcraft*," *Games and Culture* 1, no. 4 (2006): 281–317.

29. Schaap and Aupers, "'Gods in *World of Warcraft* Exist,'" 1750.

30. As comment threads like "Renewing the Horde vs Alliance Conflict?," from the gaming forum *battle.net*, indicate. The upcoming 2018 *World of Warcraft* expansion, "Battle for Azeroth," appears likely to reignite the old conflict between the Alliance and the Horde.

31. Sumerian99, "The years of ceaseless conflict we've had a test," r/wow, January 15, 2017, https://www.reddit.com/r/wow/comments/5o130q/the_years_of_ceaseless_conflict_weve_had_are_a/.

32. Nadine Brozan, "Emotional Effects of Natural Disasters," *New York Times*, June 27 (1983), accessed 1 March 2018, https://www.nytimes.com/1983/06/27/style/emotional-effects-of-natural-disasters.html.

33. Wagner, *Godwired*, 201.

34. Wagner, *Godwired*, 201.

35. Headchopperz, "I want us to lose in Legion," r/wow, November 12, 2015, https://www.reddit.com/r/wow/comments/3sjgwm/i_want_us_to_lose_in_legion/.

36. Thomas W. Malone, "Heuristics for Designing Enjoyable User Interfaces: Lessons from Computer Games," *Proceedings of the 1982 Conference on Human Factors in Computing Systems* (New York: Association for Computing Machinery, 1981): 67.

37. Wagner, *Godwired*, 202.

38. Malone, "Heuristics for Designing Enjoyable User Interfaces," 67.

39. Swineflew1, comment on Reddit thread Headchopperz, "I want us to lose in Legion."

40. Crawford, *Video Gamers*, 77.

41. Greg Costikyan, "Games, Storytelling, and Breaking the String," in *Second Person: Role-Playing and Story in Games and Playable Media*, eds Pat Harrigan and Noah Wardrip-Fruin (Cambridge, MA: MIT Press, 2007), 11. See also Sumerian99, "The years of ceaseless conflict we've had are a test."

Bibliography

Bainbridge, William Sims. *eGods: Faith versus Fantasy in Computer Gaming*. New York: Oxford University Press, 2013.

_____. *The Warcraft Civilization: Social Science in a Virtual World*. Cambridge, MA: MIT Press, 2010.

Bartle, Richard A. *Designing Virtual Worlds*. Berkeley, CA: New Riders, 2004.

Bernauer, Lauren. "'Elune be Praised!' *World of Warcraft*, Its People and Religions, and Their Real World Inspiration." *Literature and Aesthetics* 19, no. 2 (2009): 307–325.

Bolter, Jay David. "Digital Media and Cinematic Point of View." *Telepolis*. February 14 (1997). https://www.heise.de/tp/features/Digital-Media-and-Cinematic-Point-of-View-3445933.html (accessed May 9, 2018).

Brozan, Nadine. "Emotional Effects of Natural Disasters." *New York Times*. June 27, 1983. https://www.nytimes.com/1983/06/27/style/emotional-effects-of-natural-disasters.html (accessed May 9, 2018).

Castronova, Edward. *Exodus to the Virtual World: How Online Fun Is Changing Reality*. New York: Macmillan, 2007.

Chidester, David. "Moralizing Noise." *Harvard Divinity Bulletin* 32, no. 17 (2004): 16–18.

Collins, John J. *The Apocalyptic Imagination: An Introduction to the Jewish Matrix of Christianity*. New York: Crossroad, 1984.

Corneliussen, Hilde G,. and Jill Walker Rettberg. "Introduction: 'Orc Professor LFG,' or Researching in Azeroth." In *Digital Culture, Play and Identity: A World of Warcraft Reader*, edited by Hilde G. Corneliussen and Jill Walker Rettburg, 1–16. Cambridge, MA: MIT Press, 2008.

Costikyan, Greg. "Games, Storytelling, and Breaking the String." In *Second Person: Role-Playing and Story in Games and Playable Media*, edited by Pat Harrigan and Noah Wardrip-Fruin, 5–13. Cambridge, MA: MIT Press, 2007.

Crawford, Garry. *Video Gamers*. New York: Routledge, 2012.

Davidsen, Markus Altena. "Fiction-Based Religion: Conceptualizing a New Category against History-based Religion and Fandom." *Culture and Religion: An Interdisciplinary Journal* 14, no. 4 (2013): 378–395.

Dormans, Judith. "Understanding Fan Practices: A Study into Videos, Role-Play and Fanfiction Based on Pervasive Gameworlds." Paper presented at *Under the Mask 3*, University of Bedfordshire, June 2, 2010. http://underthemask.wdfiles.com/local—files/papers-2010/Judith%20Dormans.pdf (accessed May 9, 2018).

Dretzin, Rachel. "Life on the Virtual Frontier." *Digital Nation*. February 2010. http://www.pbs.org/wgbh/frontline/film/digitalnation/ (accessed May 9, 2018).

Ducheneaut, Nicolas, Nick Yee, Eric Nickell and Robert J. Moore. "Building an MMO with Mass Appeal: A Look at Gameplay in *World of Warcraft*." *Games and Culture* 1, no. 4 (2006): 281–317.

Ducheneaut, Nicolas. "The Chorus of the Dead: Roles, Identity Formation, and Ritual Processes Inside a FPS Multiplayer Online Game." In *Utopic Dreams and Apocalyptic Fantasies: Critical Approaches to Researching Video Game Play*, edited by J. Talmadge Wright, David G. Embrick, and Andras Lukacs, 199–222. Lanham, MD: Lexington Books, 2010.

Emmerson, Richard K., and Ronald B. Herzman. *The Apocalyptic Imagination in Medieval Literature*. Philadelphia: University of Pennsylvania Press, 1992.

Fine, Gary A. "Network and Meaning: An Interactionist Approach to Structure." *Symbolic Interaction* 6, no. 1 (1983): 97–110.

Frykholm, Amy. *Rapture Culture: Left Behind in Evangelical America*. New York: Oxford University Press, 2004.

Geraci, Jovita L. *Imagining the End: Apocalyptic Imagery in Visual Media*. Ph.D. thesis, University of California, 2012.

Geraci, Robert M., and Jovi L. Geraci. "Virtual Gender: How Men and Women Use Video Game Bodies." *Journal of Gaming and Virtual Worlds* 5, no. 3 (2013): 329–348.

Gilmore, David D. *Monsters: Evil Beings, Mythical Beasts, and All Manner of Imaginary Terrors*. University Park: University of Pennsylvania Press, 2003.

Hanson, Paul D. *The Dawn of Apocalyptic: The Historical and Sociological Roots of Jewish Apocalyptic Eschatology*. Philadelphia: Fortress Press, 1979.

Headchopperz. "I want us to lose in *Legion*." r/wow. November 12, 2015. https://www.reddit.com/r/wow/comments/3sjgwm/i_want_us_to_lose_in_legion/ (accessed May 9, 2018).

Jahn-Sudmann, Andreas and Ralf Stockmann (eds). *Computer Games as a Sociocultural Phenomenon*. New York: Palgrave Macmillan, 2008.

Jenkins, Henry. *Textual Poachers: Television Fans and Participatory Culture*. London: Routledge, 1992.

Lawton, David. *Faith, Text and History: The Bible in English*. Charlottesville: University of Virginia Press, 1990.

Malone, Thomas W. "Heuristics for Designing Enjoyable User Interfaces: Lessons from Computer Games." *Proceedings of the 1982 Conference on Human Factors in Computing Systems*. New York: Association for Computing Machinery (1981): 63–68.

McGinn, Bernard, John J. Collins, and Stephen J. Stein, eds. *The Encyclopedia of Apocalypticism*. New York: Continuum Press. 2000.

Nardi, Bonnie A. *My Life as a Night Elf Priest: An Anthropological Account of World of Warcraft.* Ann Arbor: University of Michigan Press, 2010.

Newman, James. *Videogames.* London: Routledge, 2004.

Schaap, Julian and Stef Aupers, "'Gods in World of Warcraft Exist': Religious Reflexivity and the Quest for Meaning in Online Computer Games." *new media & society* 19, no. 11 (2017): 1744–1760.

Sumerian99. "The years of ceaseless conflict we've had are a test." r/wow. January 15, 2017. https://www.reddit.com/r/wow/comments/5o130q/the_years_of_ceaseless_conflict_weve_had_are_a/ (accessed May 9, 2018).

"There are 1.8 Billion Gamers in the World and PC Gaming Dominates the Market." *Mygaming.* https://mygaming.co.za/news/features/89913-there-are-1-8-billion-gamers-in-the-world-and-pc-gaming-dominates-the-market.html (accessed May 9, 2018).

Wagner, Rachel. "God in the Game: Cosmopolitanism and Religious Conflict in Videogames." *Journal of the American Academy of Religion* 81, no. 1 (2013): 249–261.

_____. *Godwired: Religion, Ritual, and Virtual Reality.* New York: Routledge, 2011.

Webb, Robert L. "'Apocalyptic': Observations on a Slippery Term." *Journal of Near Eastern Studies* 49, no. 2 (1990): 115–126.

Weber, Eugen. *Apocalypses: Prophecies, Cults and Millennial Beliefs Through the Ages.* Cambridge, MA: Harvard University Press, 1999.

World of Warcraft. Created by Blizzard Entertainment. USA, 2004–.

Muslim Women Cosplayers

*Intersecting Religious, Cultural
and Fan Identities*

JULI L. GITTINGER

Introduction

This essay will explore outward markers of Muslim religious identity (such as *hijab* or modest clothing) that are both performative and transformative.[1] There is quite a bit written about the integration of hijab with Western fashion,[2] and a new slang term, "mipsterz," refers to a Muslim hipster (noted for dressing a specific way), however, the focus of the present study is how Muslim fans, and in particular female Muslim cosplayers who wear the veil, maintain this dedicated symbol of their faith in a costume-play arena. For this research, I provided open-ended questionnaires on an online survey site that kept the participants anonymous (though they provided their location), and I received responses from over 30 cosplayers from around the world. Many of their responses are included in this essay. I will be framing this discussion through Pierre Bourdieu's concept of *habitus* and capital to explore the phenomena of cosplay among "geek" or "nerd" cultures that celebrate fantasy, science fiction, genre fandoms, and comic book heroes. I argue that through the incorporation of the headscarf as part of costume, Muslim cosplayers are simultaneously subverting normative discourses within two groups: Muslim women and cosplayers/fans. By challenging perceptions of "typical" representation/participation, hijabi cosplay has the potential to both "normalize" Muslims in pop culture arenas and highlight a need for diverse representation among characters in popular literature, television, and film.

154

Cosplay in Scholarship

The term "cosplay" is a portmanteau of the words costume and roleplay, referring to the practice of donning a costume to assume the identity of a historical or fictional figure, often from literature, film, or other pop culture sources.[3] Despite the increased popularity of the phenomenon, there is remarkably little written specifically on cosplay as a form of identity-performance, or the sociological, cultural, and psychological functions of such performances. Since scholarship on the phenomenon of cosplay is limited, much of the research may be found in studies of specific fandoms (for example, on *Star Trek* fans or *Doctor Who* fans) that may not include an extensive analysis of cosplay, but address it incidentally as part of a larger conversation about fandom.[4] More detailed ethnographic studies have been done by Nicolle Lamerichs,[5] who looks at the role of the body in enacting character narratives, and by Jin-Shiow Chen who interviewed cosplayers in Taiwan.[6] On the topic of gender-bending and cross-playing, Rachel Hui-Ying Leng and Theresa Winge have explored this phenomena with particular attention to anime and manga fandoms.[7]

Robin Rosenberg and Andrea Letamendi's unique contribution to this scholarship is a psychological study on cosplayers in the United States that surveys nearly one thousand participants and reveals some worthwhile statistics.[8] In their survey, ages ranged from 13 to 74, women outnumbered men almost 3:1 (717 women and 249 men), and most of the cosplayers were white. Rosenberg and Letamendi note an unusual dominance of women in cosplay as one of the few arenas in the geek world that are not typically dominated by men (for example the information technology and gaming industries are male-dominated). They also speculate that the low number of cosplayers-of-color could indicate a lack of black or Latino characters in comics, sci-fi, and so forth, although these marginalized subgroups have spawned social media communities such as "cosplaying while black" and "hijabi cosplayers" on sites like Twitter and tumblr. The lack of diverse representation of cultures and ethnicities in many genres create hurdles for some cosplayers who want to represent characters authentically; on the other hand, creative approaches to work around these obstacles, like gender-bending, cross-playing, and "mashups" are generally lauded with positive appreciation in American cosplay arenas.

Performing Identity in Cultural and Symbolic Fields

Religious modesty is enjoined of both men and women in Muslim tradition, as prescribed in the *Qur'an*. The specificity of exactly what should be covered, however, is fairly vague. Passages that advise covering women's "charms" could refer to any number of areas on a woman's body:

> And tell believing women that they should lower their eyes, guard their private parts, and not display their charms beyond what [it is acceptable] to reveal; they should draw their coverings over their necklines and not reveal their charms except to their husbands, their fathers, their husbands' fathers, their sons, their husbands' sons, their brothers, their brothers' sons, their sisters' sons, their womenfolk, their slaves, such men as attend to them who have no desire, or children who are not yet aware of women's nakedness [*Qur'an* 24:31].

The covering of women's heads or hair was already culturally prevalent at the time of Muhammad, and not only among Jewish and Christian communities; veiling was practiced among pre–Abrahamic traditions like those found in Greece and Assyria. It is thought that the *hijab* (which could mean veil, partition, or curtain) referred in particular to Muhammad's wives, which were not to be spoken to unless they were behind a partition (*Qur'an* 33.53). Varying interpretations of both *hadith* (sayings of the Prophet) and the *Qur'an* have been used to regulate modesty since then.

To address the significance of the retention of visible symbols of religious modesty—while simultaneously signaling membership to a particular fandom or subculture—Pierre Bourdieu will be helpful for framing this discussion. He asserts that everyone has a number of social identities that help to organize our relationships within the social world, whether to individuals or to other social groups. Bourdieu refers to these varying social contexts as "social fields."

> The social field can be described as a multi-dimensional space of positions such that each actual position can be defined in terms of a multi-dimensional system of coordinates whose values correspond to the values of the different pertinent variables. Agents are thus distributed, in the first dimension, according to the overall volume of the capital they possess and, in the second dimension, according to the composition of their capital—in other words, according to the relative weight of the different kinds of capital in the total set of their assets.[9]

"Capital" can exist in the form of material properties, or in the form of power over a field at a given moment. The types of capital Bourdieu delineates are powers that exert the most influence or reward (actual material reward or social status) in any particular sphere—notably economic capital, cultural capital, social capital, and symbolic capital. The power that is held by the agent in each social field defines his or her social position within that field "commonly called prestige, reputation, fame, etc., which is the form assumed by those different kinds of capital when they are perceived and recognized as legitimate."[10] In other words, how a person is viewed in any social field or circle depends on the perceived relationship between the person and others in that field; thus their authority or reputation within that field is contextually constructed. For example, the most recognizable outward religious marker of Muslim women is the hijab, the veil or headscarf which traditionally covers the head and neck area. The social capital of the hijab could signal status, age, piety, difference, or belonging, depending on the contextual arena in which is it worn. In the present political climate of the U.S., it may have negative connotations and facilitate social "othering" where their cultural capital is de-valued. In contrast, in some Muslim countries wearing the hijab could carry great social and economic capital, and imply class status as well as piety.[11]

This is where Bourdieu's concept of *habitus* is also useful. *Habitus* is the "system of dispositions" developed in response to various social contexts. Bourdieu understands *habitus* of the individual as a habitual self-recognition that is dynamic and responsive to varying social fields. For most of my research participants, there are three identities which are in play: Muslim identity (religious/cultural), gender (female in all but one case), and cosplayer/fan. Each of these is contextually responsive and have varying understandings of "normative" behavior, which in turn delineates subversive or confirmative behavior. For example, a Muslim cosplayer in Ohio may socially identify in a way that responds to (i.e., contradicts) the normative understanding of who a cosplayer is—white/American and Christian/secular. In the American heartland, she may experience a feeling as non-belonging, her religious/cultural identity may be seen as novel, and therefore challenge preconceptions of fandom participants. On the other hand, the Muslim cosplayer in Saudi Arabia may have to negotiate her identity as a Muslim, redefining what is modest, "proper," and possibly juxtapose traditional representation against what may be perceived as very Western. Lastly, acceptance and recognition among the fan community as a member of a particular fandom relies upon the ability to represent a character in a recognizable way, even with a wardrobe modification such as adding a headscarf.

Cosplay in many ways subverts *habitus*: instead of producing and regulating social practices, *habitus* is destabilized when the field no longer offers consistent rules of gender, age or propriety. For the Muslim cosplayer who chooses to integrate a symbol of religious identity like the hijab, they are challenging the identity of "Muslim" as a fixed subject. The cultural and social capital as a Muslim in these instances is both challenging the normative, discursive constitution of the subject and allows for phenomenological changes in the social fields.

The American scholarship on Muslim identity—especially the performativity of wearing the hijab—has been well traversed, especially post–9/11 when a woman's choice to wear a headscarf in the U.S. could be seen not only as an assertion of personal and religious identity, but as a political statement. Nick Hopkins and Ronni M. Greenwood in particular have explored the

psychology behind women's willful and visible declarations of religious identity, and how such performances are consequential to their Muslim identity.
As Hopkins and Greenwood argue, wearing the headscarf is one way to
"reflect an attempt to control one's categorisation by others such that it
accorded more closely with one's self-categorisation."[12] Self-categorization
theory (SCT) provides a theoretical framework for understanding the relationship between social identification and behavior. SCT argues that in-group
norms dictate the behavior of group members through cognitive representation of such norms; group members, however, through strategic presentation, may also "display particular attributes so as to challenge outgroup
stereotypes of the in-group."[13] Through analyzing accounts of Muslim women
who choose to wear the hijab, Hopkins and Greenwood are able to explore
how their subjects choose to visibly declare their Muslim-ness and the connection between visible performance and their Muslim identity—whether
conforming to or rebelling against "in-group norms." Wearing the hijab may
be an in-group signifier among Muslim communities, but points to an out-
group/"other" in cosplay communities while simultaneously asserting belonging to a particular fandom (and to fan/geek/nerd culture in general) through
the participation of cosplaying. Again, cosplay effectively subverts *habitus* in
that habitual self-presentations are destabilized when the rules of the social
field (such as gender or propriety) are inconsistent.

I would argue that Muslim cosplay both conforms to in-group norms
of modest dress and outward markers of piety, and challenges the perceived
stereotypes of the in-group by the out-groups. That is to say, the performance
of both conservative religious dress with the "fringe" or playful nature of cosplay exhibits both dynamics of group behavior discussed in Hopkins and
Greenwood's research. Furthermore, while the wearing of the veil may reflect
an Orientalist image of the Muslim woman,[14] the manipulation of the veil in
cosplay most certainly challenges it.[15]

The commitment to wear the hijab is an act of bravery and a declaration
of identity for many young Muslim-American women, especially when challenged with new social or professional arenas that do not easily accommodate
such visible signs. Workplaces that require uniforms, such as the military,
the police force, sports organizations, and other clothing-specific occupations
or institutions have had to provide ways to accommodate religious prescrip-
tions of dress, or the religious practitioner has had to find creative work-
arounds themselves.[16] The latter is certainly the case for the Muslim cosplayer.

Conventions are a place where one can fantasize, to a large extent, and
to make believe or pretend they are in a safe environment where they are free
of judgment for their fandom. Fans are able to move among a community
that celebrates such playfulness or communal make believe. Part of that safe

environment (now enshrined in many conventions' official policies and rules for attendees) is protection from sexual harassment, regardless of what the person is wearing. Largely due to the nature and design of character costumes in videogames, anime, and comics, conventions exhibit a populous number of scantily clad men and women who are authentically representing outfits of their characters. So, in addition to negotiating a religious item like the hijab, one challenge for the Muslim cosplayer is modesty. Some of the cosplayers I interviewed addressed this struggle saying that "sometimes the outfits are harder to translate within the bounds of my dress code" (New York) or "videogame characters are often almost naked, I have a hard time with those" (Denmark). Most, however, said that they managed to adopt just about any character to modest dress, or naturally gravitated towards modest, or even Muslim characters.

The aptly named "Lolita" style is another popular trend among cosplayers in Japan, and is catching on in the U.S. and other countries. The clothing is Victorian or Edwardian influenced, but more infantilized or "cutesie" to reference the fashion worn by popular anime figures, and often comes in candy hues. Short ruffled hoop skirts, over-the-knee stockings, pinafores, parasols, and schoolgirl Mary Jane shoes are typical elements. Muslim cosplayers who wish to try this style wear an aesthetically consonant headcovering (possibly with bows or frills), and negotiate the short skirt by wearing leggings or slim pants underneath. The juxtaposition of religiously prescribed modesty with the baby-doll costuming parallel the tensions between the infantile girlishness and sexualization of Lolita fashion.

Other cosplayers struggle with simple design elements, like hair. "Hermione Granger is someone who I haven't figured out yet," my Moroccan respondent said. "I mean, I can be the 'hijabi Gryffindor student,' sure, but I'd like to be specifically her [Hermione]. Not sure how to do that." Fashioning the headscarf to replicate a hairstyle (like the auburn cascade of Ariel or the trademark buns of Princess Leia) is something well-articulated by many cosplayers. Characters who do not have a specific hallmark look or identifiable hairstyle are more difficult. Wigs were considered to compromise the integrity of hijabi cosplay and not authentically adhering to the modesty of hijab.

Hijabi Cosplayers: Interviews and Responses

Cosplay allows for both religious performativity and a mitigation of cultural stereotypes and perceptions that makes it a fascinating phenomenon to discuss. While actively researching this topic, I saw cosplay by Muslim women in various social media spaces, and therefore utilized platforms such as Facebook, Reddit, and tumblr to post a call for respondents in appropriate forums or with the "hijabi cosplay" tag. The questionnaire was open ended so the respondents could answer in their own words and with as much detail as they liked, but the surveys were anonymous—only a location was requested. During the first wave of research, I received twenty-one responses during a five-week period, coming from a wide range of locations: Malaysia, Qatar, United Arab Emirates, U.S., Saudi Arabia, Netherlands, France, Morocco, United Kingdom, and Denmark. The American respondents were from Texas, California, New Jersey, New York, Virginia, Michigan, and Illinois. I will refer to these subjects by their locations. The second wave came from a call I put out on the Japan Otaku Matsuri Convention page on Facebook, which yielded another dozen or so responses. Since those are largely from Malaysia, with a few from Brunei and Indonesia, I will refer to them by location and number.

I began with a very general question: "Why cosplay?" The consensus was that it was fun to pretend to be someone else and that the clothing or costumes offered an opportunity to dress differently from day-to-day conventions. "Because I can be anything I want. A short escape from reality" (Malaysia7). One of two male respondents replied "Becoming a badass character" as his reason for cosplaying. "Malaysia13: Imagine yourself being a character from your favorite anime/cartoon/game? It's fun! And of course some of cosplayers inspired me to be like them too. It's like you dress up, makeup, and bring the character alive in reality!" For the cosplayers I surveyed, the decision to roleplay a particular character came from a combination of physically favoring the character and the ability to integrate conventions for modesty into the outfit. They did not necessarily gravitate towards hooded or masked characters, however. A Texas cosplayer said her first consideration was, "Can I muslim-ify the look of the character?" A cosplayer from Selangor, Malaysia said, "It does not matter, as long as I like the character, I will try to transform it into a proper costume for wearing hijab." Although most of the cosplayers who responded to the questionnaire relayed that they "hijabify" characters or are able to make adjustments to costume to accommodate modesty, a respondent from the Netherlands seemed frustrated by the lack of options. She gave the example of Nico Yazawa (an anime character from *Love Live!*) as someone she would love to cosplay, but "she isn't wearing a mask and wears skirts" thus was ruled out for this particular cosplayer, who preferred masked characters. More than a few of my respondents noted that wearing a wig (like for an anime character) was "cheating" and it was better to try to interpret the hairstyle into a hijab.

Other respondents emphasized that they had to feel some sort of connection with the character, which may be inspiring, a role model, or an alterego:

CHICAGO, IL: I have to both love the character and find it plausible to either wear as is or to adapt to be appropriate for hijab.

SAUDI ARABIA: I choose characters that I like and [who] have similar physique and skin tone to myself. Accuracy of the cosplay matters a lot to me.

BROOKLYN, NY: In these times, I love characters that represent good in society and what we should strive to become. I also love characters that reflect diversity and different cultures in a positive way, like Ms Marvel.

MALAYSIA13: I like a character that gives a good vibe and inspired us to be a good leader and better person. Ex: Ayame Yomogawa from Kabaneri of The Iron Fortress.

Sometimes the desire to cosplay a particular character could just be as simple as wearing something unique: "Malaysia9: I have always wanted to do armored characters because it looks damn cool!!!" The role of religion in the practice of cosplay is something I obviously found intriguing, hence this study, although this was not shared by all of my respondents. One of the young women from Saudi Arabia noted that cosplay conventions were one place where she should be free from discussing such matters. She argued:

I like to think of cosplay as a social space where I can avoid any mention of my religion to begin with. I want people to see my costume and say "Hey, nice! I recognize that character and love the show/game it comes from!" not "hey, let's talk about the cultural representation and systemic tolerance of your faith blah blah."

The respondent from Denmark had similar thoughts, stating, "I think people should let everyone have fun and just respect the rest of us."

Several of the women from the Malaysian convention (and one of the men) discussed *aurat*, which are the intimate parts of the body to be covered under Islamic law. Genitals are the obvious area to be concealed, but for women *aurat* could also include neck, breasts, thighs, and buttocks. As with the instructions for modest dress in the *Qur'an*, guidelines are open for interpretation as to what ornaments a woman must cover, though head and bosom are most consistently understood to be among them. Again, this may or may not present challenges to the cosplayer:

MALAYSIA3: Hijab cosplay isn't something easy to commit to. I had to go out of my way to find suitable leggings that won't make my legs stick out and it was hard. In my Keith cosplay, I had to buy a bigger sized shirt to cover my behind. I even had to buy pants that are loose but still fit so that I can capture Keith's character correctly. And when it comes to suiting my tudung [hijab] to a character's hair, it's really hard. I have to think of a style where it fits the character's hair and I have to find the right color and whatnot. It's really hard.

Other cosplayers saw their costumes as more conscious acts of representation in the public sphere. Several saw cosplay as a potential for "normalizing" an otherwise exotic or foreign religion through shared fondness for the cultural practice of cosplaying:

HOUSTON, TX: I definitely think Muslim representation is important to the cosplay community in terms of religious tolerance because it normalizes my identity as a Muslim. People have a certain view of what a hijabi is supposed to be like and if they see more hijabis being actual people with personalities and not just as one group, it would lead to less generalizations about hijabis and Muslims in general. In that way, I do think cosplay is important in the way activity is important in showing that Muslims take part in it too. The Muslim representation in any activity shows people that we are just people who have different hobbies, just like them.

SAN JOSE, CA: I think it [cosplay] is incredibly important; Muslim women in particular who want to cosplay don't really have a space to do so, for a couple of reasons. We rarely (or never if we're in hijab) see characters with whom we share a similar appearance, and because so many popular female characters wear close to nothing (which is cool? Just not something I could wear), and there is not an art nor field that has been hampered by being inclusive. Also, I think it kind of breaks that barrier where people who may not know someone Muslims can get to know them. If someone who's never met a Muslim can say "oh, my favorite cosplayer happens to be Muslim," I highly doubt that same individual will turn around and hate on Muslims.

MALAYSIA5: Yes cosplay is important. I feel like it can make people be more open and understanding about our religion. It's not about covering the whole thing (except the eyes) by force.... Overall, no matter what race or religion you are, cosplay is for everyone.

Some of my respondents saw cosplaying as an opportunity for dialogue, inviting non–Muslims to interact with Muslims in a positive way. The playfulness of cosplay subverts many of these preconceptions and provides a potential forum for discussing cultural differences (as the Chicago cosplayer notes, like when curious friends ask why she does not show her arms).

CASABLANCA, MOROCCO: I want other fans to know I am a Muslim woman. I'm from Morocco, and we don't have a big cosplay culture there (that I have found yet) although I talk to Muslims on message boards in Egypt and parts of Europe who share their costumes. London [where I go to school] is pretty diverse, and you see Muslim girls all the time in street clothes, very hip, and it's not that shocking to see one dressing up in a costume I guess. But I would think in America or France where Muslims are less accepted that seeing a Muslim girl dressed up at a fan convention would show that we are just like anyone else. I'd like to hope it would open up a conversation and let them ask questions if they were curious about my faith or my culture.

CHICAGO, IL: I think it is extremely important; upon joining the anime club at my university, close to none of the members thought it was normal for hijabi Muslim girls to be in something like this, nor capable of cosplay. It enlightens people to not only tolerate religions, but be informed on them. For example, many of my [non–Muslim] friends have witnessed my habits as a hijabi, and have asked questions regarding certain cosplays: Why can't you let the arms show? Why is it important this character's tight halter become slightly looser? It's been a great way to be casual about answering questions and learning about each other.

UK: I think it shows that at the end of the day, Muslims can be geeks which is something I think is often overlooked.

MALAYSIA1: It shows that being a Muslim doesn't stop us to do what we want.

Participating in a common hobby, like cosplay, seems to be one way these young women find useful in correcting or illuminating assumptions made by outsiders who rely on Orientalist or racial stereotypes for their understanding. As the Saudi Arabian respondent noted: "The burden of breeding tolerance towards Muslims and improving Islam's public image falls on us Muslims and us alone, by being open minded, integrating well into other societies, and being as tolerant of others as we wish others to be tolerant of us." This is an attitude found widely online, with Muslim women, Muslim Americans, Muslim Brits, and other groups actively blogging, Snapchatting, and arguing online that they are not so different than any other person. Videos such as "Happy American Muslims" or "Happy British Muslims" (both using the tune of Pharrell Williams' "Happy" and available on YouTube) show Muslims dancing and smiling and doing everyday things like eating ice cream, playing baseball, playing with their kids, or being silly for a camera. They are dressed Western, for the most part, but many of the women are also wearing stylish hijab. Most importantly, it can be argued that cosplay is a way to positively assert Muslim identity in empowering ways:

> CHICAGO, IL: Cosplay has been a great way to be wholly myself: a strong Muslim who tries her best to follow her religion's guidelines but knows that those guidelines do not impose on what I love. By cosplaying and ignoring what elders in my community say about the inappropriateness or childish-ness in dressing up, I've come to terms with who I am as well as engaged in lots of respectful dialogue about Islam as well as the mutual pieces of fiction we love.

Global vs. Personal Identities

In the summer of 2016, a British Muslim cosplayer with the Facebook handle of "Hijabi Hooligan" went from a few hundred followers to several thousand once her Captain America hijabi cosplay went viral. Popular websites such as *i09* and *Buzzfeed* have run articles on "our favorite Muslim cosplayers" to showcase the phenomenon.[17] As this essay was being written, the first ever Hijabi cosplay convention in Malaysia, Japan Otaku Matsuri, was underway. Clearly the rising popularity of nerd/geek/fan culture and learning about Muslim culture are intersecting in a way that is testament to globalization.

Globalization (or what many have argued is actually "Westernization") is a valid concern for the discussion of cosplaying—although costume play and masquerading have been practiced around the world in various forms for decades, if not centuries. The earliest sci-fi convention in the U.S. was Worldcon, which took place in 1939 in New York and continues to this day. The popularity of such conventions in the U.S. notably increases in the 1960s with the rise in television and movies that featured outer-space and alien beings. Renaissance fairs and Civil War reenactments (to name just two other arenas of costume and roleplaying) can be traced back even earlier. Renaissance era masquerade balls paralleled the popularity of Commedia dell'Arte, complete with prescribed masks and costumes for each archetypal character. Mardi Gras and Carnivale are costume play spectacles that encourage fantasy and taboo, while also preceding religious holidays of austerity to highlight the duality of sacred/profane, feasting/fasting, etc. Those two holidays in particular are excellent examples where institutional power—the Church, moral propriety, class-specific behavior—is visibly subverted.

The politics of costume play, in this instance, critique categories of "normative" versus "deviant" behavior, categories which are discursively constituted through the relationship between agent/*habitus* and social field. Mardi Gras in the city of New Orleans, for example (which may arguably be devoid of its original symbolic value and more commercial now), plays with ideas of excess and austerity, and with liminality (especially regarding gender). Carnivale as celebrated in Trinidad, on the other hand, grew out of colonialism with slaves who were forbidden to participate in the European pre–Lenten celebrations and created their own (called *Canboulay*). In that instance, costumed performances not only celebrated fantasy and myth, but also highlighted the diversity of immigrant communities as well as asserting creole identities in opposition to the plantation owners.

Thus, costume play is not specifically Japanese, American, or any other nationality. The genres from which characters derive, however, may be argued to be originate from specific regions and thus, concentrated in those areas (anime and manga, in particular). Globalization is working in a more positive way, I would suggest, in that it is highlighting this practice and making a previously marginalized group-within-a-group (i.e., hijabi cosplayers) into a global phenomenon.

There may be consequences, however, of worlds colliding—East and West, modern and traditional, secular and religious—when a Muslim wishes to don a costume and participate in conventions and other cosplaying arenas. A question I had not thought to ask the first wave of respondents, but was added to the questionnaire for the Asian cosplayers, was, "How do other Muslims (family, friends, community) regard your cosplay hobby?"

MALAYSIA3: My family was okay with it. Although it becomes quite a problem as cosplay costumes are expensive and most of my family members feel like it's a complete waste of money. To the eyes of the public, however, might be quite different. Through some experience, some people actually like seeing me cosplay. I once got greeted by some people and they seemed to like me cosplaying even though I'm a Muslim.

MALAYSIA6: For my family, they don't care as long as my studies are ok. My friends, at first they're confused because the costumes were weird (and probably they never saw one especially [since] I wear hijab) but after a while they saw my cosplays, they told me that one day, they also want to go to a cosplay event to see how the even goes.

MALAYSIA7: So far my family and friends are accepting. They also help me a lot. Like sometimes accompany me to event or help me out with my costume. As for the public community, well there are [some] who can't accept us, but hey we can't always please everyone right? As long as my family accepts it, I don't mind.

BRUNEI10: In Brunei, cosplay is not very supported by government, however cosplay community we unite to show our passion in cosplay.

MALAYSIA13: At first, difficulties occur since my parents are quite strict. I'm a person who is willing to hide stuffs from parents because sacred of their "NO" about me being involved in cosplay. But it takes time too for their approval. For now it's between 50/50 support.

Overall, the consensus was that aside from some questioning looks and concerns over expenses, the practice was not regarded as *haram* (forbidden) as long as modesty was being observed. This question needs to be asked outside of the arena of the Malaysian cosplay community, however, where a cosplayer may be more isolated from other hobbyists or where the practice could be seen as a Western import or practice. That will be a consideration in my future research.

Conclusion

Cosplayers, I would argue, are not placed in a scenario to fulfill a diversity quota or appeal to some liberal sense of inclusion; they are wilfully participating in a devotional fandom and, through their own interpretations of the character, consciously altering widely held perceptions of that character, as well as perhaps perceptions of Muslim culture in general. Using Bourdieu, this study has queried what social fields are being negotiated, what cultural capital is being displayed, and how does its interpretation affect the *habitus*. In doing so and assessing the responses of cosplaying hijabis referred to in this essay, we can see that dual identities (female/Muslim, Muslim/American, Muslim/Buffy-Fan, and so forth) compete and overlap in interesting ways. This discussion has identified concerns between presentations of the "normal Muslim" and cosplaying—arguably a "non-normal" practice (in the sense that it has a specific social arena)—being used to subvert in-group/out-group paradigms.

The process of "normalization" is entirely a discursively constructed process that begins with the self-representation of the subject and continues to be shaped by members of the social fields in which they interact. Clearly "normal" is not a stable term, and has no meaning except in relation to what is perceived as its opposite. Discussing "normalization" is problematic in its terminology, but (for lack of better, more nuanced words) is a necessary discussion when addressing how Muslims are perceived on a global scale, and especially through digital media. One only has to use the image-search function on Google for "Islam" or "Muslims" to see an inundation of austere, angry, or violent images. Women in hijab (or the more complete versions, *niqab* and *burqa*) populate our media, often with the understanding that the garment is an emblem of sexism and oppression. Therefore, hijabi cosplayers succeed in both altering normative perceptions of what it means to be a Muslim woman, and challenge normative understandings of who typically cosplays. Perhaps even more interesting, it is the subversive practice of cosplaying—which we can argue to be "nerdy," "weird," or "not-normal"— that is used to "normalize" Muslims in the global social sphere. While cosplay could involve any number of costuming elements which would serve modesty or head covering requirements, the choice to synthesize pop culture characters with a recognizable religious signifier such as the Muslim headscarf illustrates a subversion of popular conceptions of both Islam and of fan culture.

NOTES

1. This field research has also resulted in an article, Juli Gittinger, "Hijabi Cosplay: Performances of Culture, Religion, and Fandom," *Journal of Religion and Popular Culture* 30, no. 2 (2018): 87–105.

2. See Heather Marie Akou, "Building a New 'World Fashion': Islamic Dress in the Twenty-First Century," *Fashion Theory* 11, no. 4 (2007): 403–21; Petra Kuppinger, "Cinderella Wears a Hijab: Neighborhoods, Islam, and the Everyday Production of Multiethnic Urban Cultures in Germany," *Space and Culture* 17, no. 1 (2013): 29–42.

3. The term (*kosupure* in Japanese) is generally understood to be coined by game designer Takahashi Noboyuki in 1980. See Theresa Winge, "Costuming the Imagination: Origins of Anime and Manga Cosplay," *Mechademia* 1 (2006): 65–76.

4. See Camille Bacon-Smith, *Enterprising Women: Television Fandom and the Creation of Popular Myth* (Philadelphia: University of Pennsylvania Press, 1992); Kurt Lancaster, "When Spectators Become Performers: Contemporary Performance—Entertainments Meet the Needs of an 'Unsettled' Audience," *The Journal of Popular Culture* 30, no. 4 (1997): 75–88; Celia Pearce, Tom Boellstorff, and Bonnie A. Nardi, *Communities of Play: Emergent Cultures in Multiplayer Games and Virtual Worlds* (Cambridge, MA: MIT Press, 2011); Tina L. Taylor, *Play Between Worlds: Exploring Online Game Culture* (Cambridge, MA: MIT Press, 2009).

5. Nicolle Lamerichs, "Stranger Than Fiction: Fan Identity in Cosplay," *Transformative Works and Cultures* no. 7 (2011); Nicolle Lamerichs, "The Cultural Dynamic of *doujinshi* and Cosplay: Local Anime Fandom in Japan, USA, and Europe," *Participations: Journal of Audience and Reception Studies* 10, no. 1 (May 2013): 154–176.

6. Jin-Shiow Chen, "A Study of Fan Culture: Adolescent Experiences with Animé/ Manga *doujinshi* and Cosplay in Taiwan," *Visual Arts Research* 33, no. 64 (2007): 14–24.

7. See Rachel Hui Ying Leng, "Gender, Sexuality, and Cosplay: A Case Study of Male-to-Female Crossplay," *Phoenix Papers* 1, no. 1 (April 2013): 89–110. Winge, "Costuming the Imagination," 65–76.

8. Robin S. Rosenberg and Andrea M. Letamendi, "Expressions of Fandom: Findings from a Psychological Survey of Cosplay and Costume Wear," *Intensities: The Journal of Cult Media* 5 (Spring/Summer 2013): 9–18.

9. Pierre Bourdieu, *Language and Symbolic Power* (Cambridge: Polity Press, 1991), 226.

10. Bourdieu, *Language and Symbolic Power*, 226.

11. Norma Claire Moruzzi has noted that, in her research on Iranian women, they often "choose their style of *hijab* as one way of publicly staking their claims to different forms of recognized social capital," Norma Claire Moruzzi, "Trying to Look Different: Hijab as the Self-Presentation of Social Distinctions," *Comparative Studies of South Asia, Africa and the Middle East* 28, no. 2 (2008): 226–227. *Varying cuts and colors of hijab may* distinguish them as fashion leaders or as aiming "for an upward social trajectory with a Western model of consumer culture and sexualized modernity."

12. Nick Hopkins and Ronni Michelle Greenwood, "Hijab, Visibility and the Performance of Identity," *European Journal of Social Psychology* 43, no. 5 (2013): 445.

13. Hopkins and Greenwood, "Hijab, Visibility and the Performance of Identity," 438.

14. Edward Said's theory of Orientalism has been widely used in both scholarship and popular media, central to which he talks about images that exotify/eroticize—women especially. In the West, the stereotypical image of the Muslim woman is a covered one, often reflective of a perception of Islam as oppressive or regressive, while simultaneously eroticizing the hidden. As Haideh Moghissi has argued, the popular clichés of Oriental veiling remained dominant into the twentieth century and continue to 'misrepresent' images as homogenous social reality. See Haideh Moghissi, ed. *Women and Islam: Images and Realities* (London and New York: Taylor and Francis, 2005).

15. While my surveys did not include questions about diaspora identity or other 'dual spheres' that might factor into Hopkins and Greenwood's research (such as nationalism, immigrant identity, and so on), I am considering geek culture/fandom as the competing identity with which Muslim identity must negotiate.

16. A few examples, but in no way an exhaustive list, of organizations that have official policies which now include religion-specific dress code modifications include: U.S. Army, Olympics, FIFA, the police departments of Washington DC and other cities, NBA, and the Pentagon.

17. See Katharine Trendacosta, "This Is Our New Favorite Captain America Cosplay Ever," *Gizmodo*, August 3 (2016), http://io9.gizmodo.com/this-is-our-new-favorite-captain-america-cosplay-ever-1784778834.

BIBLIOGRAPHY

Akou, Heather Marie. "Building a New 'World Fashion': Islamic Dress in the Twenty-First Century." *Fashion Theory* 11, no. 4 (2007): 403–21.

Bacon-Smith, Camille. *Enterprising Women: Television Fandom and the Creation of Popular Myth*. Philadelphia: University of Pennsylvania Press, 1992.

Bourdieu, Pierre. *Language and Symbolic Power*. Cambridge: Polity Press, 1991.

Chen, Jin-Shiow. "A Study of Fan Culture: Adolescent Experiences with Animé/Manga *doujinshi* and Cosplay in Taiwan." *Visual Arts Research* 33, no. 64 (2007): 14–24.

Gittinger, Juli L. "Hijabi Cosplay: Performances of Culture, Religion, and Fandom." *Journal of Religion and Popular Culture* 30, no. 2 (2018): 87–105.

Hopkins, Nick, and Ronni Michelle Greenwood. "Hijab, Visibility and the Performance of Identity." *European Journal of Social Psychology* 43, no. 5 (2013): 438–47.

Kuppinger, Petra. "Cinderella Wears a Hijab: Neighborhoods, Islam, and the Everyday Production of Multiethnic Urban Cultures in Germany." *Space and Culture* 17, no. 1 (2013): 29–42.

Lamerichs, Nicolle. "The Cultural Dynamic of *doujinshi* and Cosplay: Local Anime Fandom in Japan, USA, and Europe." *Participations: Journal of Audience and Reception Studies* 10, no. 1 (May 2013): 154–176.

_____. "Stranger Than Fiction: Fan Identity in Cosplay." *Transformative Works and Cultures* 7 (2011). DOI: http://dx.doi.org/10.3983/twc.2011.0246.

Lancaster, Kurt. "When Spectators Become Performers: Contemporary Performance-Entertainments Meet the Needs of an 'Unsettled' Audience." *The Journal of Popular Culture* 30, no. 4 (1997): 75–88.

Leng, Rachel Hui Ying. "Gender, Sexuality, and Cosplay: A Case Study of Male-to-Female Crossplay." *Phoenix Papers* 1, no. 1 (April 2013): 89–110.

Moghissi, Haideh, ed. *Women and Islam: Images and Realities*. London and New York: Taylor and Francis, 2005.

Moruzzi, Norma Claire. "Trying to Look Different: Hijab as the Self-Presentation of Social Distinctions." *Comparative Studies of South Asia, Africa and the Middle East* 28, no. 2 (2008): 225–234.

Pearce, Celia, Tom Boellstorff, and Bonnie A. Nardi. *Communities of Play: Emergent Cultures in Multiplayer Games and Virtual Worlds*. Cambridge, MA: MIT Press, 2011.

The Qur'an. Translated by M.A.S. Abdel Haleem. Oxford: Oxford University Press, 2010.

Rosenberg, Robin S., and Andrea M. Letamendi. "Expressions of Fandom: Findings from a Psychological Survey of Cosplay and Costume Wear." *Intensities: The Journal of Cult Media* 5 (Spring/Summer 2013): 9–18.

Taylor, Tina L. *Play Between Worlds: Exploring Online Game Culture*. Cambridge, MA: MIT Press, 2009.

Trendacosta, Katharine. "This Is Our New Favorite Captain America Cosplay Ever." *Gizmodo*, August 3 (2016). http://io9.gizmodo.com/this-is-our-new-favorite-captain-america-cosplay-ever-1784778834 (accessed March 15, 2018).

Wilson, G.W. *Ms. Marvel Vol. 1: No Normal*. Marvel Entertainment, 2014.

Winge, Theresa. "Costuming the Imagination: Origins of Anime and Manga Cosplay." *Mechademia* 1 (2006): 65–76.

Magical Matrimony

Romance and Enchantment
in Harry Potter–*Themed Weddings*

Venetia Laura Delano Robertson

Introduction

In June of 2017 many of its readers celebrated twenty years since *Harry Potter* first graced the shelves of their local bookstores. Like Harry himself would be, a considerable number, perhaps even the majority, of the present fans of J.K. Rowling's much-loved series are today well into adulthood. With maturity does not necessarily come a disdain for the favored texts of childhood and adolescence, nor those aimed at a younger audience. There are numerous flourishing adult fandoms based on products pitched to the juvenile or young adult demographic,[1] but the *Harry Potter* fandom is arguably the most visible and celebrated example.

C. Harrington and Denise Bielby have posited a pertinent approach to fan studies in the "life course perspective" which investigates the relationship of fandom to significant stages in identity development as fans age. "Popular media," they argue, "are, of course, thoroughly implicated in life course processes and transitions … texts and technologies help unite cohorts, define generations and cross-generational differences, and give structure and meaning to our lives as they unfold."[2] The present study seeks to explore this point of connection by looking at the use of themes from *Harry Potter* (1997–)[3] in weddings by fans of this beloved transmedial text. Through the analysis of academic work on *Harry Potter* fandom and interviews with six couples— Elizabeth and Paul, Jamie and Ian, Emily and Chris, Christabel and Alex, Ashley and Nicholas, and Tori and Scott—who had, or plan to have, *Harry Potter* themes incorporated into their weddings, this essay demonstrates how the profound relationship fans have with this franchise encourages them to enchant their own stories with references to Rowling's fantastic narrative.[4]

In recent years, myriad examples of *Harry Potter* fandom manifesting in the adult market have emerged, such as bars featuring alcoholic beverages like the "Gin Weasley" served at The Lockhart Cocktail Lounge,[5] Hogwarts-inspired escape rooms,[6] and the *Harry Potter* student societies, annual film screenings, and "muggle Quidditch" teams hosted on many a university campus. In addition, the media has been replete with stories of couples drawing on *Harry Potter* to infuse their wedding ceremonies and celebrations with the traditions, ethics, stories, characters, and charm of the Potterverse. Such fandom-themed weddings may be driven by the significant role a text has played in the romantic connection between the matrimonial parties, however, as this essay demonstrates, texts like *Harry Potter* also serve as an important source for enchantment; a sense of wonder with the world. The "romance" of *Harry Potter* is thus multilayered, offering fans both coming-of-age narratives through which they can read their own experiences of adolescence, making friends, and falling in love, and an aesthetically rich and symbol-laden realm from which they can draw inspiration when creating their own "fantasy": their wedding day.

A seminal factor in such examples of mediated enchantment is the rising secularization that has diluted the levels of religion previously found in notable life events like weddings. Weddings are becoming noticeably "de-traditionalized" in the Western world[7]: many countries no longer require religious authorities to solemnize the proceedings, the eligibility of parties has been extended to include homosexual couples and individuals of non-binary gender, and the wedding industry is supporting the culturally, and subculturally, diverse ways in which people wish to express their personalities, philosophies, and understanding of love and commitment. For those for whom fandom is central to their identity as both individuals and couples utilizing their favorite texts in the design of their wedding enables them to personalize the event and engage in creating their own traditions. In turn, the sacralization of the text through its inclusion in this milestone occasion maintains the devotional, joyful, and meaning-laden experiences we might attribute to religion for secular fans.

The Franchise and the Fandom

In a book on fandom, the *Harry Potter* franchise likely needs no introduction, however some of its facets and its dedicated fanbase need iteration here. The books are both cross-genre—John Granger, author of *Looking for God in Harry Potter* (2004) and the so-called "Dean of *Harry Potter* Studies" describes Rowling's writing as "a gathering together of schoolboy stories, hero's journey epics, alchemical drama, manners-and-morals fiction, satire, gothic romance, detective mysteries, adventure tales, coming-of-age novels, and Christian fantasy"[8]—and cross-generational, appealing to audiences young and old, and across and over time. The immensely successful films that followed, as well as the novels and film adaptations that branched-off the *Harry Potter* heptad (like *Fantastic Beasts and Where to Find Them*),[9] multi-platform games, Wizarding World theme parks, and Rowling's official *Harry Potter* fansite *Pottermore*, among other products and experiences, have sustained fan interest in the Potterverse for many years, and may do so for many more.

The films grew in maturity—as did its characters, child stars, and adolescent audience—and developed from whimsical teenage tales with pantomime-like over-performances from its veteran actors (Michael Gambon's volatile Albus Dumbledore; Emma Thompson's ditsy Professor Trelawney, Helena Bonham Carter's demented Bellatrix Lestrange) and underwhelming contributions by the awkwardly pubescent debut leads (Daniel Radcliffe as Harry Potter, Emma Watson as Hermione Granger, and Rupert Grint as Ron Weasley) to the solemn tone of the apocalyptic two-part final wherein the leading cast truly find their stride. Importantly, with the fairly consistent annual release of the films (between 2001 and 2011 only 2006 and 2008 did not see an installment), many viewers, as readers had in the years prior, progressed through school alongside Harry, Ron, and Hermione (born circa 1980). The books, famously attributed to boosts in youth literacy rates, have made appearances in many primary and secondary school curricula as prescribed readings, as well as featuring in the syllabi of a number of tertiary institutions including Georgetown, Yale, the University of Western Ontario, and Durham University.

With consistency the academy has investigated the nuances of Rowling's great success and the dedicated fandom her work has generated. Catherine Tosenberger, among others, has observed that Potterheads, as they are known, are especially avid contributors to their fan cultures: "readers who participate in the Potter fandom do not simply passively absorb the texts but actively respond to them."[10] One reason for such deep engagement with the text that has sparked discussion among scholars recently is the religious overtures of the Potterverse. Rowling's immersive fantasy world and its abundant mythology, Signe Cohen notes, involves the "blurring of religious, cultural, and historical elements that appeals to contemporary readers' postmodern sensibilities."[11] Furthermore, as Laura Feldt asserts, it has remarkable re/enchanting qualities: "*Harry Potter* has powerfully re-introduced magic and prevalent ideas from contemporary magical milieus, along with other religious fragments and a teleological, purposeful world, into the mainstream of the Western collective imaginary."[12] This essay argues that it is not just the explicitly magical but the themes of love and commitment that have generated a sense of enchantment with the novels, especially among consumers who have aged alongside the main characters.

Love in the Potterverse

Love is a central theme in the *Harry Potter* stories and in the reasoning for fan adoration of this text.[13] For Lev Grossman "the overwhelming importance of continuing to love in the face of death" is "Rowling's abiding thematic concern."[14] One of the last lines uttered by Dumbledore in the final book— "Do not pity the dead, Harry. Pity the living, and, above all, those who live without love"—cements Grossman's claim, but the closing scene—set in the future where the main characters Harry, Ron, and Hermione have all paired up successfully (Ron and Hermione marry and Harry marries Ron's sister Ginny) and are sending their children off to Hogwarts—insinuates that the strongest and therefore most magical form of love is that of the heteronormative family unit. In a critical reading of *Harry Potter* implications of the most plot-pivotal expressions of love can be revealed to be just as problematic as positive. As a fairly traditional hero tale, there are tropes in the novels that rely upon conformity to conservative gender roles and identities.[15] Female characters are typically maidens (Ginny, Hermione), mothers (Lily Potter, Molly Weasley), or crones (either wise like Professor McGonagall, or sinister like Dolores Umbridge), and act consistently as helpmeets or foils for the leading male characters. Women are most valuable as mothers, and moreso if they are also martyrs.

A mother's love, it is reiterated, is a near-invulnerable force of protection which Harry Potter's mother Lily imparts on him by sacrificing herself to save the life of her infant son. Dumbledore explains to Harry that, even as a defenseless baby, this ultimately selfless act enabled him to deflect Voldemort's devastating "Killing Curse":

> If there is one thing Voldemort cannot understand, it's love. He didn't realize that love as powerful as your mother's for you leaves its own mark. Not a scar, no visible sign ... to have been loved so deeply, even though the person who loved us is gone, will give us some protection forever.[16]

Thus, a lack of maternal devotion is as potent in effect as its opposite: Voldemort, born Tom Riddle, is revealed to have been orphaned by a mother who could not bring herself to stay alive, even for her baby boy—a stark contrast with Lily Potter's noble act of motherly martyrdom—and leaves him bereft of not only affection but of the intimate and sacred knowledge of love.[17]

While the supreme example of a mother's love is embodied in Lily Potter's death, an event which, though it only appears in the novels as recollections, is the catalyst for Harry's hero's journey, it is not the sole cause for his success. It is Professor Snape, the childhood friend and unrequited lover of Lily but sometime-nemesis of Harry, who in fact continuously and secretly rescues the titular figure during his perilous school years. This plot-twist is revealed memorably in a scene where Dumbledore realizes that Snape's "power animal" or patronus is a doe just as Lily's had been:

> "But this is touching, Severus," said Dumbledore seriously. "Have you grown to care for the boy, after all?"
> "For him?" shouted Snape. "Expecto Patronum!"
> From the tip of his wand burst the silver doe. She landed on the office floor, bounded once across the office, and soared out of the window. Dumbledore watched her fly away, and as her silvery glow faded he turned back to Snape, and his eyes were full of tears.
> "After all this time?"
> "Always," said Snape.[18]

The question, "after all this time?" and answer, "always," have become inextricably embedded in the lexicon of the Harry Potter fandom where Snape is typically treated as a redeemed, if not heroic figure. The phrase gained additional importance upon the death of Alan Rickman, who portrayed Snape in the films, but has been utilized as a symbol in the design of tattoos, jewelry, and t-shirts as a reference to one's dedication to the *Harry Potter* story, and in weddings to refer to the devotion of the couple to both the story and to one another. However, as Maria Nikolajeva aptly notes, Snape's protection of Harry is also driven by the guilt he feels for informing Voldemort of the Potters' location and therefore contributing to Lily's murder, making an already tragic figure a little more wretched:

> Ironically, the safeguard Harry has always been told was provided by his mother's love turns out to be the safeguard of her rejected devotee.... Thus the seven-volume epic can be viewed as a distressing story of a pathetic man who longs for the son he has never had.[19]

Romantic love is an ongoing motif in the stories, unsurprising since it is set for the most part at a high school. Rowling herself explained in an online post in 2005 that the *Harry Potter* books are "very character driven" and "it is important, therefore, that we see these characters fall in love, which is a necessary part of life."[20] While they are exclusively heterosexual Granger insists that "the Potter epic is not the boy-meets-girl, boy-loses-girl, lovers-unite romance formula."[21] Love triangles, obviously that of Snape-Lily-James Potter, and less explicitly that between the "Golden Trio" Harry-Hermione-Ron, give depth and complexity to the relationships that blossom in adolescence but keep truly happy endings from happening. Some characters are destined to be alone once heartbroken, including the avuncular yet mysterious headmaster Dumbledore, who is, Rowling revealed in an interview after the conclusion of the series, a celibate homosexual.[22] The chaste, straight, and somewhat unsatisfying love lives of Rowling's characters have been rewritten in the fanfiction, which demonstrates a keen interest in queer and non-canonical couplings.

Fanciful and creative extensions of Rowling's plotlines by fans have real-world motivations and consequences, as Catherine Tosenberger has argued: "in an era when representations of adolescent sexuality are both exploited and policed, Potter fandom is an arena in which fans of all ages, genders, and sexual orientations can tell stories to satisfy their own desires."[23] For example, the most popular tryst in "shipping" (relationship) or "slash" (homosexual relationship) fanfiction is that between in-world enemies Draco and Harry, and their stories are regularly erotic as well as romantic.[24] Sometimes fan desires are to see certain sexualities reflected in the literature, othertimes it is to see the emotional bonds they find most convincing—a "one true pairing," such as Harry and Hermione instead of the canonical Hermione and Ron—come to fruition.[25] In other examples, fanfiction serves to reinterpret Rowling's romantic narratives through the lens of contemporary mores and social politics. An interesting example of this evolving extra-textual contribution by fans comes in the tweets made by girlziplocked under the "Modern-Day Harry Potter" or #mdhp hashtag between 2014 and 2016, which posit alternate futures of Hogwarts alumni with a wry, feminist bent.[26] These detail, in short, pithy bursts, the passionless domesticity of Harry and Ginny—

> "And how's Harry?" "Oh, you know, still using SKYRIM to avoid engaging in our marriage," Ginny spat;

Hermione's liberating single life after she divorces an alcoholic and unambitious Ron—

> Hermione's phone vibrates. A text reads, "I miss u." She walks to the window and rearranges the stars to read: "I AM FREE NOW, RON."

scattered with humorous reflections on the dismal dating scene in both the wizard and muggle worlds—

> Hermione removes her headphones to acknowledge the man tapping her shoulder. "Hi," he says, grinning. His ass hair is set ablaze.

and the heartwarming contrast of the partnership of the quirky secondary characters/fan favorites, Neville Longbottom and Luna Lovegood—

> "Nev," Luna whispered, "I have no idea where I'm going." "It doesn't matter," Neville whispered back, "I follow you, regardless."
> "Luna," Neville spoke to the ceiling, "we travel hand-in-hand. That's what marriage is—the constant renegotiation of travel plans."

In this version of events, Luna and Neville, who, girlziplocked's Hermione notes, are the only two of their cohort to have graduated Hogwarts without post-traumatic stress disorder, are also the only ones to enjoy marital success.[27]

Despite some evident dissatisfaction with the romantic canon of the *Harry Potter* among fans, leading to the production of romantic or erotic fanon, expressive commentary like girlziplocked's, or repetitive debates over the virtues of "Dramione" (the portmanteau used by Draco/Hermione shippers) versus "Harmione" (Harry/Hermione), other fans clearly feel the storyline exemplifies the magic of true love. For example, Elizabeth, planning a *Harry Potter*/Marvel themed wedding to her fiancé Paul, commemorates her long-standing connection to *Harry Potter* with a tattoo on her forearm bearing the word "Always"—a reference to Professor Snape's fateful admission of his eternal love for Lily Potter mentioned above. This tattoo, and part of the motivation for involving this text in her wedding, is because it "encapsulates what *Harry Potter* is based on: the feeling of love and friendships."[28]

Couples who have drawn on *Harry Potter* in the themes, rituals, and aesthetics or their weddings have been increasingly visible in the past decade, and are featured, usually with image galleries and short interviews, on sites focused on the news,[29] the mainstream wedding industry,[30] the alternative wedding industry,[31] *Harry Potter* fandom,[32] and fandoms generally.[33] There are innumerable creative ways to infuse *Harry Potter* into an event, as a brief search of image-curating sites like Pinterest will attest. From subtle nods to the books in personal vows, to lavish decorations and props used in the reception space to make visual references to scenes from the films, the hundreds of photos, products, and tutorials available online indicate alone that adult fans find joy in incorporating *Harry Potter* themes into significant life events. The evident public interest and attenuating media coverage of *Harry Potter*–themed weddings is, in itself, worthy of note for scholars of popular culture and spirituality, however these sources provide little information on the interlinks of fiction, religion, and enchantment in the lives and relationships of the couple in question. Hence, I sought out married and engaged Potterheads to gain insight into the affiliation between their love of Rowling's work and their "big day."

Magical Matrimony: Harry Potter Weddings

To learn more about the impetus behind involving *Harry Potter* themes in such life events I created an online survey, and followed up willing respondents with semi-structured interviews. An invitation to participate was advertized on Facebook groups, forums, and a Reddit page for *Harry Potter* fans. Reddit, a popular user-determined content aggregator site that has different groups called subreddits, such as r/harrypotter (also called "The Great Hall"),[34] was the most productive avenue for finding fans who had posted about their weddings or wedding plans, and who were prepared to share their ideas with an inquisitive academic. r/harrypotter (which has 408,302 members) is a popular space to discuss a multitude of *Harry Potter*–related things, including questions about plot inconsistencies, advice for Hogwarts-based craft projects, deliberations over the mechanics of magical spells, the morality and motivations of characters, and alternate endings to Rowling's storylines. r/harrypotter is organized into topics and moderated to encourage discussion with image sharing limited to certain days or occasions.

Prior to circulating the survey requests, my preliminary experience of *Harry Potter* fandom, academic understanding of such fandoms broadly, and exposure to wedding industry websites (as a woman in her early 30s and an authorized civil celebrant I both fit the target market for such sites and, conveniently, find them personally and professionally interesting) had led me to anticipate trends in the responses from people who have had *Harry Potter* weddings such as:

(1) they had grown up reading *Harry Potter*;
(2) were fans of other fantasy/sci-fi media and participated in fandoms;
(3) would be atheists or non-religious, but find moral messages and enchantment in *Harry Potter*;
(4) the *Harry Potter* franchise had, in some way, brought them together, and contained inspiring messages about love.

I designed my questions to gain information on the above, and found my assumptions generally correlated with the resulting data. The six couples I received responses from were heterosexual, from the United Kingdom or United States, and had an age range of 24–34 years old, with many of the participants first encountering the *Harry Potter* stories at school, either primary or secondary. One fiancé had only seen the movies, and another was a fan of other media, but not explicitly *Harry Potter*—that is, all six brides but only four of the grooms were fans of the series.

While participation in *Harry Potter* fandom was an important part of the relationships of some couples like Tori and Scott who attend events like LeakyCon and ComicCon to meet actors from the films, other fandoms were also present, for example, Jamie and Ian told me "we plan on getting Wall-E/ Eve tattoos soon and we incorporate a lot of fiction, etc. in our day to day lives, phone case, etc." Emily and Christopher themed their wedding after several of their favorite novels, television series, films, and videogames including *Star Wars, Alice in Wonderland, The Illiad,* and *The Legend of Zelda,* as well as *Harry Potter.* These texts were referenced in the soundtrack to the ceremony and reception, their centerpieces that adorned their tables, and their wedding favors, designed to look like miniature books. Making their fan lives a central part of their wedding day was a way of acknowledging this shared and important part of their relationship:

> Our favorite stories influence many of the ways we interact. We have spent a fair amount of time watching speculative fiction shows together.... He says part of it is having a shared lexicon, knowing references helps communication, and is just part of getting to know each other and taking an interest in each other's fandoms.

As well as having their favorite literature play a central part in their wedding décor, Emily and Christopher added "We also dressed up as characters for our engagement photos [from] *Firefly* (Zoe/Wash), *Star Wars* (Leia/Han), and *Doctor Who* (River/11th Doctor)." Elizabeth and Paul will be including both the *Harry Potter* and the Marvel franchise in their wedding, the first to represent her interests, and the second for his. All the participants who answered the question regarding religion described themselves as being non-religious or atheists, with the exception of one who discussed maintaining their identity as a Christian following a struggle with the conservative back-lash against Rowling's books from people in her church circle. The following section will focus on what I found to be the most interesting aspect of this research, the impact of *Harry Potter* on the identity formation of both indi-viduals and couples and the inspiration they took for their wedding day from the text's motifs of love and magic.

We start with Elizabeth, whose fiancé Paul is not as enamored with *Harry Potter* as she but acknowledges it is "such a big part" of her life. She further explains: "I just feel a close connection to the franchise. It was my childhood all the way into my teenage years and hasn't left me during my adulthood." Like Elizabeth, many of the survey participants noted growing up with *Harry Potter* (or HP) as relevant to their ongoing engagement with the text well into adulthood. Emily explains that, for her, aging alongside Harry and his friends was a valuable experience:

> I am of the perfect generation that roughly grew up perfectly to match the age of Harry in each book as they came out—it meant that the series grew up with me. The early books were perfectly escapist and full of magic delights, while the later ones appealed to my older desire for more meaningful speculation.

Tori and Scott both read the books when they were juveniles, and even then Tori identified strongly as a fan:

> HP was a huge part of my life growing up. I have never been more excited than I was on the release days of the books.... I spent every day of my life on theleakycauldron. org and mugglenet.com growing up speculating.

Christabel and Alex, who met playing Quidditch at University, were also introduced to the books when they were young and found reading them a formative period: "Harry Potter means a lot to us because we grew up with it.... It's been important to our lives as we are both dyslexic and it was the first book that we could read with interest and helped us to enjoy reading." In their wedding, pages from the books were folded into paper flowers and inserted into the floral arrangements, the house colors of Hogwarts were used in their bunting, a cake was made in the shape of the school by the groom's family, and a tiny snitch decorated one of the bride's nails. Simply put, Christabel and Alex said, "we used it as a theme to symbolize how our relationship started and a common interest that brought us together."

For Jamie and Ian, *Harry Potter* has played a seminal role in their lives as individuals and in the development of their relationship. Again, aging in tandem with the main characters allowed for a strong connection to the series to form:

> We both grew up with *Harry Potter* and experienced his growth as we grew. In a lot of ways, he helped us cope with various things. For example, when he got angsty in the *Order of the Phoenix*, I [Jamie] was in an angsty place. He realized his friends were there for him though and came around to the truth eventually. This helped me to do the same.... The memories that we created making friends and discovering ourselves through the HP community helped to shape us as adults.

Harry Potter is truly embedded in the love story of Jamie and Ian: "Ian and I shared a love of HP and shared our first kiss watching the HP Musical on YouTube. Ian first decided he was going to marry me when we went to HP World in Orlando. Bringing this story full-circle, Ian adds: "When we got married, we talked a lot about how we wanted to make this a memory that we could carry forward in our lives, and we recognized how much of our formative years were influenced by the *Harry Potter* story. In her assessment of fans using *Doctor Who* themes in their weddings, Jessica Johnston observes corresponding findings, stating, "fans are able to blend the various memories they have of fandom into a meaningful performance narrative that extends beyond fandom and into other corners that make up their lives."[35] That, as adults, these couples decided to include *Harry Potter* themes in their wedding day is not only due to their sustained adoration of the text however, but because of the meaningful messages they regard as inherent in the text. In planning for their upcoming wedding, Ashley and Nicholas have used pages from the novels to create paper-flower boutonnieres. Having the books as part of their décor is a reminder of what they love about the narrative: "The whole story is essentially about how love & friendship is the main factor in the characters survival. Nothing to do with skill set, nothing to do with your background, or how much money you had. Simply being a good person." Correspondingly, Elizabeth says it is "the magic and relationships" in *Harry Potter* that so to her. Jamie elaborates on finding inspiration in the narrative's depiction of love: "*Harry Potter* is not a story of love between two people but rather the love between many people. It is a story of creating your own family of friends and loved ones and surrounding yourself with those people and allowing them to strengthen you. Her husband Ian makes the connection between romance and enchantment via the text even more explicit in his explanation:

> I think that overall the aspect of the *Harry Potter* stories that drew us to include it in our wedding is the idea that magic is real and love is the greatest magic of all. Obviously we recognize that you can't make things levitate, or that spells aren't actually real, but we have each had moments in our lives that made us think that there was an unseen power that was making things work out for the best, and in that sense, the world is full of magic.

Jamie and Ian's wedding invitation was designed to look like the bewitched Marauder's Map, during the ceremony the bride, groom, and celebrant made frequent reference to the text, included quotes from the books and Rowling in their speeches, and incorporated the notion of the "unbreakable vow" from *The Half-Blood Prince* into their wedding vows.[36] Finally, their toast was made using their version of "felix felicis," a good luck potion.

    That *Harry Potter* provides imaginative fodder for the constructing of unique and personalized wedding decorations, rituals, and vows is especially notable when religion is no longer a binding or authoritative source for understanding and articulating messages about love, marriage, and the sacred. Tori and Scott had mild concerns about using *Harry Potter* so prodigiously in their wedding, with some of the older guests unfamiliar with the text. Nonetheless, elements were sprinkled throughout the styling, with their tables named after school houses and locations from the books, songs from the film's soundtrack featuring on their playlist, and "Bertie Bott's Every Flavor Beans" as favors for their guests. Theming was important as a way to express their fan identities and to demonstrate the profundity of their fandom:

> Another part of incorporating it into our wedding was because both of us are atheist and weren't willing to have any religious themes in our wedding, so it felt like we needed something to tie it together. It also represents to our family and friends that we are unique and like to do things our own way.

Similarly, Jamie and Ian note:

> Neither one of us is particularly religious, so when we wanted to find a shared belief that we could center our ceremony on, our love for the story of *Harry Potter* was a clear choice.... There's something truly beautiful about *Harry Potter* and we wanted to share that with our friends and family.

Emily and Christopher were the only couple I spoke to with religious beliefs, but even in their Christian ceremony the importance of *Harry Potter* was highlighted. This is reflected in Emily's description of the proceedings:

we did have some Christian stuff in the wedding in the form of a Bible reading by my grandmother, the service conducted with religious themes by Chris's friend who is a children's hospital chaplain, and a prayer before dinner by Chris's mom ([a] HP fan!) who is a Episcopal Reverend.

In her fandom, Emily has found cause to contrast her religious faith with the enchanting experiences that can be derived from deep engagement with cherished texts: "I personally believe in taking a lot of lessons about empathy from stories like HP … religion can be just as inspirational, but also has that dark side that books less often fall prey to. It makes me more trusting of stories, and less of religion." Feldt has commented that "the heterogeneity and equivocality of the representation of religion and magic" in *Harry Potter* appeals to readers "who may enjoy the fascination of religious representations freed of any dogmatic or institutional binds."[37] This presumption seems to have been played out by several of the people I spoke to and others who have had *Harry Potter*–themed weddings, for example, Meredith and Joshua whose ceremony was officiated by a celebrant dressed as Snape,[38] and Christine and Andy who had their guests perform a "spell" over them with customized wands they gave as favors.[39] In civil ceremonies, but also in religious ones, we see a renegotiation of where and how sources of enchantment can be found and represented in the utilization of popular culture products as wedding themes.

Fandom-themed weddings are not unique to Potterheads—and Johnston's work on weddings of *Doctor Who* fans[40] provides an interesting comparative study—but the rich aesthetic and narrative offerings of the Potterverse do appear to have leant themselves especially to the decorative, performative, and ritual design elements of Western wedding planning. In an industry that promotes a fairly homogenous vision of what a wedding entails, couples must be innovative if they want to carve out a space for an authentic expression of their personalities. As Bird summarizes (noting also the gendered nature of the wedding and wedding-planning), the internet offers the modern bride "a smorgasbord of options, most saturated with the imagery of movies, television, celebrity discourse, and advertising" from which she must devise "an event that expresses her uniqueness, yet is staged in a way that will be recognized and appreciated by her guests."[41] However, as Cele Otnes and Elizabeth Pleck have argued, the wedding, "a temporary dreamworld," has become "one of the few recently democratized portals to re-enchantment in life"[42] and so we are seeing innovation and imagination in wedding styling and theming that display what enchantment, love, and fandom mean to different people.

There are a variety of motivators behind the trend in using popular culture products in wedding ceremonies and receptions aside from the reason of the connubial couple feeling greatly attached and represented by certain texts. For example, in the multi-billion dollar wedding industry, where anything from underwear to forks can be marked up in price for the "big day,"[43] many couples seek cheaper ways to achieve their desired look. The current trend in DIY or "do it yourself" aesthetics encourages participants to make their own decorations or purchase those that have been hand-made, often repurposing materials, as a budget and environmentally-friendly gesture. Additionally, couples who identify as "offbeat," a label affiliated with "alternative" lifestyles, may not find resonance with classic bridal color schemes, traditions, and ideologies and will likely also require custom-made materials to embody their values and tastes. These cultural currents dovetail with the "maker" community many fandoms support and the vested interest in creating fan-products that enable consumers to show their allegiance to their text of choice.

In essence, what these things have in common is they respond to the need for visible and practical options for people who wish to participate in typical social rituals, whether its getting married or wearing a t-shirt sporting your favorite brand's logo to indicate your support, but whose cultural interests are not represented in the mainstream market for goods and services. Thus, articles like "45+ ways to make your *Harry Potter* weddings MAGIC" featured on the website *Offbeat Bride* seek to respond to all of these requirements by providing couples with inspiration and practical advice for how they can employ the texts they adore in their non-traditional, yet nonetheless meaningful and enchanted, ceremonies.

Conclusion

This essay holds with the contention shared by the other essays in this volume, that popular culture functions in a multitude of meaningful ways in the lives of its consumers, and that its affordances in the development of personal and communal identity, worldviews and beliefs, and enchantment with life fulfill a role once traditionally performed by religion. Trends in the data from my study of the six heterosexual couples that had, or were planning to have, *Harry Potter* themes included in their wedding day explored here include that they often grew up reading the novels and watching the movies, bonded over the franchise (and/or fandom surrounding other fantasy and science fiction texts), and found that *Harry Potter* represented, in some profound way, their matrimonial commitment. That the majority of the subjects whose experiences I draw on in this paper self-identified as being atheists or non-religious—one participant identified as Christian—has interesting implications for the findings of my research and the study of religion and fandom generally, however as a preliminary foray into the area this discussion has focused on how the motifs of "magic," "love," and "friendship" from Harry

Potter have resonated with fans and moved them to theme their weddings around this text.

With the modern world becoming increasingly secular such uses of popular culture can some to replace or compliment traditional religious and spiritual elements that have historically been integral to life events such as weddings. Theming a wedding after a favorite text is a playful approach to injecting a personality trait that stands outside the norm—in this case highlighting one's status as a fan and attenuating devotion to a fantasy world—into an event that is still regularly treated as solemn, formal, and sacred. As Tori succinctly stated, "I also like to do things a little out of the ordinary, so having a themed wedding was right up our alley." Significantly, media-themed weddings open the notion of sacrality up for re-examination, as such convergences indicate, as Feldt argues, "how pertinent deeper considerations of various types of literature as media are in the general study of religions today,"[44] and in turn how pertinent reconsiderations of previously religious rituals, commitments, and texts are in light of the meaningful place of fandom in the philosophies, motivations, and manifestations of life events today.

NOTES

1. See for example, Venetia Laura Delano Robertson, "Of Ponies and Men: *My Little Pony: Friendship Is Magic* and the Brony Fandom," *International Journal of Cultural Studies* 17, no. 1 (2014): 21–37.

2. C. Lee Harrington and Denise Bielby, "A Life Course Perspective on Fandom," *International Journal of Cultural Studies* 13 (2010): 431.

3. "*Harry Potter*" will be used herein to refer not just to Rowling's seven-part series (1997–2007) but also to the films (2001–2011) and franchise generally.

4. Quotations from interviewees have been adjusted for spelling errors and punctuation.

5. For example, see Canada's Lockhart bars, named after the dilettante-ish character Gilderoy Lockhart from J.K. Rowling, *Harry Potter and the Chamber of Secrets* (London: Bloomsbury, 1998).

6. Bradley Johnston, "A 'Harry Potter'–Inspired Escape Room Has Opened In Melbourne," *AWOL*, March 21 2018, https://awol.junkee.com/harry-potter-escape-room-melbourne/59465.

7. See, for example: Dusty Hoesly, "Your Wedding, Your Way: Personalized, Nonreligious Weddings Through the Universal Life Church," in *Organized Secularism in the United States: New Directions in Research*, eds. Ryan T. Cragun, Lori L. Fazzino, and Christel Manning (DeGruyter: Leck, 2017), 253–287.

8. John Granger, *Harry Potters Bookshelf: The Great Books Behind the Hogwarts Adventures* (New York: Berkley Books, 2009), e-book.

9. J.K. Rowling, *Fantastic Beasts and Where to Find Them* (London: Bloomsbury: 2001); *Fantastic Beasts and Where to Find Them*, dir. David Yates (Warner Bros. Films, UK/U.S., 2016).

10. Catherine Tosenberger, "'Oh my God, the Fanfiction!': Dumbledore's Outing and the Online *Harry Potter* Fandom," *Children's Literature Association Quarterly* 33, no. 2 (Summer 2008): 200.

11. Signe Cohen, "A Postmodern Wizard: The Religious Bricolage of the *Harry Potter* Series," *Journal of Religion and Popular Culture* 28, no. 1 (Spring 2016): 55.

12. Laura Feldt, "*Harry Potter* and Contemporary Magic: Fantasy Literature, Popular

Culture, and the Representation of Religion," *Journal of Contemporary Religion* 31, no. 1 (2016): 109–110.

13. For an assessment of how younger readers have responded to these themes see Ranjana Das, "'To Be Number One in Someone's Eyes...': Children's Introspections About Close Relationships in Reading *Harry Potter*," *European Journal of Communication* 28, no. 4 (2013): 454–469. See also Carole Cusack's chapter in this volume.

14. Lev Grossman, "Harry Potter's Last Adventure," *TIME*, July 21, 2007, http://content. time.com/time/world/article/0,8599,1645771,00.html.

15. Tison Pugh and David L. Wallace, "Heteronormative Heroism and Queering the School Story in J.K. Rowling's *Harry Potter* Series," *Children's Literature Association Quarterly* 31, no. 3 (Fall 2006): 263.

16. J.K. Rowling, *Harry Potter and the Sorcerer's Stone* (New York: Bloomsbury, 1998), 299.

17. J.K. Rowling, *Harry Potter and the Half-Blood Prince* (New York: Scholastic, 2005), 262, 275. See Elizabeth E. Heilman and Trevor Donaldson, "From Sexist to (sort-of) Feminist: Representations of Gender in the Harry Potter Series," in *Critical Perspectives on* Harry Potter, ed. Elizabeth E. Heilman (New York: Routledge, 2009), 152–3 for more on mothers in the Potterverse.

18. J.K. Rowling, *Harry Potter and the Deathly Hallows* (New York: Scholastic, 2007), 687.

19. Maria Nikolajeva, "Harry Potter and the Secrets of Children's Literature," in *Critical Perspectives on Harry Potter*, ed. Elizabeth E. Heilman (New York: Routledge, 2009), 240.

20. Granger, *Harry Potters Bookshelf*, n.p.

21. Granger, *Harry Potters Bookshelf*, n.p.

22. EdwardTLC, "J.K. Rowling at Carnegie Hall Reveals Dumbledore Is Gay; Neville Marries Hannah Abbott, and Much More," *The Leaky Cauldron*, October 20, 2007, http://www.the-leaky-cauldron.org/2007/10/20/j-k-rowling-at-carnegie-hall-reveals-dumbledore-is-gay-neville-marries-hannah-abbott-and-scores-more/.

23. Catherine Tosenberger, "Homosexuality at the Online Hogwarts: Harry Potter Slash Fanfiction," *Children's Literature* 36 (2008), 203.

24. Darlene Hampton, "Bound Princes and Monogamy Warnings: *Harry Potter*, Slash, and Queer Performance in LiveJournal Communities," *Transformative Works and Cultures* 18 (2015), n.p.; Tosenberger, "Homosexuality at the Online Hogwarts," 192.

25. Tosenberger, "Homosexuality at the Online Hogwarts," 191.

26. Girlziplocked, "Modern Day Harry Potter," *Medium*, November 3, 2014, https://medium.com/@hollywood/modern-day-harry-potter-e7e3c02fb9a4;
"Modern Day Harry Potter: Part II," *Medium*, August 8, 2016, https://medium.com/@girlziplocked/modern-day-harry-potter-part-ii-e7b521178017.

27. According to Rowling, there is good reason to expect Ron and Hermione of having an unsuccessful marriage. See: Andrew Sims, "J.K. Rowling and Emma Watson discuss Ron, Hermione, and Harry: The full interview," *Hypable*, February 7, 2014, https://www.hypable.com/jk-rowling-ron-hermione-interview/. While in the film version of *Deathly Hallows* Part II a relationship between Luna and Neville is implied, elsewhere Rowling has been adamant that the two would not make a good couple: J.K. Rowling, "Luna and Neville will hook up in HP&THBP," *J.K. Rowling Official Site*, http://web.archive.org/web/20110623030508/http://www.jkrowling.com/textonly/en/rumours_view.cfm?id=24.

28. As is popular among Harry Potter fans, the "A" in "Always" is made up of the "Deathly Hallows" symbol, ⚠, an image that has come to act totemically for Potterheads who wear it conspicuously to signal their devotion to their text. "One simply uses the symbol to reveal oneself to other believers" explains Xenophilius Lovegood in Rowling's *The Deathly Hallows*, 405. For more on bonding over Deathly Hallows tattoos, see: Margaret Kaminski, "Why I got the same Harry Potter tattoo as hundreds of strangers," *Hello Giggles*, September 2, 2016, https://hellogiggles.com/lifestyle/harry-potter-tattoo-fandom/.

29. Kelsey Borresen, "This DIY 'Harry Potter' Wedding Will Leave You Positively Spellbound," *The Huffington Post*, April 30, 2015 (last updated July 12, 2017), https://www.huffingtonpost.com.au/entry/best-diy-harry-potter-wedding_n_7164320.

30. Kaitlin Jones, "Harry Potter–Themed Wedding Brings Hogwarts to Life: See the Owl Ring Bearer!" *The Knot*, April 12, 2016, http://www.theknotnews.com/harry-potter-wedding-owl-ring-bearer-8416.

31. "Harry Potter" tag, *Offbeat Bride*, https://offbeatbride.com/tag/harry-potter/.

32. "Potter Weddings," *Mugglenet*, http://www.mugglenet.com/fans-fun/potter-weddings/.

33. Alanna Bennett, "People Have Harry Potter–Themed Weddings, and Here Are the Highlights," *The Mary Sue*, July 25, 2011, https://www.themarysue.com/harry-potter-weddings/.

34. r/harrypotter, www.reddit.com/r/harrypotter/.

35. Jessica Johnston, "*Doctor Who*–themed Weddings and the Performance of Fandom," *Transformative Works & Cultures* 18 (2015), n.p.

36. J.K. Rowling, *Harry Potter and the Half-Blood Prince* (New York: Scholastic, 2005).

37. Laura Feldt, "Harry Potter and Contemporary Magic: Fantasy Literature, Popular Culture, and the Representation of Religion," *Journal of Contemporary Religion* 31, no. 1 (2016): 110.

38. Keith Hawk, "Congratulations to Joshua and Meredith on their "Potter"-themed wedding celebration," Mugglenet.com, May 20, 2014, http://www.mugglenet.com/2014/05/congratulations-to-meredith-and-joshua-on-their-potter-themed-wedding-celebration/.

39. "Harry Potter Theme Wedding: Christine & Andy," *Bridal Guide*, n.d., https://www.bridalguide.com/photos/get-inspired/real-weddings/harry-potter-wedding-christine-andy.

40. Johnston, "*Doctor Who*–themed Weddings."

41. S. Elizabeth Bird, "From Fan Practice to Mediated Moments: The Value of Practice Theory in the Understanding of Media Audiences," in *Theorising Media and Practice*, eds. Birgit Bräuchler and John Postill (New York: Berghan, 2010), 93.

42. Cele Otnes and Elizabeth Pleck, *Cinderella Dreams: The Allure of the Lavish Wedding* (Berkeley and Los Angeles: University of California Press, 2003), 15.

43. One study shows vendors can charge up to 28 percent more for a good or service for a wedding rather than a different kind of event. See Kristin Wong, "Wedding Markup Is Real, So Don't Be Afraid to Call It Out and Haggle," *Life Hacker*, April 28, 2016, https://lifehacker.com/wedding-markup-is-real-so-dont-be-afraid-to-call-it-ou-1773506685?IR=T.

44. Feldt, "Harry Potter and Contemporary Magic," 110.

Bibliography

Bennett, Alanna. "People Have Harry Potter–Themed Weddings, and Here Are the Highlights." *The Mary Sue*, July 25, 2011. https://www.themarysue.com/harry-potter-weddings/ (accessed May 9, 2018).

Bird, S. Elizabeth. "From Fan Practice to Mediated Moments: The Value of Practice Theory in the Understanding of Media Audiences." In *Theorising Media and Practice*, edited by Birgit Bräuchler and John Postill, 85–104. New York: Berghan, 2010.

Borresen, Kelsey. "This DIY *Harry Potter* Wedding Will Leave You Positively Spellbound." *The Huffington Post*, April 30, 2015 (last updated July 12, 2017). https://www.huffingtonpost.com.au/entry/best-diy-harry-potter-wedding_n_7164320 (accessed May 9, 2018).

Das, Ranjana. "'To be number one in someone's eyes...': Children's introspections about close relationships in reading Harry Potter." *European Journal of Communication* 28, no. 4 (2013): 454–469.

EdwardTLC. "J.K. Rowling at Carnegie Hall Reveals Dumbledore Is Gay; Neville Marries Hannah Abbott, and Much More." *The Leaky Cauldron*, October 20, 2007. http://www.the-leaky-cauldron.org/2007/10/20/j-k-rowling-at-carnegie-hall-reveals-dumbledore-is-gay-neville-marries-hannah-abbott-and-scores-more/(accessed May 9, 2018).

Feldt, Laura. "Harry Potter and Contemporary Magic: Fantasy Literature, Popular Culture, and the Representation of Religion." *Journal of Contemporary Religion* 31, no. 1 (2016): 101–114.

Girlziplocked. "Modern Day Harry Potter." *Medium*, November 3, 2014, https://medium. com/@hollywood/modern-day-harry-potter-e7e3c02fb9a4 (accessed May 9, 2018).

Girlziplocked. "Modern Day Harry Potter: Part II." *Medium*, August 8, 2016, https://medium. com/@girlziplocked/modern-day-harry-potter-part-ii-e7b521178017 (accessed May 9, 2018).

Granger, John. *Harry Potters Bookshelf: The Great Books Behind the Hogwarts Adventures.* Berkley Books: New York, 2009. E-book.

Grossman, Lev. "Harry Potter's Last Adventure." *TIME*, July 21, 2007. http://content.time. com/time/world/article/0,8599,1645771,00.html (accessed May 9, 2018).

Hampton, Darlene. "Bound Princes and Monogamy Warnings: *Harry Potter*, Slash, and Queer Performance in LiveJournal Communities." *Transformative Works and Cultures* 18 (2015). DOI: 10.3983/twc.2015.0609.

Harrington, C. Lee, and Denise D. Bielby. "A Life Course Perspective on Fandom." *International Journal of Cultural Studies* 13 (2010): 429–450.

"Harry Potter Theme Wedding: Christine & Andy." *Bridal Guide*, n.d. https://www.bridal guide.com/photos/get-inspired/real-weddings/harry-potter-wedding-christine-andy (accessed May 9, 2018).

Hawk, Keith. "Congratulations to Joshua and Meredith on Their 'Potter'-Themed Wedding Celebration." Mugglenet.com, May 20, 2014 http://www.mugglenet.com/2014/05/ congratulations-to-meredith-and-joshua-on-their-potter-themed-wedding-celebration/ (accessed May 9, 2018).

Heilman, Elizabeth E., and Trevor Donaldson. "From Sexist to (sort-of) Feminist: Representations of Gender in the Harry Potter Series." In *Critical Perspectives on Harry Potter*, edited by Elizabeth E. Heilman, 139–162. New York: Routledge, 2009.

Hoesly, Dusty. "Your Wedding, Your Way: Personalized, Nonreligious Weddings Through the Universal Life Church." In *Organized Secularism in the United States: New Directions in Research*, edited by Ryan T. Cragun, Lori L. Fazzino, and Christel Manning, 253–287. DeGruyter: Leck, 2017.

Johnston, Bradley. "A 'Harry Potter'–Inspired Escape Room Has Opened in Melbourne." *AWOL*, March 21 2018. https://awol.junkee.com/harry-potter-escape-room-melbourne/ 59465 (accessed May 9, 2018).

Johnston, Jessica. "*Doctor Who*–Themed Weddings and the Performance of Fandom." *Transformative Works & Cultures* 18 (2015). DOI: 10.3983/twc.2015.0637.

Jones, Kaitlin. "Harry Potter–Themed Wedding Brings Hogwarts to Life: See the Owl Ring Bearer!" *The Knot*, April 12, 2016. http://www.theknotnews.com/harry-potter-wedding-owl-ring-bearer-8416 (accessed May 9, 2018).

Kaminski, Margaret. "Why I got the same Harry Potter tattoo as hundreds of strangers." *Hello Giggles*, September 2, 2016. https://hellogiggles.com/lifestyle/harry-potter-tattoo-fan dom/ (accessed May 9, 2018).

Nikolajeva, Maria. "Harry Potter and the Secrets of Children's Literature." In *Critical Perspectives on Harry Potter*, edited by Elizabeth E. Heilman, 225–242. New York: Routledge, 2009.

Otnes, Cele and Elizabeth Pleck. *Cinderella Dreams: The Allure of the Lavish Wedding.* Berkeley and Los Angeles: University of California Press, 2003.

Otter Bickerdike, J. *The Secular Religion of Fandom.* London: Sage, 2016.

"Potter Weddings." *Mugglenet.* http://www.mugglenet.com/fans-fun/potter-weddings/ (accessed May 9, 2018).

Pugh, Tison, and David L. Wallace. "Heteronormative Heroism and Queering the School Story in J.K. Rowling's Harry Potter Series." *Children's Literature Association Quarterly* 31, no. 3 (Fall 2006): 260–281.

r/harrypotter. www.reddit.com/r/harrypotter/ (accessed May 9, 2018).

Robertson, Venetia Laura Delano. "Of Ponies and Men: *My Little Pony: Friendship Is Magic* and the Brony Fandom." *International Journal of Cultural Studies* 17, no. 1 (2014): 21–37.

Rowling, J.K. *Harry Potter and the Sorcerer's Stone.* New York: Bloomsbury, 1998.

_____. *Harry Potter and the Chamber of Secrets.* London: Bloomsbury, 1998.

_____. *Harry Potter and the Half-Blood Prince*. New York: Scholastic, 2005.

_____. *Harry Potter and the Deathly Hallows*. New York: Scholastic, 2007.

_____. "Luna and Neville will hook up in HP & THBP." *J.K. Rowling Official Site*. http://web. archive.org/web/20110623030508/http://www.jkrowling.com/textonly/en/rumours_ view.cfm?id=24 (accessed May 9, 2018).

Sims, Andrew. "J.K. Rowling and Emma Watson Discuss Ron, Hermione, and Harry: The Full Interview." *Hypable*, February 7, 2014, https://www.hypable.com/jk-rowling-ron-hermione-interview/(accessed May 9, 2018).

"tag: harry potter." *Offbeat Bride*. 2008–2018. https://offbeatbride.com/tag/harry-potter/ (accessed May 9, 2018).

Tosenberger, Catherine. "Homosexuality at the Online Hogwarts: Harry Potter Slash Fanfiction." *Children's Literature* 36 (2008): 185–207.

_____. "'Oh My God, the Fanfiction!': Dumbledore's Outing and the Online *Harry Potter* Fandom." *Children's Literature Association Quarterly* 33, no. 2 (Summer 2008): 200–206.

Wong, Kristin. "Wedding Markup Is Real, So Don't Be Afraid to Call It Out and Haggle." *Life Hacker*, April 28, 2016. https://lifehacker.com/wedding-markup-is-real-so-dont-be-afraid-to-call-it-ou-1773506685?IR=T (accessed May 9, 2018).

Afterword

Fantastic Fan Conventions and Transformational Festivals

John W. Morehead

Introduction

At first glance, a science fiction and fantasy convention may seem unrelated to Burning Man, a transformational festival that creates a temporary experimental art community. Yet these events have much in common. In this essay, I draw upon festival studies to explore two phenomena that fantastic fan conventions and transformational festivals share: the crafting of a shared mythos, and engagement with ritual, which when united constitute a quest for the sacred.[1] James Combs has argued that as Christianity retreated and popular culture became a major contributor to individual identity in the contemporary West, formal religious rituals were supplanted by "a plurality of celebrations, popular groupings around various things, old and new, familiar and bizarre, sanctioned and condemned, the sacred profaned and the profane made sacred."[2]

Fandom gatherings and transformational festivals are two forms of contemporary celebration that emerged in the mid-twentieth century and gained momentum as fringe subcultures gradually mainstreamed from the 1980s onwards, in the context of neoliberal consumer culture.[3] This culture encourages individualist and consumerist strategies in the crafting of personal and group identity. This essay discusses myth and ritual at Burning Man and in the *Star Trek* fandom, and the fan practice of cosplay (costume play), as manifestations of the quest for, and creation of, spaces of freedom in which experiences of non-ordinary reality can occur. In these spaces, festival participants and fans alike are modern pilgrims departing profane existence to encounter the sacred and subsequently return to everyday life transformed.

Transformational Festivals

Transformational festivals and fantastic fan conventions take place within a cultural context of contemporary festivals, carnivals, and fairs as the latest manifestation of gatherings that are "important forms of social and cultural participation, used to articulate and communicate shared values, ideologies and mythologies central to the world-view of relatively localized communities."[4] Throughout history, such events have functioned to bring members of a community together to in order to define, reinforce, and promote specific bonds, be they religious, social, ethnic or based on some other common denominator. These traditional functions of festival persist, but contemporary individuals come together to express concerns such as shared culture, lifestyle, and identity, affirming their elective affinities. This is often linked to playful engagement with alternative possibilities. Festivals provide temporary utopian ("no place") spaces in which participants can experiment, rehearse, discover and recover identity through performance and celebration of the shared passions that briefly unite them.[5]

Transformational festivals and fantastic fan conventions can be understood as expression of "weekend societies." In his analysis of electronic dance music festivals, Graham St John defines weekend societies as "event-centred cultures that provide their memberships with identification and recognition independent from traditional sources (e.g., ethnicity, faith, class)" that are also "diverse in their organization, intention and populations."[6] However, the term "weekend societies" may raise fan hackles, given the conflict that has existed since the 1950s between those who proclaim "Fandom Is A Way of Life" (FIAWOL) and those for whom "Fandom Is Just A Goddam Hobby" (FIJAGH).[7] This essay links fan conventions to transformational festivals, a term popularized by Jeet-Kei Leung in a 2010 TEDx Talk in Vancouver.[8] Leung considered the term useful, while acknowledging the difficulty in specifying anything "that could guarantee a festival to be transformational.... There's no doubt that many participants *are* having life-altering experiences at festivals and an increasingly coherent culture is emerging that fosters and supports these experiences."[9]

Thus, there is no agreed checklist of elements that constitute an "authentic" transformational festival, and several distinct subcultures are involved in devising and maintaining these temporary communities. However, scholars have provided helpful models and genealogies; St John argues that transformational festivals are based on "countercultural event models" that coalesce in the gnostic and shamanic streams of the New Age milieu, involving

healing arts and the human potential movement; egalitarianism, civic engagement and direct democracy; the back to the land movement, sustainability practices and permaculture; the visionary arts movement and entheogens; embracing and appropriation of indigeneity (ritual and symbolism).[10]

Additionally, transformational festivals generally have several features in common. These include an outdoor location (although this is not always the case), music and dance, workshops, visionary art, costuming, "an ethos of community building ... and creative expressionism,"[11] and a festival space and experience where participants view themselves as co-creators rather than passive recipients.

Transformational festivals are a global phenomenon, with the West Coast of North America having a special environment that is conducive to such gatherings. Jason Winslade writes, "the science fiction convention is a direct influence on the indoor [Pagan] festival"[12]; Pantheacon, an indoor Pagan festival held in California's Bay Area is structured on the science fiction convention model. San Francisco, California is also the birthplace of one of the best known transformational festivals, Burning Man, which is held annually in the Black Rock Desert of neighboring Nevada state. Other examples include: the Symbiosis Gathering in Oakdale, California; Lightning in a Bottle in Bradley, California; Beloved in Tidewater, Oregon; Envision in Rancho la Merced, Costa Rica; and Shambhala Gathering in Salmo, British Columbia, Canada.[13] These festivals are a part of a long history of carnival, and for Leung, represent the "rejoining of the sacred ritual and the secular festival."[14] It is therefore appropriate to consider fantastic fan conventions and transformational festivals as "weekend societies" (connecting them, unintentionally, to FIJAGH) but also as pilgrimages, in which pilgrims journey to a sacred center, returning to profane, everyday life transformed by the experience.[15]

Mythos, Ritual and the Sacred

Leung has explored the phenomenon of transformational festivals further in a four-part webseries called *The Bloom: A Journey Through Transformational Festivals*.[16] *The Bloom* is comprised of video segments of transformational festival participants and key spokespersons taken from events around the world. Through the series, the viewer witness the experiences of participants, and gain insights from spokespersons as to the significance of particular elements. "Episode 3: New Ways of the Sacred,"[17] is focused on mythos and ritual in connection with the sacred. Leung is both host and narrator, and "New Ways of the Sacred" opens with a discussion of the simultaneous rise of rationality and consumerism, which has left many contemporary Westerners feeling spiritually empty. This process of disenchantment was initially articulated by sociologist Max Weber in the early twentieth century. For Weber, the disenchantment of the world (*die Entzauberung der Welt*) was a process in which religion declined and science became the master narrative of the West, resulting in the modern world becoming less magical.

In "New Ways of the Sacred," Jason Pitzl-Waters, former editor of the Pagan blog *The Wild Hunt* and Program Director of Faerieworlds festival in Oregon, notes that,

> people stopped believing in God and where rationalism and secularism sort of became the dominant narrative. So, what happens in this void where organized religion used to dominate everything? What's happened is that now is that we are going through a process of re-enchantment, where into this void people have started to create their own sense of the sacred, and of myth, and legend to fill their lives with these things that used to be dictated to them.[18]

For humans as *homo narrans*, storytelling people,[19] this overemphasis on the rational and scientific led to the collapse of the mythic narratives that had provided an understanding of humanity and its relation to the world. Re-enchantment develops in response, and new myths and rituals emerge to re-enchant the world against the "iron cage" of secularism.

Various scholars have theorized the process of re-enchantment. Adam Possamai argues that "there is a collective move away from the over-rationalisation of everyday life to re-enchanted forms.... Westerners are facing the return of spiritual/magical thinking ... which produces a sense of the mysterious, the weird and the uncanny."[20] Possamai draws on David Tacey's model of "reconnection with nature" and Michel Maffesoli's idea of neo-tribalism, in which "the identification with our fellow humans practiced in the culture of festivities where people play with multiple identities" that re-enchants.[21] Tacey's and Maffesoli's ideas combine in transformational festivals, whereas in indoor fantastic fan conventions Maffesoli's concept of neo-tribalism is most relevant.

Fantastic fan conventions and transformational festivals tap into both mythos and ritual, and in the context of latter, an individualized, consumer approach is applied to various religions and spiritualities, resulting in an eclectic synthesis as personal myths are constructed. These subjective myths are then lived out by participants and expressed in variety of ways, from music to art to dance to costuming.[22] Fantastic fan conventions also draw upon mythos, but in different ways. For participants in festivals, sacred mythos is subjectively created out of a collection of spiritualities and fused together. By contrast, fans at science fiction and fantasy conventions draw upon various pre-existing stories from their favorite literature, films, television programs, comics, animation, and anime. This can be creative, with fans producing fiction and art, to name but two products, that complement or supplement the "canon."

Star Trek *Fandom and the Sacred*

Robert Ellwood has argued that from the 1960s onward "new mythologies from the fabrics of science fiction and fantasy" emerged.[23] David Hartwell concurs, asserting

SF is a uniquely modern incarnation of an ancient tradition: the tale of wonder. Tales of miracles, tales of great powers and consequences beyond the experience of people in your neighborhood, tales of the gods who inhabit other worlds and sometimes descend to visit ours, tales of humans traveling to the abode of the gods, tales of the uncanny: all exist now as science fiction. Science fiction's appeal lies it its combination of the rational, the believable, with the miraculous. It is an appeal to the sense of wonder.[24]

As science fiction can be understood to function as a myth, it also has a connection to the religious. Fandoms are a site for the development of new forms of the sacred. *Star Trek* fandom was the first such phenomenon to be analyzed using a religious or spiritual lens by anthropologist Michael Jindra. Jindra argued that *Star Trek* pointed to an idealized other world, the plot narratives functioned as mythology, the ethical message was strong, the fandom was a "church-like" community, and attendance at conventions was a form of pilgrimage.[25] William Shatner, the actor who played Captain James T. Kirk in *Star Trek* and was thus a key figure at the center of the *Star Trek* mythos, wondered why fans had such devotion to the franchise: he produced a book and a documentary film exploring this question.[26] In the documentary Shatner interviews Robert Walter, President of the Joseph Campbell Foundation, associated with the noted mythologist and author of *The Hero with a Thousand Faces* (1949). Walter's analysis of fan devotion is that *Star Trek* functions as a powerful mythology from which people craft their own personal narratives, and through a dynamic participatory process, live out the mythos in various ways, from the hope of a united humanity, to its drawing upon its ethical framework, to performative and ritual aspects.[27]

Star Trek's stories capture the imagination, and fans shift from passive viewers of television and film to active participants who go out and embody the mythos. The fandom is multi-faceted; there are those who cosplay as Starfleet officers and others who have created a functional language in Klingon, which they speak while meeting costumed as Klingons, the enemy race that became an ally in *The Next Generation*.[28] *Get a Life!* is bookended with the moving story of David Sparks, known as "Captain Dave," who first appeared in Shatner's earlier film, *The Captains* (2011). Captain Dave was severely incapacitated by Duchenne Muscular Dystrophy yet attended *Star Trek* conventions with the help of his mother and a nurse. *Star Trek* provided him with a meaningful mythos and community in which to live his brief life of forty years.[29] So, while transformational festivals and fantastic fan conventions may seem light years apart, both draw upon mythos as an important facet of individual and community life.

Cosplay as Fan Ritual

In the context of transformational festivals, it is claimed that ceremony or ritual provides meaning and purpose and may be understood as mythology embodied and enacted. Transformational festivals include a variety of ritual performance, individual and collective, such as dance, stage shows, music, the construction of altars and temples, and costuming. Costuming is a major part of transformational festivals, as clothing is an important way of presenting oneself as an individual and in making a statement about being part of a community. At festivals like Burning Man nudity is common, and while it may seem strange to consider this a form of costuming, since it is outside the mainstream forms of public presentation of the self, it can be understood in this context.[30] Yet other forms of costuming more common, and there is great diversity in the forms these take. Participants at Faerieworlds, for example, which describes itself as the "largest mythic, fantasy and faerie themed event in the US,"[31] may put on fairy wings or wear an animal mask. In all such festivals, the primary dynamic relates to play and crafting self-identity.

Sarah Pike has written extensively on festivals, particularly Burning Man and various Pagan events, and she addresses how costuming involves a form of "serious play" and experimentation with concepts of the self:

> [i]n the limited time and space of festivals, participants replace mundania's ideals of beauty with a reality characterized by dress up, personal creativity, body art, and erotic dancing. By bringing out their hidden identities and marketing their bodies with the signs of festival culture, Neopagans express identities that contrast sharply to the outside world.[32]

Humans are *homo narrans*, storytelling creatures, but it has also been suggested by theologian Harvey Cox that we are also *homo festivus* or *homo fantasia*, humanity at play, and "essentially festive and ritual creatures."[33] Through this process of "serious play," festival goers experiment with new senses of identity. This involves a utilization of the festival space and costuming as an opportunity to tap into the childhood self and play with this in the creation of a new identity, even if only temporarily.

Costuming is also important at fantastic fan conventions. Fans publicly declare their loyalty to a particular fandom by wearing t-shirts, and serious fans engage in the far more dramatic and time-consuming phenomenon of cosplay. While the type of costuming is different at fan convention from that at transformational festivals, the function of costuming is similar. First, costuming at fantastic fan conventions is related to mythos.

In her analyis of science fiction culture, Camille Bacon-Smith considered clothing in relation to the geographical space of the convention. She argues that costuming provides for "boundary maintenance, enculturation, and rituals of solidarity and identity."[34] This involves the "dress code" of fan conventions and its importance for concepts of inclusion. She says that, "Costume marks the territory of the convention as more clearly "other" than science fiction fashion..."[35] Costume is both actual and symbolic, with fans performing as characters from their beloved films, television series or comics, making the convention a performative event.

Much of this discussion of costuming and ritual at fantastic fan conventions applies to transformational festivals. It is less clear that costuming at conventions can be understood to have a connection to the sacred; but that can be argued with reference to cosplay. This type of costume play began at the first World Science Fiction convention in 1939, where Forrest J Ackerman, who claimed to have invented the term sci-fi, attended the event dressed in a "futuristicostume" based on the science fiction film *Things to Come* (1936). Ackerman attended with his girlfriend, fellow cosplayer Myrtle R. Jones, who designed the costumes that both she and Ackerman wore.[36] The term "cosplay" was coined in 1983 by Nobuyuki Takahashi,[37] and it has now become a major facet of fantastic fan conventions, and even a fan industry with its own celebrities. It is associated with a range of fantastic fandom characters and stories, but its connection to Japanese anime and manga was what led to it becoming a pop culture phenomenon.

Katharine Buljan identifies cosplay as a type of "religio-spiritual devotional practice" for some fans.[38] Buljan provides examples of fans dressing as various anime characters in a process of personal transformation, often with a sense of becoming "a supernatural being or a human character with supernatural abilities."[39] abilities. Following Eliade, Buljan argues that from this a form of cosplay ritual is active that involves "the re-enactment of myth(s) in the sense of episodes from anime featuring supernatural plotlines and characters with superhuman powers."[40] While acknowledging that there are differences in the degree to which individual cosplayers are committed to such mythic enactment, Buljan argues that the costuming ritual provides the ability to transcend the profane and to cross over into the supernatural "through the vehicle of myth."[41] Research into anime and manga cosplay thus demonstrates that, in some circumstances for some fans and convention attendees, cosplay can be understood as an expression of a quest for the sacred.

That cosplay is meaningful and moving for those who participate in it is the theme of Adam Savage's TED Talk, "My Love Letter to Cosplay."[42] Savage, a celebrity due to his part in the Mythbusters television series, shares how he was a lonely child who often played alone and created his own toys and costumes, including a space helmet, complete with a spaceship console.

Eventually he attended San Diego's Comic-Con to participate in cosplay dressed as Hellboy after crafting his outfit of prosthetics and contact lenses. In spite of the discomfort of the suit, Savage found the experience exhilarating. He also describes cosplaying the character No-Face from the Hayao Miyazaki's *Spirited Away* (2001) at Comic-Con:

> This isn't a performer-audience relationship. This is cosplay. We are all of us on that floor injecting ourselves into a narrative that meant something to us, and we are making it our own. We are connecting with something important inside of us and the costumes are how we reveal ourselves to each other.

For Savage, the process of cosplay is deeply meaningful, an embodiment of mythic narratives that allows participants to look into themselves through the process of playing with other identities. In so doing we also connect with others.

Conclusion

I have been a fan of science fiction, fantasy, and horror, the genres of the fantastic, for most of my life, having caught the "bug" in elementary school, somewhere between kindergarten and third grade. I still remember the evening when my father gave my younger brother and me the opportunity to choose between watching our more standard family entertainment or a scary movie on television. We eagerly, if gingerly, chose the latter, which happened to be *The Creature from the Black Lagoon* (1954). My reaction was a mixture of shock and awe, fear and fascination. I haven't been the same since. That began a regular diet of consumption of the fantastic through film and television. I have also participated in fan cultures, from attendance and speaking at Salt Lake Comic Con, to interactions with other fans online on blogs and other forums.

This book is a part of my journey as a fan and scholar of the fantastic. For several decades, scholars have been exploring various facets of popular culture and fandom, including science fiction, fantasy, and horror. This volume seeks to add to that body of scholarship in ways that are informed by good academic study, but in a manner that is accessible to fans with no academic background. The desire is to find a middle ground so that in this book both scholars and fans can find something of value that they can learn from. I would like to thank the contributors to this volume, and McFarland & Company for their continued support and partnership in exploring various facets of the fantastic, popular culture, and religion. I hope this volume adds value to the ongoing scholarly discussion of fandom and religion, and that fans of the fantastic might gain new insights into the depths of meaning that comes through enjoying what they love.

NOTES

1. I would like to acknowledge a blog post by Jason Pitzl-Waters that sparked this line of research for me. See Jason Pitzl-Waters, "Transformational Festival Culture," *The Wild Hunt: Modern Pagan News & Commentary*, 2 October, 2011, http://wildhunt.org/2011/10/trans formational-festival-culture.html.

2. James Combs, "Celebrations: Rituals of Popular Veneration," *Journal of Popular Culture* 22, no. 4 (1989): 71–72.

3. Thomas Frank, *The Conquest of Cool: Business Culture, Counter Culture, and the Rise of Hip Consumerism* (Chicago and London: University of Chicago Press, 1997), 233–235.

4. Andy Bennett, Jodie Taylor and Ian Woodward, "Introduction," in Andy Bennett, Jodie Taylor and Ian Woodward (eds.), *The Festivalization of Culture* (London and New York: Routledge, 2016), 1.

5. Jennifer E. Porter, "To Boldly Go: *Star Trek* Convention as Pilgrimage," in Jennifer E. Porter and Darcee L. McLaren (eds.), Star Trek *and Sacred Ground: Explorations of* Star Trek, *Religion and American Culture* (Albany: State University of New York Press, 1999), 252–256.

6. Graham St John, "Introduction to Weekend Societies: EDM Festivals and Event-Cultures," *dancecult: Journal of Electronic Dance Music Culture* 7, no. 1 (2015): 3. While research on "weekend societies" has not to date included fan conventions, a case can be made that such conventions meet St John's definition as event-cultures.

7. Jeff Prucher (ed.), *Brave New Words: The Oxford Dictionary of Science Fiction* (New York: Oxford University Press, 2007), 63.

8. Jeet-Kei Leung, "Transformational Festivals and the New Evolutionary Culture," *TEDxVancouver,* 2010, https://youtu.be/Q8tDpQp6m0A.

9. Kitt Doucette, "7 Wildest Transformational Festivals," *Rolling Stone*, May 11, 2016, http://www.rollingstone.com/culture/lists/7-wildest-transformational-festivals-20160511.

10. St John, "Introduction to Weekend Societies," 7.

11. Andrew Johner, "Transformational Festivals: A New Religious Movement?," in *Exploring Psychedelic Trance and Electronic Music in Modern Culture*, ed. Emilia Simão (Hershey, PA: IGI Global, 2015), 59.

12. J. Lawton Winslade, "Alchemical Rhythms: Fire Circle Culture and The Pagan Festival," in *Handbook of Contemporary Paganism*, ed. James R. Lewis and Murphy Pizza (Leiden and Boston: Brill, 2009), 249.

13. Doucette, "7 Wildest Transformational Festivals."

14. Leung, "Transformational Festivals and the New Evolutionary Culture."

15. Victor Turner, "The Centre Out There: Pilgrim's Goal," *History of Religions* 12, no. 3 (1972): 191–230.

16. Jeet-Kei Leung and Akira Chang, *The Bloom Series* (Elevate Films, Keyframe Entertainment, Multi Music & Grounded TV, 2014), http://series.thebloom.tv.

17. "Episode 3: New Ways of the Sacred," *The Bloom Series*, http://www.filmsforaction. org/watch/the-bloom-episode-3/.

18. "Episode 3: New Ways of the Sacred."

19. Jonathan Gotschall, *The Storytelling Animal: How Stories Make Us Human* (New York: Mifflin Harcourt Publishing Company, 2012).

20. Adam Possamai, *Religion and Popular Culture: A Hyper-Real Testament* (Brussels, Belgium: Peter Lang, 2005), 103.

21. Possamai, *Religion and Popular Culture*, 103.

22. David Lyon, *Jesus in Disneyland: Religion in Postmodern Times* (Cambridge and Malden, MA: Polity, 2000), 76.

23. Robert Ellwood, *The Sixties Spiritual Awakening: American Religion Moving from Modern to Postmodern* (New Brunswick, NJ: Rutgers University Press, 1994), 309.

24. David Hartwell, *Age of Wonders: Exploring the World of Science Fiction* (New York: Walker and Company, 1984), 42.

25. Michael Jindra, "*Star Trek* Fandom as a Religious Phenomenon," *Sociology of Religion* 55, no. 1 (1994): 27–51.

26. William Shatner with Chris Chris Kreski, *Get a Life!* (New York: Atria Books, 1999).

27. William Shatner (dir.), *Get a Life!*, EPIX Original, 2012, https://www.epix.com/movie/william-shatners-get-a-life.

28. Jeff Greenwald, *Future Perfect: How Star Trek Conquered Planet Earth* (New York and London: Penguin Books, 1998), 31, 75.

29. In relation to *Star Trek* functioning as sacred mythology, there is a certain irony here in that *Star Trek*'s creator, Gene Roddenberry, was a noted Secular Humanist.

30. Robert V. Kozinets, "Can Consumers Escape the Market? Emancipatory Illuminations from Burning Man," *Journal of Consumer Research* 29, no. 1 (2002), 21.

31. *Faerieworlds: A Gathering of the Tribes* website, "About the Event," http://faerieworlds.com/about-the-event/.

32. Sarah M. Pike, *Earthly Bodies, Magical Selves: Contemporary Pagans and the Search for Community* (Berkeley and Los Angeles: University of California Press, 2001), 203.

33. Harvey Cox, *The Feast of Fools: A Theological Essay on Feasting and Festivity* (New York: Harper & Row, 1969), 8.

34. Camille Bacon-Smith, *Science Fiction Culture* (Philadelphia: University of Philadelphia Press, 2000), 32.

35. Bacon-Smith, *Science Fiction Culture*, 35.

36. Cristen Conger, "The First Lady of Cosplay," *Stuff Mom Never Told You*, August 27, 2014, http://www.stuffmomnevertoldyou.com/blogs/the-first-lady-of-cosplay.htm.

37. Erica McGillivray, "The Future's Been Here Since 1939: Female Fans, Cosplay, and Conventions," *Uncanny* 2 (January/ February 2015), http://uncannymagazine.com/article/futures-since-1939-female-fans-cosplay-conventions/.

38. Katharine Buljan, "Spirituality-Struck: Anime and Religio-Spiritual Devotional Practices," in *Fiction, Invention and Hyper-reality: From Popular Culture to Religion*, ed. Carole M. Cusack and Pavol Kosnáč (New York: Routledge, 2017), 107.

39. Buljan, "Spirituality-Struck," 107.

40. Buljan, "Spirituality-Struck," 108.

41. Buljan, "Spirituality-Struck," 108.

42. Adam Savage, *Adam Savage: My Love Letter to Cosplay*, TEDTalk, 2016, https://www.ted.com/talks/adam_savage_my_love_letter_to_cosplay#t-116447.

BIBLIOGRAPHY

Bacon-Smith, Camille. *Science Fiction Culture*. Philadelphia: University of Philadelphia Press, 2000.

Bennett, Andy, and Ian Woodward. "Festival Spaces, Identity, Experience and Belonging." In *The Festivalization of Culture*, edited by Andy Bennett, Jodie Taylor and Ian Woodward, 11–26. London and New York: Routledge, 2016.

Bennett, Andy, Jodie Taylor, and Ian Woodward. "Introduction." In *The Festivalization of Culture*, edited by Andy Bennett, Jodie Taylor and Ian Woodward, 1–8. London and New York: Routledge, 2016.

Buljan, Katharine. "Spirituality-Struck: Anime and Religio-Spiritual Devotional Practices." In *Fiction, Invention and Hyper-reality: From Popular Culture to Religion* edited by Carole M. Cusack and Pavol Kosnáč, 101–118. New York: Routledge, 2017.

Combs, James. "Celebrations: Rituals of Popular Veneration." *Journal of Popular Culture* 22, no. 4 (1989): 71–77.

Conger, Cristen. "The First Lady of Cosplay." *Stuff Mom Never Told You.* August 27, 2014. http://www.stuffmomnevertoldyou.com/blogs/the-first-lady-of-cosplay.htm (accessed March 15, 2018).

Cox, Harvey. *The Feast of Fools: A Theological Essay on Feasting and Festivity*. New York: Harper & Row, 1969.

Doucette, Kitt. "7 Wildest Transformational Festivals." *Rolling Stone*. May 11, 2016. http://www.rollingstone.com/culture/lists/7-wildest-transformational-festivals-20160511 (accessed March 15, 2018).

Ellwood, Robert. *The Sixties Spiritual Awakening: American Religion Moving from Modern to Postmodern*. New Brunswick, NJ: Rutgers University Press, 1994.

Frank, Thomas. *The Conquest of Cool: Business Culture, Counter Culture, and the Rise of Hip Consumerism*. Chicago and London: University of Chicago Press, 1997.

Gotschall, Jonathan. *The Storytelling Animal: How Stories Make Us Human*. New York: Mifflin Harcourt, 2012.

Greenwald, Jeff. *Future Perfect: How Star Trek Conquered Planet Earth*. New York and London: Penguin Books, 1998.

Hartwell, David. *Age of Wonders: Exploring the World of Science Fiction*. New York: Walker and Company, 1984.

Jindra, Michael. "Star Trek Fandom as a Religious Phenomenon." *Sociology of Religion* 55, no. 1 (1994): 27–51.

Johner, Andrew. "Transformational Festivals: A New Religious Movement?" In *Exploring Psychedelic Trance and Electronic Music in Modern Culture*, edited by Emilia Simão, 58–86. Hershey, PA: IGI Global, 2015.

Kozinets, Robert V. "Can Consumers Escape the Market? Emancipatory Illuminations from Burning Man." *Journal of Consumer Research* 29, no. 1 (2002): 20–38.

Leung, Jeet-Kei. "Transformational Festivals and the New Evolutionary Culture." *TEDxVancouver*, 2010. https://youtu.be/Q8tDpQp6m0A (accessed March 15, 2018).

Leung, Jeet-Kei and Akira Chang. "Episode 3: New Ways of the Sacred." *The Bloom Series*. Elevate Films, Keyframe Entertainment, Multi Music & Grounded TV, 2014. http://series.thebloom.tv (accessed March 15, 2018).

McGillivray, Erica. "The Future's Been Here Since 1939: Female Fans, Cosplay, and Conventions." *Uncanny* 2, January/ February 2015. http://uncannymagazine.com/article/futures-since-1939-female-fans-cosplay-conventions/ (accessed March 15, 2018).

Morehead, John W. *Burning Man Festival: A Life-Enhancing, Post-Christendom, "Middle Way."* Masters thesis, Salt Lake City: Salt Lake Theological Seminary, 2007.

Pike, Sarah M. *Earthly Bodies, Magical Selves: Contemporary Pagans and the Search for Community*. Berkeley and Los Angeles: University of California Press, 2001.

Pitzl-Waters, Jason. Transformational Festival Culture," *The Wild Hunt*, October 2, 2011, http://wildhunt.org/2011/10/transformational-festival-culture.html (accessed March 15, 2018).

Porter, Jennifer E. "To Boldly Go: *Star Trek* Convention as Pilgrimage." In Star Trek *and Sacred Ground: Explorations of* Star Trek, *Religion and American Culture*, edited by Jennifer E. Porter and Darcee L. McLaren, 245–270. Albany: State University of New York Press, 1999.

Possamai, Adam. *Religion and Popular Culture: A Hyper-Real Testament*. Brussels: Peter Lang, 2005.

Prucher, Jeff (ed.), *Brave New Words: The Oxford Dictionary of Science Fiction*. New York: Oxford University Press, 2007.

Savage, Adam. "My Love Letter to Cosplay." *TEDTalk*, 2016. https://www.ted.com/talks/adam_savage_my_love_letter_to_cosplay (accessed March 15, 2018).

Shatner, William (with Chris Chris Kreski). *Get a Life!* New York: Atria Books, 1999.

Shatner, William (dir.). *Get a Life!* EPIX Original, 2012. https://www.epix.com/movie/william-shatners-get-a-life (accessed March 15. 2018).

St. John, Graham. "Introduction to Weekend Societies: EDM Festivals and Event-Cultures." *dancecult: Journal of Electronic Dance Music Culture* 7, no. 1 (2015): 1–14.

Turner, Victor. "The Centre Out There: Pilgrim's Goal." *History of Religions* 12, no. 3 (1972): 191–230.

Weber, Max. *Max Weber: Essays in Sociology*. Translated by Hans H. Gerth and Charles Wright Mills. Abingdon: Routledge, 2001 [1948].

About the Contributors

Greg **Conley** received his Ph.D. focusing on speculative fiction from the University of Memphis in 2013. He teaches comparative humanities at Eastern Kentucky University and English at Bluegrass Community and Technical College. His research includes Gothic fiction, science fiction, and fantasy, as well as scientific and religious themes in speculative fiction.

Carole M. **Cusack** is a professor of religious studies at the University of Sydney. She researches and teaches on contemporary religious trends. Her books include *Invented Religions* (2010) and (with Katharine Buljan) *Anime, Religion, and Spirituality* (2015).

Jovi L. **Geraci** is an instructor in religious studies at Manhattan College. Her research interests include religion in popular culture, material religion, and indigenous religions. She is coauthor (with Robert M. Geraci) of "Virtual Gender" in *Journal of Gaming and Virtual Worlds* (2013).

Juli L. **Gittinger** is a lecturer in South Asian religions at Georgia College. Hinduism and Islam are her primary areas of expertise, with emphasis on contemporary issues (nationalism, media, gender, culture). Religion and new media, popular culture, and cosplay are of particular interest to her, and a focus of future research.

Rhiannon **Grant** is a lecturer in modern Quaker thought and a tutor for Quaker roles at Woodbrooke, Birmingham, UK. Her work explores issues of religious language, identity, and belonging, and the relationships between religious practice and belief, using interdisciplinary approaches.

Irma **Hirsjärvi**, Ph.D., works at the University of Jyväskylä's Research Center for Contemporary Culture and was a coordinator of the Global Comparative Youth Media Participation project (Academy of Finland, 2009–2013). She is part of The World Hobbit reception project and also of the Media Fuzz project, funded by the Kone Foundation.

Linda **Howell**, Ph.D., is an instructor and director at the University of North Florida. She teaches writing, media, and fan studies classes. She has taught classes on *Supernatural*, Marvel, and various fan-centric texts. Her research centers on digital literacy practices and concepts of plagiarism and citation, which informs her fan studies scholarship.

Marc **Joly-Corcoran** has a Ph.D. in film studies. He is parttime lecturer at the University of Montreal and a film director. He has published articles and given papers in international panels (Istanbul, Salzburg, Rotterdam, Los Angeles). His main research concerns fan culture and fan creations. He is also the cofounder and co-chief editor of the online journal *Kinephanos*.

Jyrki **Korpua**, Ph.D., is a researcher at the University of Oulu, Finland. He is editor-in-chief of *Fafnir: Nordic Journal of Science Fiction and Fantasy Research* and Chair of the Board of Finfar (The Finnish Society for Science Fiction and Fantasy Research). His interest in literary and cultural studies focuses on fantasy, myth, the Bible, and utopias and dystopias.

John W. **Morehead** works in religion and pop culture as expressed in science fiction, fantasy and horror. He has coedited, edited, and contributed to *Handbook of Hyper-Real Religions* (2012), *The Undead and Theology* (2012), *Joss Whedon and Religion* (2013), and *The Supernatural Cinema of Guillermo del Toro* (2015).

James **Reynolds** is a senior lecturer in drama at Kingston University, London. His Ph.D. research investigated performance practices in Robert Lepage's theater. His book *Robert Lepage/Ex Machina* will be published in 2019. His other research interests include Howard Barker's theater, the cinematic adaptation of graphic novels, theater for recovery, and adapting children's literature for the stage.

Venetia Laura Delano **Robertson** received her Ph.D. in studies in religion from the University of Sydney in 2017. She has written about identity and spirituality in relation to subcultures and fandoms for *Nova Religio,* the *International Journal of Cultural Studies*, and *Fiction, Invention, and Hyper-Reality* (ed. Cusack and Kosnáč, 2017).

Maria **Ruotsalainen** is a doctoral student in digital culture studies at the University of Jyväskylä, Finland. She is interested in how current technologies and digital mediums change everyday experience of the public and private, time and location, as well as self and identity. Her thesis applies Gilles Deleuze and Félix Guattari to the experience of play in digital games.

Minna **Siikilä-Laitila** is a Ph.D. student in contemporary culture at the University of Jyvaskyla, Finland. Her thesis examines intertextual online conversations about fantasy literature, focusing especially in intertextuality, plagiarism and fandom. She considers herself an interdisciplinary researcher and likes to combine communication studies with literature studies.

Tanja **Välisalo** is a doctoral student in contemporary culture at the University of Jyväskylä. Her research interests include transmedia audiences, media fandom and the ludification of culture. She is at work on a dissertation about audience reception and fan practices relating to fictional characters.

Index